When We Were Your Age

When We Were Your Age

A Peek at New England Childhoods of the 1920s, 30s, and 40s

ANNE G. D. SMITH

Contact information: BookLocker.com

Printed in the United States of America
Paperback ISBN: 978-1-63492-769-7
Epub ISBN: 978-1-63492-770-3
Mobi ISBN: 978-1-63492-771-0

Cover and book design, book production: Julie Gallagher
Photo restoration and colorization: DejaViewPhotos.com

Photo Credits

Front cover: Shirl, far left, at age 7 with her entry for the doll carriage parade [photo courtesy of Shirley Schofield]

Back cover: (clockwise from left) Ellen at age 4 with her dog, Polly [photo courtesy of Ellen Downing]; Edith at age 2 or 3 [photo courtesy of Edith Warner]; Vicki (left) with her sister Jessie, early 1930s [photo courtesy of Victoria Bradley]; Pumpie at age 10 with friends on a Sunday morning [photo courtesy of Pearl Perry]

CONTENTS

PART ONE
Glimpses

CONTENTS

PART TWO

Lives and Times

CONTENTS

CONTENTS

Once Upon
a Time

"WHEN *I* WAS YOUR AGE, *Sonny-boy,* we *walked* to school. Ten miles, barefoot, in the snow. Uphill both ways."

When I was your age . . . We don't hear that expression very much anymore. On one hand, that's a relief. It was usually met with a lot of eye-rolling, especially by children: *Here we go again about the good old days. Bor-ing.* And who could blame them, if what they heard underneath the words, perhaps in the tone of voice, was *We were better than you. We weren't soft and lazy, like you.* Who wants to be told that? And how does just being born in a hardier and harder time automatically make some any better than others? They just grew up then; did what they had to do. On the other hand, if we never hear about those old days, good ones or bad, how will we ever know about them? How will we have a sense of ourselves as products of history, as players in history? How will we understand how today's realities came about? Will we see ourselves simply as meaningless blobs of self-aware organic structures plopped into a society for a short time without an awareness of where it came from?

The truth is, a lot of things *were* harder back in the day. But some things were *easier.* And an awful lot about childhood wasn't much different than it is now.

Children today have more comforts, but less freedom. More conveniences, but maybe more stress. Like almost all Americans before them, they argue with their siblings and complain about school. There used to be bullies, and there still are. There were kids who were nice, who tried to include everyone; there still are. There were some great parents, and some rotten ones. But mostly there were just kids and adults who, in the course of a few days or a few weeks, did some things right and some things wrong, forgot something important, saved the day, made silly mistakes, didn't like the food they were served, did something really well, looked like an idiot, said something quite wise, got a lucky break, got blamed for something that wasn't their fault, wasted their time, spilled something, worked hard, were grumpy, mean, tired, and kind. Just like today.

Some things never change. Take these excerpts from the chapter "Children" in the book *How to Behave,* which was published in the United States. When do you think it was written?

> *"American children . . . are not, as a general rule, well behaved. They are rude and disrespectful . . . They inspire terror rather than love . . . generally and particularly disagreeable . . . 'Young America' . . . is born with a full comprehension of his own individual rights, but is slow in learning his social duties . . . In the days of our grandfathers, children were taught manners at school . . . better than the no manners at all of the present day. We must blame parents in this matter . . . If you would have your children grow up . . . respected by their elders as well as their contemporaries, teach them good manners in their childhood."**

Anything sound familiar? But the author is referring to neither today's generation, nor the one featured in this book. No; this was written back in 1857. Those ill-mannered kids with the negligent parents belonged to the generation of children brought up just before the Civil War—perhaps your great-great-great-great-grandparents. (Did you notice how the author wrote, *"In the days of our grandfathers, blah blah blah . . . ?"* Even in 1857 they were referencing those elusive "good old days!") People have been complaining about how children were being brought up for a long, long time. Maybe that's because some of the

---

* From "How to Behave" by Samuel R. Wells, 2013 edition, F & W Media, Inc., pp. 75-76. Original text from "How to Behave: A Pocket Manual of Republican Etiquette and Guide to Correct Personal Habits"—*originally published in 1857* by Fowler & Wells, Co., Publishers, New York, New York.

things about kids that have always irritated adults so much, just haven't changed. Kids are still kids, for good or for bad.

Much has changed in the world, and much has not. One thing that hasn't is how difficult it is for young people to understand, really *know*, that the elderly people they meet were once young and strong; and that someday they themselves will be old and weak. We know, instinctively, that we will always be the same person deep inside, the same being, but we struggle to understand how that bent and wrinkled 90-year old could once have been a toddler saying "NO!" to her mother, a girl whispering to her best friend, or a thirteen-year old with a crush on the boy next door; can still, inside, *be* that very same person right now.

Once upon a time the people featured in this book were newborn babies, just as each of you once was. The only difference between them and you is that they opened their eyes on the world at a different point in time. They learned to function in their world, as you did in yours. If they'd been frozen in time soon after birth—possible only in science fiction, of course—and awakened to be brought up when you were born, they would have taken on the habits and knowledge of *your* world. We are products of our own age.

If we are going to learn about yesterday's world with any enthusiasm, it probably won't be from school history books, no matter how appealingly they've been written, how cool they try to appear. There seems to be an odd, universal aversion to textbooks—perceived, for some reason, as not *real*—and kids especially can sniff them out two blocks away. Of course, the best way to learn about that world is by talking directly with elderly people, asking questions about what they did as kids, listening to their stories. I hope you do that. I also hope that you'll see this book as the next-best thing to it, because it *is* real. Twenty-five former children have generously shared their childhood memories in interviews that took place in 2013 and 2014. These are their stories, along with some background information that we need in order to understand their times. They hope that everybody who picks up this book will understand their generation's world a little better. And will have fun doing it.

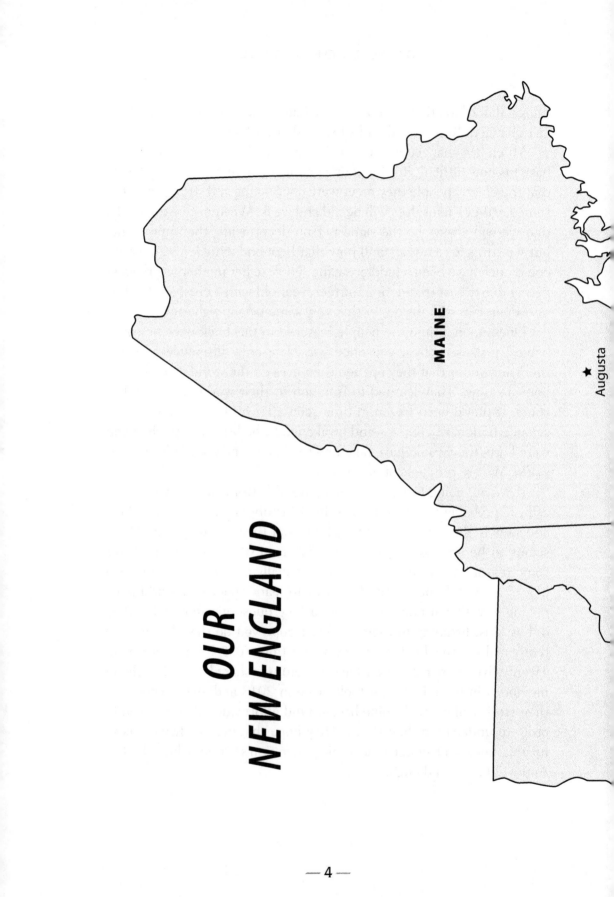

OUR
NEW ENGLAND

MAINE

★ Augusta

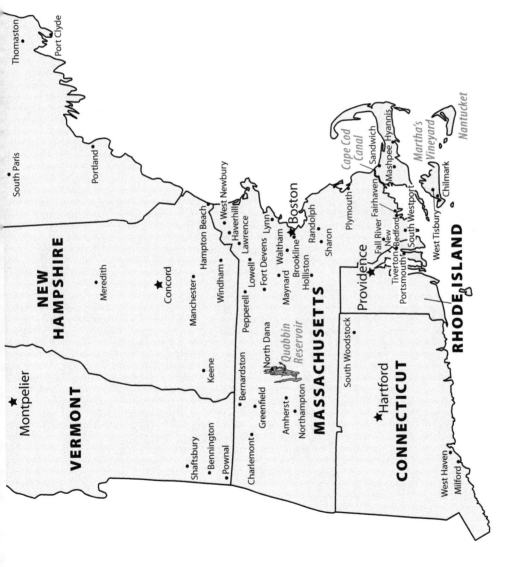

Glimpses

Only glimpses.

Some fully true,

Couple? mostly not,

Most mostly true.

But all and each

Of a wink, of a breathing,

A twinkle, a flash

When *we* stood shivering

On muddy grass,

Slurping raindrops into heads
crammed with dreams,

Fully alive.

Firm on this ground.

This very same earth.

1

Okie

OKIE TIGHTENED HER GRIP on her lunch pail, gathered her books snugly against her coat, and slid to the end of the bench. *We're almost there. Get ready.* The younger girl beside her moved to the other end. They turned to face each other, gazing unblinkingly into each other's eyes in a silent challenge.

"Remember," recited Kay mockingly, "no standing up until he says, 'Go!'"

"I know that!" her older sister snapped hotly. "I'm not stupid!" She immediately regretted it.

Kay was pleased with herself. Okie had taken the bait. She flashed a ha-ha smile of satisfaction through her stare. *Okie is scared of me. Scared, scared, scared.* But her sister had regained her composure and wiped her face of emotion. Just a slight roll of the eyes that said it all: "*I'm* not afraid of *babies.* Last time you got lucky." Inwardly she was shaking. She had to, just *had to,* win. Kay was two whole years younger. She would be insufferable if she won again.

"Girls!" Their father's voice broke through. "All set?" The horse had stopped and was standing patiently, waiting for her load to get lighter. "1–2–3 — GO!"

Kay and Okie jumped out of the sleigh on opposite sides and raced up to the schoolhouse. Okie was in the lead by several feet as she reached out for the doorknob. But the heavy door suddenly swung outward as the teacher stepped outside, bell in hand, to ring the final warning. Okie swerved to the right just in time to avoid being hit, and Kay, watching from behind, ran to the left and behind the open door. She slapped the knob.

"I WIN!" she shouted. "I WIN *AGAIN!*" she screamed, dancing and laughing, leaping into the snow piled up beside the path, while her sister stomped inside.

The teacher finished ringing and looked over at her. "I don't know what else you've won, but since you're not inside, you're late. You've won extra homework!"

2

Adrianne

ADRIANNE MARGARET GRAY was only three years old, so she wasn't at the Devon School in Milford that day. If it had been a few years later, after she had started school, she would have been there, because Adrianne went to the Devon from second through eighth grade. But that's got nothing to do with this. At all. She just wasn't there on that special day in the late 1920s. The day that her resourceful, clever mother saved Laurids Thomas Lauridsen from an unjust beating in the third-grade cloakroom.

Laurids was never called by his first name, of course. What a name for an American child! He went by either Tom or his nickname, Buddy. "Buddy" because his older sister couldn't pronounce "brother." And later he was Bud. And then, in college, Teapot Tom, because he signed his incredible paintings of still lifes with a tiny teapot. Wait. Getting off track again, so let's move on. Oh, and by the way, Adrianne herself never had a nickname until she was married and her husband started calling her Ade. She was named for her mother's brother, Uncle Adrian, who was a sculptor and . . . *Sorry!!!* No more interruptions. That's a promise. Well, Buddy was on his way to school one day. Probably he was wishing he were on his way *home* instead, because he was not at all interested in what school offered. He had already stayed back in first grade, and Mrs. Gray—Adrianne's mother—would be keeping him back again at the end of this year. Not because he was unintelligent. After all, in high school he eventually buckled down to his schoolwork, even though he didn't enjoy it, and did well enough to go on to college, at a time when not a lot of others did. And graduate. It wasn't just any old college, either. *Yale University.* But when he was a boy, school took time away from what he liked to do at home. He always had interesting projects going on. The good stuff. He built tree houses and forts with his friends, restored junk cars. So anyway, Buddy was walking to school. He was almost there, and he needed to cross the street. So he did.

Miss Hutchinson walked quickly into the school, her expression grim and determined. Without even stopping to take off her coat in her own classroom, she marched across the hall to confront Mrs. Gray. Young Lauridsen, she complained, had just now crossed the street right in front of her car, and she had come within an inch of hitting him. It was careless and irresponsible of him, and she demanded that he be punished.

A few minutes later, the bell rang. Mrs. Gray's third graders entered the building, hung their coats in their cloakroom, and then went straight to their desks, where they sat down and waited to start the day. Adrianne's mother picked up her discipline "ruler"—in reality, an old wooden slat from an auditorium seat—and summoned Buddy to the now-empty cloakroom. The rest of the class sat in hushed astonishment. *What had Buddy done?! they whispered to each other. He **never** got the ruler!* She got right to the point. Had he cut in front of a car this morning? Well, sure, he said, there were cars on the street when he crossed. But they were way far away from *him*. There had been *lots* of space to cross safely, and *plenty* of time! Mrs. Gray thought fast. She knew Buddy well, and she knew Miss Hutchinson well. Well enough to know that the truth lay somewhere between the two accounts. The politics were tricky here. Mrs. Gray was young, and she was new to the school. The older teacher was powerful and domineering, and she absolutely had to be appeased. But Mrs. Gray also suspected that she unfairly "had it in" for Buddy. What should she do? An answer came quickly. She grabbed a student's leather jacket off a hook. This had to be good and loud, loud enough to be heard in the room across the hall. She gave Buddy a long look as she said, "I'm going to need your cooperation here." Then she poised her ruler over the coat and told him, "Every time I give this jacket a whack, you holler for all you're worth." She held his gaze until his face told her he understood. After several good swats and a nice job of howling, the mission was complete. The conspirators left the cloakroom together.

In the end, everyone was satisfied. Miss Hutchinson thought that justice had been served. Mrs. Gray *knew* that justice had been served. And Buddy? He grew up to marry Adrianne, and they lived happily ever after. He adored his kind, wise mother-in-law, and both of them loved to tell the story of the beating that never was.

3

Sonny

Louis Dominic Miconi was at it again. He stepped off the sidewalk and strode up the pavement leading to the New Haven YMCA, glancing casually from side to side. Deciding he wasn't being watched (and who would be suspicious of this purposeful young man, books under arm, steadily approaching the building?), he veered from the path before reaching the entrance and sauntered off to his right. Rounding the building, he dashed to his left and dropped nimbly into the space between a low wall and the building. He was met with hushed cheers. "Where ya been, Sonny? We thought the truant guy grabbed ya." Sonny looked around at his friends and relaxed. He settled into a spot on the ground. Skipping school was fun. It was going to be a great day.

4

Shirl

HALLOWEEN! Shirley Ann Harris grabbed a bar of soap and ran outside to join the waiting group of giggling girls. They had graduated from little-kid Halloween parties, and this year they would roam on their own. Shirl's mother smiled as she watched the laughing teens stroll away, soap tucked into pockets. She knew very well what they were up to and didn't mind a bit. Neither did the storeowners up in the Square who were about to have their display windows soaped; nor the police. Better to keep some control on the night by allowing some harmless fun, rather than risking real rowdiness by irritating everyone with a crackdown on silliness. Who would rather end up with broken windows than soapy ones? Goodness! Mrs. Harris remembered last year, when her husband had answered a knock at the door and been greeted by a bag of flour thrown all over him. She laughed again. Mr. Harris was very well liked, and the kids had meant the prank only for fun. And he hadn't held it against them.

5

Bella

To Bella—Isabella Cairnie Monroe—the stars had never looked so . . . so . . . delightfully enchanting. They twinkled, they sparkled, they danced and shimmered over the fields and houses. The brilliance! She couldn't stop staring as she dragged Johnnie Smith's toboggan up, up, and up through the streets of Andover. And the moon! She stopped, entranced. *It almost blazed!* Bella held her mittened hand to her forehead, shielding her eyes as she gazed at that moon, marveling at how it lit up the countryside. *Might be three in the afternoon instead of a midwinter night. Simply . . .*

"Hey, Bella! Keep moving. We can't stay out all night." Okie, as they called Johnnie, sounded annoyed. Bella snapped to. He was right. They'd all get in trouble if they were late. And they wanted to get two runs in tonight. "Hurry up," he ordered, "or I won't let you on." Bella tugged at the heavy sled and crunched on as fast as her freezing legs would carry her. Further up School Street she handed the toboggan off to her sister. They could sled here only at night, when hardly any cars were on the streets, but there was never time for more than two runs before they had to be home. When they reached the Academy, all eight kids could pile on and go flying downhill for over half a mile of bliss. And then they'd do it again—shoot all the way down from the school, tearing between the two cemeteries, zipping clear across the railroad tracks. To home. Then Bella would race over to Baker Lane to a warm stove and to bed, the thrill playing in her head all night.

6

Beena

Verena Rose Davis sprinted back to the harbor. "Where's Polly?" she called to her cousin up on the dock as she raced by, heading for a fishing shack.

"Still getting her bathing suit on. Taking her time about it, too," Joe replied before muttering, "As usual."

Beena, as everyone called Verena, emerged with two oars and two extra bailers. As she dashed to the dock she could see Polly finally strolling into view. Joe started to work on the rope holding the dory in place as Beena climbed down into the boat. "Hey!" he objected. "Those are my father's oars!"

"So what?" Beena laughed. "We're in a hurry. And this is my father's skiff."

"Yeah, but we all know you aren't going to get in trouble if anything goes wrong." He turned and yelled to his dawdling twin sister. "Will you hurry up? You've only got to the count of five, and then we're going without you."

Polly knew he meant it. She started running full speed as Joe and Beena shouted together, "ONE . . . TWO . . . THREE . . . FOUR . . . FIVE!" Just as his sister reached him, Joe leapt from the dock into the waiting vessel. He slipped the remaining rope off its post and flipped it into the boat.

"Hey, you meanies! I was here!" Polly complained. "Hold it for me."

Beena reached out and grabbed a piling so the dory would stay in place. "No, you weren't. Not by five. So now you have to row," she said, handing her the oars.

The children settled themselves in the boat, and Polly headed toward the middle of the harbor. "Where do you think we should stop?"

Joe and Beena both took a good look around before answering at the same moment. "Right next to the buoy," Beena said, pointing, as Joe murmured, "Maybe nowhere."

"What are you talking about?" gasped Beena. "We came out here to play Sink!"

"I mean," Joe said, "that maybe we shouldn't. The water's getting rougher."

"Yeah, a little rougher," Beena conceded warily. Five minutes ago it had been still and glassy, and now it was a bit choppy. The air had also changed. It was heavier, and a light breeze had replaced the dead calm. But nothing to worry about. It had been so awful this summer. Cold, rainy, or stormy every single day. They were finally having a chance for some fun, and today had looked perfect. "It's fine. We can swim back in this."

Joe shook his head. "Fine maybe for us, but not for the boat. I'm afraid this wind is going to take her way off." The breeze had suddenly strengthened. Whitecaps were lapping the dory's sides.

"But Daddy doesn't mind! He'll get it back," she objected.

"Yeah," agreed her cousin, "but not necessarily with my father's oars still inside."

Beena was horrified. No Sink today? They hadn't swamped the boat in the harbor yet this summer, and she wasn't going to pass up this chance. She reached out quickly to grab two of the bailers so she could start bringing seawater into their dory, but Joe was too fast for her and scooped them all up. "Let's take a vote," she suggested, in a last-ditch effort to save Sink. "How about you, Polly?"

Thwack. The whitecaps had turned into waves and were hitting them broadside. Polly shook her head and maneuvered the boat into a better position. The steady breeze had shifted and become a strong easterly wind. She started rowing back. She was just as afraid of losing the oars and getting in trouble as her brother was.

Beena gave up. She stared at the approaching shoreline, pouting. Nuts. Maybe tomorrow they'd be luckier.

7

Helen

HELEN ELAINE SANFORD was leaving home. She snapped her small case shut. It hadn't taken long to pack: one dress, one coat, some socks, a book, a few small items. It was everything she owned in the world besides what she was wearing—one blouse, one skirt, one pair of shoes. She lifted the bag off the bed and stepped out of the little room where the older girls slept. Her younger sisters were in the hallway, crying. Doubts trickled into her mind as she made her way down the stairs and through the first-floor rooms, little girls clinging to her skirt, weeping. "Don't go away, Helen! Don't go!" Was she really doing this; really leaving? She looked around in a silent goodbye. The kerosene lamp she had done her homework by. The radio. The kitchen table. Her mother's chair. The stove she had polished every Saturday night. *Who was going to do that now?* Guilt stabbed at her heart. Helen's aunts from Sagamore appeared from a side room. *Were all her relatives going to show up today?* Over and over they scolded, trying to get her to change her mind. *Who did she think she was, running out on her mother when she needed so much help? Who was going to take her place? help take care of the new baby and the other little ones, look after them, change their diapers, feed them? What a burden for her mother and sisters! How could she think only of herself?* Were they right? *Maybe I don't belong in college anyway.*

Because she left, Helen was able to be much more of a help to her family over the years that followed than she ever could have had she stayed. But nobody knew that on this crisp and sunny September morning in 1942. It seemed to everyone she was being just plain selfish.

She opened the front door and stepped out. A procession of sobbing children followed her onto the sandy path that led to the street. Once more Helen had to banish the doubts that tugged at her—had to remind herself that she had everything she needed: a suitcase, a scholarship, and a mission. She said a final goodbye and set off walking to meet her ride. Two miles later she climbed into a car. And in less than an hour she was at the dormitory at Hyannis State Teachers College. She had arrived in another world.

8

Butch

. . . No, Sister, Francis hasn't been sick. Why do you . . . What do you mean, then where *is* he? He's in *school,* of course! . . . Well, if *anyone* should know, it's *you!* . . . He left for school right after breakfa . . . Oh, yes, he *did.* Same as every day this week . . . What?! He hasn't shown up at St. Francis at *all?* . . . Yes, that's right: Fran-cis Fred-e-rick Cor-bett. Are there two . . . No? . . . Yes, of *course* he's in the fifth grade! . . . Oh, this is ridiculous. Listen, he's bringing back homework, and we're making sure he . . . Yes, I know th . . . He . . . Well, I don't know, either . . . Yes, this certainly *is* very strange . . . He is *not* skipping sch . . . I certainly wi . . . I will talk with . . .

The girl sitting in front of Francis swung around and deposited a stack of books on his desk. He took one off the top for himself, then picked up the rest, turned, and thumped them onto the desk behind. From across the aisle, Skip shot his leg out and gave him a quick kick. As soon as Francis—better known as Butch—looked over, Skip took *his* pile in both hands, stretched back, and lifted his arms over his head. Another boy received the stack and repeated the process. Butch made a mental note: only girls turn around to pass stuff down the aisle. There was some important stuff he needed to learn in this place. Good thing he had Skip to help.

Butch hadn't cared much for the nun he'd had in fourth grade. She was always whacking people. Or sending them to the office to "get the ruler" from the principal. They didn't do that stuff here at the public school. Skip had told him all about it. They gave you detention instead. Just made you stay after school, which sounded a lot better. That's when he had made the decision. He was surprised how easy it had been. Walked into the office, told the lady at the desk he was enrolling for school. She had called over to someone, "Where'd ya put those address cards?" Then it was just his name and address, phone, birth date, what grade he was in last year. And, "School starts Wednesday. You'll be in Room 15. Be in line by five to nine." He should tell the other boys back at St. Francis. Maybe they'd sign up, too.

9

Ellen

THREE-YEAR OLD Ellen Mayhew Gifford sat at the breakfast table. She clutched a baby doll and finished her corn flakes as she listened for footsteps on the stairs behind the kitchen wall. Polly, her huge St. Bernard, lay beside her, massive paws resting on the faded linoleum. At the first clatter, Ellen put down her spoon, quickly drank the rest of her tomato juice, and slid off her chair. Polly rose to her feet. Wherever Ellen was going, she was going too. They hurried along, Polly nearly as tall as her mistress, past Ellen's mother, who was clearing the table. No need to say anything. She knew where they would be. Ellen lifted her sweater off a hook, and girl, doll, and dog headed out the door.

Dorothy and William were already waiting at the road when Ellen came outside to join them. William had set his lunchbox on the ground. He picked up a handful of gray stones and started whipping them, one by one, at a target he'd carved into a tree on the other side of the roadway. Dorothy stood silently, lunchbox in hand, her face impassive. Ellen seated herself on a patch of grass, Polly beside her, and put on her sweater. *What's it like to go to school?* she wondered. *To ride the bus? And learn to read?* Her baby's covering had worked itself loose. She lifted the doll out of the blanket and rewrapped her tightly. *William and Dorothy are so lucky. When do I get to go?* The school bus rumbled into sight on the rutted dirt road. William slipped the rest of his rocks into his pocket and picked up his lunch box.

As the bus sputtered and lurched off, Ellen and Polly turned and ran. Across the yard, past the henhouse and through the flock, to a little hillside grove they raced, a soft May breeze puffing at Ellen's cotton dress. They stepped into a clearing, their own special space, their secret house. Towering trees formed the outer walls. Low boughs and branches swept pine-scented rooms into focus. Twigs, sticks, and leaves mingled with cones and needles on the grassy floor, ready to be imagined with. Everything was still, peaceful. Waiting. Waiting for Ellen, Polly, and dolly to come home and play. Ellen knelt on the prickly floor and unwrapped her doll. She laid her down and smoothed the blanket over her. She would make some lunch while the baby napped.

10

Rosanna

THERE WERE THINGS Rosanna Cecile Descoteaux never did when she was growing up, and some things she did do. For instance, she never learned to play piano with two hands. But she could play with one hand at a time, and when friends came over they'd gather around their upright to sing and harmonize. She never learned to swim. In fact, she was afraid of the water. But that didn't stop her from going to Lake Spofford, Swanzey Lake, or Hampton Beach with her teen friends and wading up to her waist. She never learned to knit, or to type. But she did take long bike rides with friends; those who didn't have bicycles rented them. And she loved to dance to "big band" music. Every Saturday night she'd be at a dance hall or a barn dance.

She didn't like to read, so sometimes she cheated on book reports. She'd rummage through her sister's old reports, choose one, get a copy of the book and read the first, middle, and last chapter, then copy the report in her own handwriting. One time her sister pointed out a spelling error right before she turned in one of these plagiarized reports. Rosanna had written the title on her report cover as "A Tail of Two Cities" [and just in case you don't know, that should have been Tale]. When she grew up and taught school, though, she had to deal with dishonest students from the other side of the desk.

Rosanna didn't learn to drive when she was young, although the family owned a car. Her mother, like most other women of her day, didn't drive; her father did, but hated to. In 1951, at the age of thirty, Rosanna got her license. She loved driving and didn't stop until she was eighty-nine years old. She was still an excellent driver, but after hearing of so many accidents caused by elderly people she worried she might cause one as well.

She says that sixteen or seventeen was the respectable age to start dating. But she was only about fourteen herself when she went on her first date. She liked to smoke. Her father smoked only rarely, but always kept a pack of cigarettes in a suit coat pocket. Rosanna would sometimes sneak into his closet to snitch one.

Then, right after she graduated from Keene High School in 1939, Rosanna gave up dancing, smoking, and boyfriends. Why? Well, those were the rules. She had entered a convent to become a nun!

11

Ellie

ELVIRA JESSIE SMITH sat at the wheel of her father's pickup as it bounced along the road to Swansea. She turned to her mother. "I don't get it. Why don't you get your license?"

Mrs. Smith laughed. "Why do I need one, Ellie? I get along fine."

"Well, so you could go places by yourself."

"I already do. I hitch up the wagon and away we trot, the horse and I."

Ellie groaned in exasperation. "You know what I mean, Ma. Places a ways off, that take forever by wagon. "

"Oh, like high school games in Swansea or Somerset? I can always get my seventeen-year old daughter to drive me. She's terribly clever."

The seventeen-year old chose to ignore how lightly her mother was treating this. "Or even just up to the Head for a church supper or to visit your friends. Four miles, Ma. It takes you an hour to go that far. Almost as long as it takes to walk. It could take eight minutes." She paused for effect. "Eight minutes, Ma," she pleaded.

Mrs. Smith laughed again. "Exactly! Only eight minutes. I'll have barely started to enjoy myself before I'll have to jump out and be somewhere with someone, doing something, when I could have had sixty whole minutes to myself to just sit, relax, daydream, ponder . . . If I tried that at home I'd be thinking, 'You know you really should be cleaning all the lamp chimneys. Or mending the somethings. Or tending the something-elses. Travel time, it's time off. Sixty delightful minutes up, sixty glorious minutes back.

"Well, when I graduate and start working, I'm going to buy my own car. And look! There's the field up ahead, and it took only . . ."

They were startled by a loud HONK coming from their left. Ellie jumped and glanced over. A convertible touring car with its top down had pulled alongside them, filled with her classmates. They were leaning toward her and shouting something. She started to roll down her window to hear what they were saying, but their voices were drowned out by her mother's.

"Don't let them get ahead and beat ya!" she was yelling.

"Honestly, Ma!" Ellie spurted as she pressed the gas pedal to the floor. "How about all your relaxing ride talk?"

"There's a time and a place for everything, dear," her mother answered, leaning forward anxiously. "Hurry up! I think we can still win!"

12

Rozzy

WOULD SHE LIKE a chocolate bar for her kindness? *Would she?* Yes, Rosamond Knapp Hutchinson certainly would! For real? She held her breath as her neighbor, Mrs. Morris, slipped a gloved hand into a pocket of her black woolen coat. It reappeared holding a Hershey bar. She was amazed. A whole candy bar, and all of it just for her! Clutching her snow shovel in one hand and pressing the chocolate to her heart with the other, she flew up the path to her door. Little Rozzy left the shovel in the entry and dashed up the stairs to her apartment. "Mum! Mum!"

Where was she? She could smell tonight's supper cooking. Macaroni and cheese. Her mother always baked it slowly, all day long, in the oven of their big, black, polished stove. Rozzy laid her precious treat on the table before yanking off her boots and placing them in a corner of the kitchen. Then she took off her mittens, coat, and snow pants and hung them to dry. It had taken her a long, long time to shovel out Mrs. Morris's car. The snow was packed solid, and it was hard work. But she had never expected such a wonderful reward.

Rozzy looked over her prize thoughtfully. *Who would she share it with?* Well, probably everyone in the whole family. Her brothers and sisters could each have two pieces—and Mum could have even more, of course, *if* she wanted them, but she probably *wouldn't*—which would leave about, oh, eight or nine for herself. She tore the paper open at one end, broke off a section, and popped it into her mouth.

She was sitting at the table, savoring the first morsel and trying to decide whether to have another bite now or save it all for later, when Mrs. Hutchinson appeared carrying a mop and a pail. She rinsed the mop in the sink as she listened happily to the whole joyous tale. Then it happened. When Mum picked up the candy bar, she noticed something. Noticed that it was . . . full of little *worms*.

Rozzy was heartbroken. If only she'd never been given that chocolate. Such an unexpected joy, and such a cruel sorrow. She cried and cried and cried.

13

Tom

Thomas Joseph McGarr was making a real scene. He kicked, screamed, and punched, and his poor parents were perplexed. Their Tom never behaved like this! Etta and Thomas stood in their front room, bewildered, trying to decide what to do. If he kept this up he would wake his little sisters. Then suddenly Tom calmed down. "There you go. That's more like it!" encouraged Etta. "Remember, if something comes up you can't handle, go next door. Mrs. Mulligan knows you're alone over here." She and her husband moved toward the door again. "We'll see you in a couple of hours. Be a good boy, and take care of your sisters." Etta put her hand on the doorknob. And as soon as she started to turn it, Tom started throwing a fit again. He had thought maybe they had changed their minds and wouldn't be going out. But they were! He resumed his tantrum. Etta sighed and looked at her husband. How could they leave now?

Mr. McGarr was not pleased. "What is wrong with you? You know how to behave! You're a responsible boy! You're not a baby! You're in school! You'll be six in a couple of months! What is going on here?"

Etta sighed again. Her shoulders drooped as she took off her coat and hung it back on its hook. "One of us needs to go over and tell the Mulligans we're not going out." Tom quieted down again, relief flooding over him. He didn't care if his parents spanked him, or sent him to bed early for being naughty. At least they were home.

14

Edith

HAVE YOU EVER DONE something ridiculous? Something so dumb you can't believe you really did it? I sure have. Too many times to count. Well, Edith Lucille Ringwall did something pretty silly once when she was a girl.

Edith had been roller-skating. When she finished skating she went home and, as usual, ran to the back of her house and up to the back door. This time, though, the door was locked and she couldn't get in. Who knows why? It doesn't matter. She could have gone around to the front door. If that had been locked she could have knocked, knowing that one of her parents would answer. Or she could have just knocked on the door she had found locked. Well, she actually *did*, but for some reason she didn't knock in the ordinary way; in other words, she didn't rap on the wooden section of the door with her knuckles. No. She chose its glass window. And she knocked on it with . . . a roller skate.

Of course the glass broke.

Now, Edith lived in a pretty calm household. She and her parents and brother generally got along well. And neither of her parents believed in spanking. They never even raised their voices. Her father was an especially gentle man. But when he saw what had happened, he did something he had never done before and never did again. He stepped through the broken glass, opened the door, and brought Edith through. Then he took her right down to the cellar. To the extra coal bin, which was always empty. He put her inside, closed the door, and locked her in.

Edith hadn't been there for more than a few minutes when her mother came down and let her out. But she never, ever, used a skate as a door knocker again.

15

Charlotte

CHARLOTTE COHEN'S MOTHER frowned as she tried to smooth out the last of the wrinkles on her husband's shirt. She gave up. The iron was too cool now to press the fabric properly, so she set it down on the hot surface of the big kitchen stove, where it could regain its fiery heat. "Come on, Charlotte," she said, smiling. "Let's take a little break." Her young daughter laid aside the garment she was pressing and placed her own iron next to her mother's. Sarah Cohen lifted a basket of rumpled clothes off her favorite chair as Charlotte pulled over two more seats. They made themselves comfortable in front of the stove, Mrs. Cohen propping her tired feet up on the extra chair. "I don't suppose you would like a story today, my precious girl?" "Oh, yes I would, Ma!" breathed Charlotte. "Will you tell me about the mermaids again? How they used to talk to you?" And her mother brought her to those magical times back in the Old Country when she was a child herself. How she went down to the river to help her own mother scrub their laundry in the shallows. How sometimes the mermaids came up from their homes in the depths and sunned themselves on the riverbank, the sea creatures and the people on the shore paying no attention to each other. How one of the mermaid children especially liked her, little Sarah Bendremer. She told her all about life under the water, and Sarah told her about houses and horses and fire. Charlotte wasn't sure which parts of the stories were real and which were made up, but it didn't matter. Inside, she felt as warm as their irons heating on the stove. She was with her mother. Her mother who made everything wonderful.

16

Louise

Louise Emily Hammond was curled up on her bedroom window seat, reading. She just loved to read. Almost as much as she loved to play nurse with her dolls. Or go barefoot. Or play in the brook, wading, jumping from rock to rock, catching chubs with fishing poles she fashioned herself with bent pins, or splashing in the swimming hole she'd helped dam up. Maybe even more. Hmm. It was hard to say. Just now she didn't care. All her attention was focused on the page in front of her.

"Louise!" Her mother's voice broke her reverie. "Louise! Are you dressed?" *Nuts. Time to get going.* She hopped down from her perch, tossed the book onto her bed, and sang out, "Yes, Mom!" Then she pulled off her nightgown and slipped into her clothes.

17

Pumpie

PEARL ELLSTINE QUICKLEY smoothed the front of her dress, nudged her hat back into place, and grasped the doorknob. Calling, "They're here! bye!" over her shoulder, she drew the door open, stepped onto the stoop, and smiled. She was named for "Aunt" Pearl, a neighbor who had no children. Every week on Dish Night Aunt Pearl and her husband would pay for a Quickley child to go to the Strand Theater and bring them back that night's free offering. If you went often enough you could collect an entire set of dishes. But today she wasn't headed for the Strand. She was on her way to church.

"Hi, Pumpie!" Her friends had arrived for the walk to church. Pearl's mother had always called her Pumpkin, but her friends had shortened it. She joined them and they all set off for Mass. Not that Pumpie was Catholic. Far from it! She was a devout Baptist. But her parents believed in keeping the seventh day holy and allowed only church activities. The children stayed in their Sunday best all day and couldn't play with their friends. They could attend church with them, though, even a Catholic church! After the St. James service, where Pumpie didn't understand most of what went on, the group made the half-mile walk back together, and she joined her family for church at Calvary Baptist, right on her own street—Ashland Street in Haverhill, Massachusetts. Her friends went home, since Catholics weren't allowed to go to Protestant services. Church was followed by Sunday school, and afterwards there was a big dinner at home. By two o'clock she was at another Sunday school at the Salvation Army. At five she went to Baptist Youth back at Calvary. Supper wasn't until seven, and by the time she'd helped with the dishes it was eight o'clock and time for bed.

18

Walt

WALTER WILLIAM KANGAS had been lulled to sleep by the steady purr of the bus's engines, and he awoke now that they were slowing. They were making a sharp turn. He lifted his head off his mother's shoulder and looked around. His bus was pulling into a parking space between two other big buses. They were at a bus station, then. Another bus station. Was this Boston? Wally pressed his face against the window, looking for something familiar. He couldn't remember what Boston looked like. It was so long ago, and he had been just a little boy. People were getting up, taking bags off the overhead racks, shuffling wearily down the aisle. His father shook his mother's shoulder. "Ellen. Wake up, Ellen. We're in Philadelphia." Philadelphia? Oh, no. They still weren't home. His father stood in the aisle and waited for his wife and son to step in front of him. They walked off the bus and into the station. Wally's stomach hurt, and his head, too. He looked up at his mother. "Ma, I'm hungry. Can I have something to eat?" She looked down at him, and Wally worried when he saw a tear in her eye. But her voice was steady. "No, Wally. Go over to the water fountain and drink as much as you can. It will make you feel better." They had eaten the last of their food, and spent the last of their money. There would be nothing to eat until they reached Boston.

When the bus pulled into the final station at last, the little family was right back where they had started two years before.

19

Elaine

DORIS ELAINE WALMSLEY, of Tiverton, Rhode Island, had a few chores at home. She washed dishes, she took care of her own room, and occasionally she cooked. Her mother's parents lived nearby, and they hired her to wash *their* dishes every night. She was paid fifteen cents a week. And she got fifteen cents per *hour* for cleaning the house. So she did learn to work. Mostly, though, Elaine played, played, and played some more. At all sorts of things.

She played piano. So did all her neighborhood friends. They all took from the same teacher and performed in two recitals every year. But Doris and her brother, younger by seventeen months, were especially accomplished. When she was in fourth grade at the North Gardner School—now the North Tiverton Fire Department building—Doris played "The Connecticut March" every single school day as the other students marched into or out of the building. (At dismissal, they left their classrooms in lines, and once they had passed through the schoolyard and reached the sidewalk they were allowed to scatter.) Her bothersome brother, who argued with their parents a lot and was a "problem" at school, was a mischief maker even at the keyboard. During piano duets with his sister, right in the middle of formal recitals, he would sometimes purposely leave his hands in her way. Oh, and by the way, Doris was never, ever called Doris. That was her mother's name. Everyone called her Elaine, her middle name. She still uses

"D. Elaine" as her signature. So I'm going to start referring to her as Elaine now.

Anyway, Elaine also played by herself, and with her small family. When she was alone she enjoyed playing with her dolls and reading. With her brother and parents she played board games such as Chinese checkers, Monopoly, and Parcheesi. She listened to radio programs like The Green Hornet, Ma Perkins, and The Lone Ranger. In 1939, when she was ten, the family took the Fall River Line boat from Providence to New York City to visit the World's Fair. For two or three summers she enjoyed a week of overnight scout camp at Camp Hoffman in West Kingston, Rhode Island, where the girls slept in tents and had primitive facilities.

Out in her back yard were raspberry bushes, and pear and apple trees to eat from and climb. And a flock of chickens. (Elaine's father and brother fed them, cleaned their coop, and gathered their eggs.) And also a doll house her father built for her, big enough for her to stand up in. One of Elaine's friends had another kind of doll house in her yard—an imaginary one that was actually just a grape arbor. The girls used both houses to pretend they were Mommies, going to the store, taking care of their babies.

Mostly, though, Elaine played with the neighborhood kids, both boys and girls, including her "pain-in-the-neck" brother. They were always outside, except Saturdays when they were at the movies in Fall River. The group spent most of the summer swimming at spots along the shore of Mount Hope Bay. They flew kites on empty lots. They played marbles and hopscotch on the dirt sidewalks, cops and robbers in the woods. Softball and dodge ball. Hide 'n' seek in the evenings. They ice skated on Duck Pond. Roller-skated on the road. Sledded. Girls pushed their doll carriages around, and boys pulled their wagons; Elaine's brother once took a white chicken from home, painted it green, and paraded it through the neighborhood in his little red wagon. The gang brought brown bag lunches to school, and when they were dismissed at noon they hopped onto their bikes and spent the hour riding, playing, and eating together. The fun and freedom just never stopped in Elaine's world.

20

Vicki

VICTORIA ANNA BRADLEY was, in her own words, "very timid." She didn't like to rock the boat. She tried hard, almost every minute of every day, to never do anything wrong or be disobedient. Otherwise, Vicki knew, she'd "get it" from her mother, meaning that she would be yelled at. She hated being yelled at.

Vicki's mother was the "boss" in the family and a very strong disciplinarian. Her father, on the other hand, was easygoing. Vicki was spanked only once in her entire life. Strangely enough, it was by her father.

She was four or five years old and had gone up a back lane that cut through the meadows in back of her house to meet her father returning from work, something she did almost every day. Sometimes—not often, but occasionally—he would take her to a little candy shop after he got home. Soon she saw him up ahead, walking with a neighbor who was also coming back from work, and she ran toward them. Mr. Bradley welcomed his little girl with a smile, but today that wasn't enough for her. Vicki's thoughts were only on candy. She asked him if they could go to the candy store, and he said no. She asked again and got the same answer. Then she did something she'd never done before: she threw a temper tantrum. She made such a scene that her father put her over his knee and spanked her.

She never had another tantrum, ever.

21

Shirley

SHIRLEY LOUISE GALE was supposed to be asleep. Instead, she was creeping into the hall and listening for sounds from downstairs. Silence. Silence. Then a low voice, followed by what sounded like the heavy kettle being placed on the stove. Good. They were both in the kitchen, then. She turned and tiptoed back toward her room. Creeeeak. Darn! Why couldn't she remember to avoid that one silly place? She froze, listening again. Nothing. They hadn't heard. Shirley slipped into her room and closed the door behind her, softly, slowly. Then she felt for the string that hung from the ceiling and pulled it. The electric bulb lit up. "All clear!" she whispered to her sisters waiting on her bed. "Who has the cards?"

"Are you sure? You know you can see light in here from under the door. I wish we had one of those little lamps you can move around. We could put it under the covers, and they'd never know!"

"Positive," Shirley answered. "They're in the kitchen. Someone start dealing."

But the game was not to be. No sooner had everyone gotten cards than they were startled by a roar coming from the bottom of the stairs. "Turn that light out!" Dad hollered. Silence. Maybe he was just guessing. "Do I have to come up there?" Nope.

The girls sprang and scattered, scurrying to their beds as Shirley yanked the light string. Rats. Maybe tomorrow night.

22

Lucy

Lucy Santo Christo had just enough time before her stepmother got home. She plunged her scrub brush back into the soapy water next to her and swished it around. Lifting it out, Lucy held the brush over the pail so the excess water could drip back in. She was tempted for a moment to rest, to look at the falling droplets plink into the water in an ever-slowing rhythm, to watch the patterns, the perfect little circular waves, appear and then fade away. *No.* Why ask for trouble? Lucy moved her brush to the next section of the pantry floor and bore down hard, scrubbing away all the dirt she could see. Her weak eyes strained to find every speck. Spotless. Spic and span. *Or else.* As she bent over her work, she heard footsteps from the other side of the wall. Someone was coming up to the apartment. Lucy froze in fear. *It wasn't fair!* She was supposed to have a whole hour to finish, and now . . . but it *wasn't* her! *She* wouldn't have knocked. *Who? Nobody ever comes up here. Who would want to?* She turned her head toward the door as her brother opened it. It was . . . !!!!!!! What on earth was her *teacher* doing here?!?!? Lucy had never, ever been so astonished. She struggled awkwardly up off her knees to greet her, but she couldn't speak as their eyes met. Neither could her teacher. She was as amazed as Lucy. She had been so sure that the girl was lying.

It was that essay. That's what Lucy learned later from her brother. Her class had been assigned to write about "what you do at home to help your parents." Well, that had been easy. Hadn't taken much thought for Lucy to come up with words to detail the tasks she was responsible for. If she and her sisters were home, they were either working or sleeping. And they wouldn't have minded the work if only they had felt loved and appreciated. They tended their stepmother's children so she could relax. And did all the housework. Every bit of it. Except for the fun stuff, like hanging curtains and "decorating." Those things she could somehow manage. But Lucy hadn't dared put that in her essay. Thank goodness she wasn't home when the teacher stopped by. She would have told the teacher Lucy had made it all up, that she only helped once in a while, that she was lazy and unreliable. And what a beating she would have given her! Lucy smiled, and closed her eyes to sleep. Finally, something had gone right for her.

23

Stillman

It was Sunday afternoon. Stillman David Haynes had been to church and had eaten a big dinner with his family. Now he was enjoying his favorite Sunday activity. "Just taking it easy," he called it. The house was quiet. His parents were resting upstairs, and nobody else was home. Stillman glanced at the living room clock and then drifted over to the radio. He twisted the power knob on and fiddled with the tuning dial, trying to guess where his station would come in best today. Then he stood by the set, watching the clock, waiting impatiently for the tubes to warm up. Three minutes. Four minutes. Four-and-a-half. Suddenly, BING! Loud and clear, no fine-tuning needed. And just in time for the announcement of the afternoon selections by the New York Philharmonic. Stillman returned to the couch, kicked off his shoes, and stretched himself out as the orchestra started to play. He closed his eyes, and music washed over him in wave after wave of refined elegance. Exquisite. Magnificent. Excitement built, the low strings were louder, faster . . . It all stopped. Nothing. Stillman waited. Then an announcement. WHAT? An American ship transporting lumber had been torpedoed and sunk, only three hundred miles off the coast of San Francisco. "That's very strange," thought the 12-year old. A moment later the music resumed, and he forgot about the peculiar news. But at intermission Stillman heard something even stranger, something so astonishing that he didn't connect it with the sinking right away. "The Japanese have attacked Pear Harbor, Hawaii, by air, President Roosevelt has just announced. The attack also was made on all naval and military facilities on the principal island of Oahu." The war! So. Now America was in it, too.

24

Nancy

NANCY HOUGHTON ELDREDGE stood in formation with her Girl Scout troop in the cool May air, lilac bunch in hand, waiting. Her gaze wandered over to the Unitarian Church, gift of oil tycoon and town benefactor Henry Huttleston Rogers and marvel of Gothic Revival style. When was it going to start, for Pete's sake? She was raising the flowers to her face for another long whiff of their heady sweetness when a whistle brought her to attention. Finally! the Memorial Day parade was getting underway. The troop inched up Green Street toward Center but within a few blocks was marching full stride to the thump and cadence of the drums from the high school band. Taking a left onto Route 6, the marchers passed the magnificent high school, another of the lavish Gothic offerings from Fairhaven's favorite son. They proceeded onto the Fairhaven-New Bedford bridge over the Acushnet River, where strong gusts blowing in from the ocean replaced the light land breeze. Nancy stepped over to the railing with the other Scouts, the stiff green fabric of her uniform flapping against her legs. It was time to release the flowers, offered in memory of fallen Navy sailors. The girls leaned over and threw their small bouquets over the side, a flurry of rushing colors. Nancy watched her lilacs fall, get caught in an updraft, and start to circle back toward her. A swooping draft intruded and carried them toward the shore until a sudden calm allowed all the blossoms to drop into the choppy water, floating and bobbing in their briny resting place.

25

Claire

FINALLY! FINALLY, FINALLY, *finally!* moving day was here. Four-teen-year-old Clairina Loretta Dube was so excited, she was having trouble keeping her mind on her work. A house! A real house. A whole building for just their own family, and nobody else. She removed the packing material from another teacup and placed it carefully on a cup-board shelf. She could hardly believe it. Heat in every room. Hot water from the faucet. Goodbye, dingy firetrap of a tenement. A refrigerator! A wash room with an electric washing machine! No more iceboxes or . . . *"Clairina! That's not where I told you to put them! Hang them on the hooks! Honestly! What is wrong with you today?"* Well, come on, Mum, what do you *think* is wrong with me? she thought as she moved the china cups. And how can *you* be so calm? Just think! No more . . . *"No, no, no! Hang them all in the same direction, like this."* Oh. Yes, of course. All day yesterday they had been here, scouring, polishing, cleaning, sweeping. Claire listened to her father and brothers clomp down the stairs from the second floor and head out to the truck for more furni-ture. She glanced into the living room. More brothers carrying in the carpet. Claire returned to the china and tried to concentrate. One of her sisters slipped a roast into the oven and started peeling potatoes. By tonight all the work would be done and they would sit down to the big Sunday meal they usually had at noontime. Was it really only this morning they had all dressed up and gone to church together from the apartment for the last time? And on returning had changed into work clothes, eaten a quick lunch, loaded furniture, swept and scrubbed the rooms, locked up, given the key to the landlord, driven away? It seemed so long ago. Part of a different life. She was a new person now, someone who lived in a real house. *Why was her mother frowning?* Claire scurried over behind her and craned her neck for a peek. The carpet had been laid; the parlor furniture carefully placed; the radio plugged in, turned on, warming up. And one of her brothers was . . . lounging in his father's armchair with his feet plunked on the ottoman, as the others returned to the truck! Just as her mother opened her mouth to scold him, the radio came to life. *Pearl Harbor. Japan. War.* Claire didn't notice as her brothers and sisters raced to the room to stand in shocked silence, listening *for how long? two minutes? two hours? two days?* She couldn't say. Suddenly, her new life had disappeared. It was part of yesterday, a yesterday far in the past. A carefree life. Without a war.

PART

TWO

Lives and Times

Psst! The beginnings of a few of our stories won't make sense unless you have read our Glimpse . . .

Oh, and no fiction from here on. All true. Through and through.

26

Kids Back in the Day

WHEN WE WERE YOUR AGE is the story of twenty-five of us, back in the day. *Our* day, long ago, when *we* were kids. Now we are in our eighties and nineties, and the oldest of us is ninety-nine. We agreed to be interviewed, to share what we remembered of our growing-up years in New England. We remembered a lot.

We were born over a span of eighteen years, from 1914 through 1932. Three of us were born before America entered the First World War, and one had graduated from high school before the youngest two were born. The seven youngest did not graduate until after the end of the Second World War. We were witnesses to a wide range of world, national, and regional events.

During the years of our childhoods, America was experiencing an explosion of technological advances. People were abandoning the slower, simpler ways of living, some of which had been around for most of human history. They were adopting devices, machinery, and technology that made their lives easier and more comfortable. The standard of living was rising. Horses were being replaced by automobiles, scrub boards by washing machines. Indoor plumbing, central heating, electricity, and telephones were becoming increasingly common. Many of our families transitioned to the use of some or all of these conveniences during our childhoods.

Hospital births were replacing home deliveries. This trend is shown clearly in our small sample. The oldest half—the thirteen born from 1914 through 1926—were all delivered at home. But nine of the twelve youngest—those born from 1927 through 1932—had hospital deliveries, including all of the 1930s births.

It was a time of nicknames. Half of us—and all but one of the boys—went by a name other than our "real" one on a daily basis. Some were common—**Tom** for Thomas, **Vicki** for Victoria—and others less so. Pearl became **Pumpie** (short for Pumpkin!) and Daisy, **Okie**.

It was also an age of immigration, but it followed several decades of even greater immigration. Although none of us were born outside the United States, fourteen—over one fourth—of our fifty collective parents were. And nine more parents were first-generation Americans.

Finally, at least twenty-one of those fifty parents were considered Yankees in full or in part. The term "Yankee" has many different definitions. In this book it is used to refer to those whose ancestors had immigrated to New England—almost always from "old" England—centuries before, or at least by the time of the Revolutionary War.

27

In Our Families
and Homes

THE TWENTY-FIVE OF US were a fortunate bunch. Although we were children during all or part of the Great Depression, our food, shelter, clothing, and education were at least minimally adequate. We all survived into adulthood, at a time when childhood mortality was much higher than it is today. Ten of us—forty percent—had brothers or sisters who died in their infancy, childhood, or teens. These deaths claimed at least twenty, or sixteen percent, of our one hundred twenty-four total siblings.

Most of us came from families that stayed together. None were split by divorce, though some were impacted by death, alcoholism, or abandonment. Five of our parents—three mothers and two fathers—died when we were between ten and eighteen years old, four due to cancer. All but four of us married, and most of us stayed married until parted by death. Only three of us were ever divorced. All but three of our spouses had passed away by the time of our interviews.

Pretty much, apart from brief periods of living with relatives at their homes or ours, we shared living quarters with only our parents and siblings. The number of children in our families ranged between one and fifteen, with an average of six. The most common number of children in our families was four.

We called our fathers Dad, Daddy, Pa, Papa, or Pop; Dad was the most popular, with Daddy in second place. Our mothers were Ma, Mother, Mom, Mama, Momma, or Mum; Ma came in first, with Mother and Mom tied for second. Fathers were almost always the sole breadwinners. Only in **Walt**'s family did both parents always work outside the home. In four others, the mother or an older sister supported the family after her husband's illness, death, or abandonment. In a few others our mothers worked seasonally or sporadically. Some of our fathers had two jobs. Ten were self-employed. Eleven were factory workers, farmers, or salesmen. Other fathers were employed as farm manager, fisherman, school administrator, fireman, tailor, truck driver, policeman, cook, executive, painter/paperer, government inspector, building contractor, custodian, barber, butcher, elevator operator, and laundry owner/operator. **Rozzy**'s oldest sister supported the family as a secretary. **Walt**'s mother was a seamstress, and the other employed mothers worked in factories, cleaned houses, or taught school. Many of our mothers had worked outside the home before marriage—some in more than one type of work. Five had worked in factories, four had done office work, and three had been teachers. Another had been a seamstress, and one had worked in a hotel.

Compared to young people today, we married young. The median age of first marriage for the four men who married was twenty-five; for the seventeen women it was twenty-one. Five were teens; two were only seventeen, but none were pregnant or already had children. Almost half married someone very close in age, within a year or less. It may come as a surprise that in only thirteen of the twenty-one first marriages was the wife younger than the husband; over one-third of the women married younger men. There was some precedence for this in previous generations: both **Tom**'s and **Beena**'s mothers were older than their husbands by nine years!

When we were interviewed, fourteen of us referred to ourselves as having been "poor" as children. But even the poor were buying homes. Sixteen of us started out in rented housing, but only eight ended our childhoods in it. Although the poorer families were more likely to rent than to own, one of the very poorest was **Okie**, whose parents owned their own house and farm, and one of the better-offs was **Ellen**, whose family always rented.

Our standard of living, as measured by how modern or primitive our facilities were, had more to do with urban versus rural locations than poverty versus affluence. We grew up at a time of rapidly growing modernization, but some segments of housing lagged behind others. Those who lived out in the country or in city tenements were the least likely to have hot water heaters, but tenements did usually have toilets. Only nine of us had both indoor plumbing and hot running water throughout our entire childhoods. Forty percent had only outhouse toilets at some point; sixty-eight percent eventually had both indoor toilets and hot water heaters.

Rural homes were more apt to be heated with stoves than furnaces, and many city tenements also lacked central heating. Just over half of us always lived in homes with furnaces; almost three-quarters of us had them by the end of childhood. Wood, gas, coal, and oil were used as fuel for furnaces and stoves. These same fuels were used in cooking. Just over half the families started with wood-fueled cook stoves. Some were upgraded to burn more than one type of fuel. One family upgraded to electric, but only in reaction to a gas explosion in their home.

Electricity had made its way into most New England homes, and on its heels was coming the convenience of electric- or gas-powered refrigerators. Seventy-two percent of our families started out without refrigerators and used a combination of iceboxes and other cold storage methods: outside sheds, cold pantries, cellar floors, and spring houses. Only forty-four percent never switched to powered cooling.

Finally, electric power was replacing "elbow grease" in the area of laundry. At some point, sixty percent of our mothers scrubbed our clothing manually in sinks or tubs. By the end of childhood the number with electric washing machines had risen to over half. Some of these were fitted with hand-cranked wringers (to "wring" the water from the dripping clothes; there was no "spin cycle"), and others had modern electric wringers. Everyone hung all the laundry on clotheslines—except **Elaine**'s parents, who bought a clothes dryer when she was in high school in the 1940s. Almost everything coming off the line needed to be ironed. Two families owned mangles, machines that simplified and improved ironing. **Beena**'s family was too poor to have even a proper ironing board; her mother had to substitute a table leaf. And we had to iron *everything*. Synthetic fabrics didn't start to be worn until the late 40s, and wrinkle-free cotton cloth wasn't invented until the 50s. Our freshly dried clothing, whether it emerged from a dryer or came off the clothesline, was an unpresentable mass of wrinkles until it was ironed.

28

Okie

Daisy Elizabeth Carleton was nicknamed "Okie" by her grandfather because she was born in Okanogan, in the state of Washington. Her parents returned to New Hampshire soon after her birth, and she spent the rest of her childhood on a farm in Meredith, near the Sanbornton town line.

Okanogan was in the far north of Washington, only fifty miles from the Canadian province of British Columbia. Okie's father, Frank Simpson Carleton, was a farmer who went west to claim a homestead tract. His first wife died giving birth to their daughter, Vada, in 1896, and his wife's parents brought the girl to Connecticut to raise. Later, Frank was joined by Okie's mother, Gertrude May North, also from Connecticut, who traveled by train across Canada to marry him. Their first child, Esther, was born in 1914, and Okie followed in 1916. A third daughter, Kathleen, or Kay, was born in 1918 after they had returned to the East. Gertrude was a Yankee whose ancestors on her father's side were traced back to the Mayflower. She dropped out of high school in New Britain to take a job on the manufacturing floor of a factory, but someone noticed she had beautiful penmanship and transferred her to the office.

Frank Carleton, also a Yankee, was born in the Sanbornton area. He hadn't graduated from high school but was intelligent and well-read, and he had attended New Hampton Literary Institute for a year.

Born *at home in Okanogan, Washington in October 1916*

When I was your age, *I had only the bare necessities. But my father had such a remarkable way of making things fun, that we found great joy in small things.*

What were your very favorite foods to eat? *I loved creamed codfish and codfish cakes.*

What else did you eat? *Corn, peas, potatoes, cooked tomatoes, cooked carrots. A rooster on Thanksgiving. One simple treat was a lettuce leaf wrap, with sugar and vinegar on the inside.*

What did you call your parents when you were young? *Daddy and Momma*

You did not attend church growing up. Is religion important to you now? *No*

How old were you when you went on your first date? *I had already graduated from high school.*

How old were you when you got married? *I was 29, and he was 30.*

What was your first full-time job? *Waitress*

What was your occupation for most of your working life? *Farm wife*

Do you think you would enjoy being a kid today? *I'm glad I'm not a kid today.*

In general, today we have many more possessions than when you were a child. Do you think this has affected our happiness? *Yes; we are less content now.*

What is your name now? *Daisy "Okie" Howe*

Did you eat beans and franks for Saturday night supper? *Yes; baked beans with salt pork.*

He left the West out of homesickness for the East, even though he insisted for the rest of his days that he preferred the open-hearted, more-accepting westerners to what he saw as New Hampshire's prim, cold-blooded population. With money from the sale of the homestead, he bought a farm in Meredith where he grew kidney beans and pop-corn as cash crops and also cut and sold just enough wood to pay his property taxes.

Okie says that she was "a skinny, freckled tomboy on a backwoods farm." She also describes herself as having been "a pretty good stu-dent, but completely lacking in being part of the social world. I had a lot of common sense but no social sense." Perhaps this was due to the isolation of the Carletons' farm: ten miles by road to the village of Meredith, and several miles to their nearest neighbor. The area was so remote that there were no churches near enough to attend, the clos-est being a summer-only in North Sanbornton. Okie doubts that they would have gone anyway: certainly not her father, but possibly her mother, who had been very religious at one time. The girls were given no religious training at all at home. However, they usually didn't do any work on Sundays, but just did "quiet things."

Even school didn't bring them into contact with many others. The closest had just one room for grades one through six. There were very few students: one year about ten kids, another couple of years eight, and, in Okie's sixth grade year, only three: Okie, Kay, and another girl. The schoolhouse was over two miles away, and the town paid their father to transport his children. But if the Carletons were isolated physically, they still felt connected to the rest of society. Okie's parents were not only well-read but also had lived for many years clear on the other side of the continent. They were aware of the world beyond their own corner.

Frank had a wonderful way of making everything fun for his girls, even farm work. He told stories as they hoed crops or brought in the hay. His daughters helped in every aspect of running the farm, but there was still plenty of time for them to play. Okie liked to be out-side. She especially enjoyed building huts in the woods with bushes and sticks. Indoors, she memorized poetry or played with the one toy she remembers having: a doll, Virginia. Her mother made clothes for

Virginia with her foot treadle sewing machine. Mr. Carleton entertained the girls by reciting long poems and inventing games for them. They also had some store-bought board games and card games, of which Authors was their favorite. Okie's parents often played chess with each other; usually Frank won, but not always.

One thing almost completely lacking in their lives was music. Every day at school the children stood to sing from their Civil War songbooks, but there were no instruments at all in the school. Okie saw a piano for the first time when she walked a few miles with her father to a neighbor's house to use their telephone. She wasn't impressed; it sounded harsh, and she didn't like it at all. (In defense of pianos, it may have been in poor condition and out of tune.)

The Carletons' farmhouse was fairly small. There were three rooms downstairs, and the girls slept upstairs. It had no electricity. They had a battery-powered radio, and Frank was very interested in world affairs and liked to hear the news. Their water source was a well that wasn't just outside, but across the road. In their outhouse, they engaged in the widespread American practice of using the Sears Roebuck catalog for toilet paper. At some point before they bought the farm, during a more prosperous time in their region, the house had been outfitted with both a telephone line and running water, but by the time they moved in there was something wrong with the pipes. Okie thinks that perhaps they hadn't been kept warm one winter and had frozen. There was no money to get the plumbing fixed, and Frank didn't have the inclination to try it himself. He preferred spending his free time reading Shakespeare and English history to making practical improvements. At least he did fix up a "well sweep" to make it a bit easier to draw water. Their sources of heat were a wood stove in the kitchen and a "chunk" stove in the living room. (Chunk stoves could take large pieces of wood and logs, so they burned longer than kitchen stoves and did not have to be tended as often.) There was no ice box; Gertrude's "refrigerator" was the bottom section of the cellar, which stayed cool year-round.

At some point the family bought a 1928 Model T Ford. Mr. Carleton didn't do particularly well at driving it, so Mrs. Carleton learned. Her husband enjoyed giving her lots of advice as she drove, though. He especially liked to tell her to "keep her spark plugs on neutral"—an expression that made no sense whatsoever. But he liked the sound of it so much he started saying it even when they weren't in the car.

After Okie graduated from Meredith High School she enrolled in a year-long course to become a dental assistant. To make ends meet, she lived with a family outside Boston as a mother's helper, something she now refers to as "a dumb job." When the course ended, she and a friend from the school went to Florida and worked as waitresses. There they met a Russian cook who offered them a ride to California in a new car he had just bought. They went, but after America entered the war Okie returned to New England. She and her sister Kay got jobs in East Hartford, Connecticut, at Pratt & Whitney, the nation's leading manufacturer of aircraft engines. Then Okie decided to join the service. In 1942, when she was twenty-five, she enlisted in the newly-formed Women's Army Corps. She was trained as a radio operator and stayed in the military for four years on assignments in the U.S., England, France, and Belgium. Okie was stationed in Belgium when word came that the war had ended. She rejoiced alongside the Belgians, who were wild with joy, literally dancing in the streets. After the war she came home, married a farmer—a local boy who had also been in the service—and had three sons and one daughter.

At ninety-seven, Okie still remembers "volumes" of poetry she memorized in her youth, but she finds it extremely difficult to add new material, as memorization is "much, much harder now." One of her greatest joys is putting her thoughts and poems onto paper. At the New Hampshire Veterans Home in Tilton, where she resides, she attends a weekly writers' group and posts her writing on her own web site.

29

Adrianne

ADRIANNE WAS BORN in Pepperell, Massachusetts, the youngest of three children. Betty was four years older, and Philip two years. Her father, Harold Frederick Gray, who was probably of Scottish descent, was born in Waltham, Massachusetts, the fourth of five children. His great-grandfather Gray had immigrated to Canada in 1813. Both of his parents had been born in Nova Scotia and moved to Prince Edward Island as children so their families could take advantage of a government program that opened up land for settlement. Harold's father, Adney, came from a family of eleven children. Only six of them lived to adulthood, consistent with the mortality rate of the time. One brother died after being caught in a hay baler, and another as a baby, probably from what is known today as sudden infant death syndrome. One evening he was "playing before the fire" at their open hearth. He seemed healthy and happy when put to bed, but the next morning he was found dead. Adney left Canada for the Boston area when he was in his late teens. He was a big man, with big hands, and very industrious. First he worked as a logger and then he got a job delivering ice, which was how he met Harold's redheaded mother, Hannah Elizabeth Williams. Hannah had also left Canada in her late teens, and she had found a job in a doctor's household in Waltham as an upstairs maid. When she and the ice delivery boy decided to marry, her employers offered their living room for the ceremony. Adney later became an engineer on the

Born *at home in Pepperell, Massachusetts in July 1925.*

When I was your age, *my mother would say, "Use it up, wear it out, make do, do without."*

What were your very favorite foods to eat? *Lobster and ice cream*

Did you or your friends ever eat out at restaurants or diners? *No*

You were required to attend church growing up. Is religion important to you now? *Yes*

Did you ever address adults by their first names? *No*

What did you call your parents? *Daddy and Mamma*

What was your first job while you were still in school? *I delivered newspapers and weekly grocery fliers, and I babysat.*

How old were you when you went on your first date, and where did you go? *I was in high school and my future husband, Bud, was at Yale. I went with him to a Christian Endeavor meeting at his church.*

How old were you when you got married? *I was almost 20, and he was 25.*

What was your first full-time job? *I was a secretary at Chance Vought Aircraft, which later became Sikorsky Aircraft.*

What was your occupation for most of your working life? *I ran an antiques business and ski school with my husband.*

Many things have been invented since you were a child. What has given you the most pleasure, or been the most valuable to you? *Cell phones*

What do you think you would most enjoy about being a kid today? *Texting!*

What would you most dislike? *Having so little free time*

Today we hear that the lives of many American children are very stressful. Was yours stressful in any way? *No. We weren't programmed. We had time to ourselves.*

What is your name now? *Adrianne "Ade" Lauridsen*

Did you eat beans and franks for Saturday night supper? *Yes, and the practice was very widespread at the time. Our beans were usually canned, but sometimes homemade. My mother had a very good recipe.*

Boston and Maine Railroad, and later still the general manager of a leatherboard factory in Townsend, Massachusetts.

Mary Augusta Scharff, Adrianne's mother, was of Dutch, English, and Yankee descent. She was born in 1894 in Tacoma, Washington and moved to Connecticut as a young girl. She later graduated from a "normal school"—a college for training teachers—in New Haven. Her parents, Augustus (Gus) Scharff and Annie Curtis, had met as teachers in the Washington Territory before it became a state. When they returned East with their three young children they settled in Orange, Connecticut. Gus worked in the laboratories at Yale Medical School, and at home he tended his big garden, smoked a pipe, and drank tea out of a saucer after pouring it from his cup. He was born in Newark, New Jersey in 1863. His father, Christian Henry Scharff, had come to New Jersey from Harlem, in the Netherlands, where he had been born in 1834. Christian's mother—Gus's Dutch grandmother—was the model for the old Dutch grandmother in the original illustrations of the children's book *Hans Brinker or The Silver Skates* by the American author Mary Mapes Dodge, which was published in 1865.

Gus's mother was Adeline Seward. Her father had died young, and she became the ward of his brother and grew up in his family home in the town of Florida, New York. This brother was one of the most powerful men in the nation, William H. Seward. He was Abraham Lincoln's Secretary of State and a former United States senator.

Mary's mother, Annie Curtis, was born in Connecticut, but the family was originally from Vermont. Her father, Henry Curtis, was an engraver. Adrianne has both Annie's and Henry's school slates. In one-room country schools of their day, most of the written work was done on these, as paper was expensive. Annie's is ten by fourteen inches. Her name is carved into the wood frame, probably by her engraver father. But slates must have been costly as well. Henry's smaller seven-by-eleven board has his name beautifully lettered with white paint on one side, and his cousin's—H.W. Hubbard—on the other! They shared a desk and held the slate between them so they could both write on it.

Harold Gray, Adrianne's father, served in the U.S. Army during World War I, and he received the Purple Heart. He was wounded twice, and his health was also permanently damaged in an attack of poison gas. He had inherited from his mother a bleeding disorder, von Willebrand disease, which Adrianne inherited as well. This condition was made even worse by the gas attack and war wounds. All this added up to a lifetime of health problems, and he was constantly in and out of hospitals for treatments and operations.

At the time of Adrianne's birth in 1925, Harold owned and operated the Brookside Laundry in Pepperell with his brother Willard. By 1928, however, the business was in trouble. Bleach had been introduced to the laundry business and had quickly become popular among customers, who appreciated the fresh, clean appearance it gave their laundry. Willard refused to use bleach, perhaps objecting to its harsh chemical nature, so they started losing customers. The brothers held on to the business by a thread, but the thread broke one very cold night in 1928 when the boilers froze and the pipes burst. The equipment was ruined and there was no money for repairs, so that was the end of the laundry. That summer, Harold moved his family to Milford, Connecticut, on Long Island Sound, and his father took over the home that Harold owned in Massachusetts. Mrs. Gray had relatives in neighboring West Haven and Orange and had found a teaching job in Milford. She would now be the main breadwinner in the family. On moving day she made the long drive in a pouring rain in their car with the two older children, and Adrianne kept her father company in his big white laundry truck.

Until they bought a home in the summer of 1936, the family lived in four different rentals. The first, a brick house on North Street in Milford, had no insulation and was terribly cold. It had a coal furnace but no pump to circulate the heated air. There was only a large grate on the first floor, opening directly into the furnace, and another grate on the second floor that helped heat to rise upstairs. Of course items were accidentally dropped through the grate into the furnace. On one occasion, Mr. Gray removed the first-floor grate, fastened a rope to Betty, and lowered her right into the furnace (which currently had no hot coals in it). She picked up whatever she was sent to retrieve and then scooped up some extras that former inhabitants had dropped as well, such as coins and jewelry! Next they moved to a home on Housatonic Avenue, but in 1930, Mrs. Gray's parents' rural cottage in Orange became available, and they took that over for a couple of years. Her sixty-four-year old father had recently died, and her mother had gone "out West" to care for a cousin in San Francisco. In 1932, when Adrianne was in the second grade, they moved back to Milford: to Devon, a shorefront section of town. They rented a home on Hackett Avenue, close to her mother's school, until finally being able to buy a house just around the corner, on Judson Place.

The new house was only a few years old and very modern. There was central heating from a coal furnace that they soon converted to oil, and a full bathroom on the second floor. It was quite a contrast to the cottage they'd rented from Adrianne's grandmother, with its outhouse in the back yard and a "bathroom" inside that was only for baths. Water for those baths had to heated on the stove and then dumped into the tub. This house, however, had a gas hot water heater in the basement that would . . . explode! if not properly handled. It built up too much steam if left on for more than fifteen or twenty minutes, so they had to be very careful. As soon as they could afford to, they replaced it with a hot water system that worked off the furnace. In 1937 they replaced the icebox with a refrigerator. Then they made one more change. They had always had gas stoves. One day Mr. Gray had struck a match to light the oven (the standard way to start it up). He hadn't realized that gas had built up inside; perhaps there was a small leak he didn't know about. The gas exploded in his face and blew him across the room. Fortunately he was not injured, but he yelled, "That's it!" and went out and bought a Westinghouse electric. They had a very modern home in one other way. Adrianne's father had enjoyed operating his business. He was always interested in the latest laundry conveniences, so they had a "mangle" to make the ironing easier, and in 1939 they also installed a Bendix washing machine, which had been introduced in 1937 as the first automatic washer for home use.

The Grays had a comfortable home. They had a telephone, and they owned a car, although Mrs. Gray walked to work, as she enjoyed the exercise. Like most families, they had one radio. Theirs was a small Zenith with a mysterious button on it. It was labeled as the place to hook up something nobody (including them) had: a television! It might have seemed to a casual observer that they were well-to-do, but they were not. The Grays were extremely careful with their money and used it wisely. Teachers, especially females, didn't make much. Harold was occasionally able to work and also received a small income from an insurance policy.

Philip was responsible for shoveling the snow and for emptying the tray under the ice box every morning so it wouldn't overflow. (As the ice melted and dripped from the big blocks of ice, water collected in this tray.) Little girls wore starched cotton dresses to school, and by the age of eight Adrianne had learned to iron hers all by herself. She was also expected to do the dishes daily and to make her bed. On Saturdays she swept, vacuumed, or scrubbed all the floors and hung the wash on the line. Then she was free to play or go to the movies.

Adrianne's parents enjoyed playing bridge with friends, and taking the family to the beach and to civic celebrations. She remembers a 1936 ceremony marking the three hundredth anniversary of the town of Milford. Mr. Gray belonged to the Masonic Lodge, and Mrs. Gray to the Eastern Star, and they were active in the Episcopal church. After church on Sundays they ate a big dinner and then might have friends over for bridge. The couples' children would spend the afternoon playing with each other.

The family enjoyed card games and board games and participating in the Devon Fife and Drum Corps. The two sisters were on fife, Philip played bugle, and Mr. Gray was the organization's treasurer. Adrianne was also a Girl Scout and sometimes went on camping weekends with her troop. Mostly, though, she had plenty of free time to spend as she wished. Normally she played outside with her friends, who all lived nearby. They did gymnastics together in their yards, played hopscotch and marbles, rode their scooters and bikes, sledded, and skated. Sometimes the girls joined the boys for hide 'n' seek or ringalevio. They also watched the construction of new houses, where horses pulled equipment to excavate sites. There was always a huge mound of dirt left around from the latest excavation, making a great place for a game of "king of the hill." She also enjoyed playing with paper dolls, reading, and playing her violin. One summer she learned to knit, because she had a problem with her knee and couldn't do much outside.

The family ate all their meals together, and the children had to eat everything, even what they didn't like, and finish everything on their plates. Mrs. Gray left soon after breakfast and was home again for a lunch of soup or sandwiches. Supper was usually meat, potato, and a vegetable. (Occasionally Adrianne's mother would prepare a salad and then forget to serve it; it would be found in the ice box after the meal.) Holiday meals were special. Her mother loved to have a goose at Christmas, but if money were too tight they'd have a turkey instead.

Adrianne started school in 1931, at the age of six. She liked school very much and preferred the strict teachers, who "had good guide-lines and kept better control." Rulers were used for corporal punish-ment, and sometimes they had a metal strip on them, which could cut students' hands. One crazy thing happened to her in about the third grade. A girl in her class named Edna came up to her at recess and, for no apparent reason, pulled Adrianne's skirt up to her neck. It was horribly humiliating. Edna was punished, and hopefully she never did it to anyone again.

It was about a ten-minute walk to the Devon school using a short-cut Adrianne took through back yards. It would have taken longer sticking to streets, but cutting through yards was an acceptable practice. She rode a bus when she attended Milford High School, which was a couple of miles away. School was occasionally canceled for severe weather. After a blizzard in 1934 school was out for days. In 1938 it was out for weeks after a hurricane.

After high school, Adrianne took a two-year secretarial course at The Booth & Bayliss Commercial School in Bridgeport. After working for a few months, she married Bud, the boy you met in Adrianne's Glimpse. He had been a good friend of her sister and had stayed in close touch with the family in the years after her untimely death. Bud was a student at Yale when war was declared. He tried to join the service but was rejected because an x-ray revealed a spot on his lungs that was thought to indicate tuberculosis. However, he never did develop the disease, and the spot was probably just scarring from where he had broken his collarbone as a child.

Adrianne had a happy childhood and home life with her brother, sister, and parents. She is grateful that it was not "programmed" and that she had time to herself. She felt "so lucky, so loved." When she was very young, her brother had teased her mercilessly, which bothered her until her mother explained that he only did it because he liked her so much. But her family endured two great sorrows. First her sister and then, three years later, her brother, died in tragic accidents: Betty at fifteen, and Philip at sixteen. Now an eighty-eight-year old widow living in New Hampshire she feels, not surprisingly, that the most important thing in life is love, and the least important, money. She learned young to appreciate how precious and fragile life is.

30

Sonny

AT EIGHTY-ONE YEARS OLD, Mr. Miconi shakes his head as he remembers his hooky-playing past: the days spent crouched in hiding with his wayward pals, trying to evade the truant officer. Sometimes the boys won, and sometimes the Law.

Louis was the third of four boys, and the fifth child of nine. Since he had the same name as his father, he was called Sonny from the time he was born. His parents, hardworking immigrants, spoke both Italian and English at home. Anna Scivone, Sonny's mother, was born in either Italy or Sicily. She came to Connecticut with her parents at the age of six, and her father died when she was young. Before marriage she worked in a candy factory in New Haven. Louis Miconi came to America by himself at about sixteen from Italy, where his parents owned an olive farm in a small village outside Rome. He did painting and papering for a living.

Louis and Anna scrimped and sacrificed for years, raising nine children in a cramped, uncomfortable New Haven tenement on Legion Avenue while saving for the American Dream: owning a home. At last they were able to buy a seven-room house in neighboring West Haven. It needed to be completely gutted and sheet rocked, but they all worked at the task. In 1941 the family moved into the home on the corner of North Union and Richards that they had rebuilt with their own hands. The comfort differences were huge. The apartment had been heated

Born *in a hospital in New Haven, Connecticut in October 1932*

When I was your age, *I didn't have much money to spend so I earned it wherever I could.*

What was your very favorite food to eat? *Spaghetti and meatballs*

Did you ever eat at restaurants or diners? Did your friends? *No*

You were required to attend church growing up. Is religion important to you now? *Yes. As an adult, I opened a Bible at random one day to the book of Romans and started reading. I kept reading the Bible and became an Evangelical. My oldest brother and four of my sisters also became born again after having been staunch Catholics.*

Did you ever address adults by their first names? *No*

What did you call your parents? *Papa and Mama*

What was your first job while still in school? *Shining shoes, at age 7*

How old were you when you went on your first date, and where did you go? *I was about 16, and I had a car. We went to a theater in Hartford. We all usually went to movies at theaters or drive-ins for dates. I took my sister's friend to the prom at West Haven High. Proms were held in the gym, and everyone would go out afterward.*

How old were you when you got married? *I was 28, and my wife was 21.*

What was your first full-time job? *U.S. Army*

What was your occupation for most of your working life? *Electronics technician/electrician*

Many things have been invented since you were a child. What has given you the most pleasure, or been the most valuable to you? *Television, computers*

Is there anything you wish had never been invented? *The atomic bomb*

How would you like to be a kid today? *I wouldn't like the peer pressure to do drugs.*

By *today's standards*, did you have a lot of "stuff" growing up? *No, I had very little.*

In general, today we have many more possessions than when you were a child. Do you think this has affected our happiness? *It has made us more comfortable, but not necessarily happier.*

Did you eat beans and franks for Saturday night supper? *No*

with small oil stoves in the front room and the kitchen. In the coldest weather, Anna lit the oven and kept its door open for added warmth, but it was still so chilly that the four boys, who all slept in the same bed, kept their clothes on and piled their coats over the covers as well. Hot water was heated on the stove and poured into the bathtub for the girls' baths, but the boys were sent weekly to a nearby shower house where they could get clean for a nickel. The new house, on the other hand, boasted a coal/wood furnace and hot water heater. A refrigerator replaced the ice box. No more washing clothes on a scrub board in the bathtub, because they had an electric washer with a hand-operated wringer attachment. Perhaps best of all for a large family were the two full bathrooms, and three-quarter bath in the basement. And at last Sonny's father had space for a garden, and for a wine cellar. He made his own wine from grapes he bought at Long Wharf. The children ground them and put them into barrels to ferment. Louis also made sausages, which he hung in the wine cellar. They had a car, which he needed for work, a radio, and, for the first time, a telephone.

Much as he enjoyed the new house, Sonny was sad to leave New Haven. In the tenement, his sister had told them scary stories at night, out in the dark hallway at the top of the long stairway. And outside he loved the noise, the action, the feeling that something was always going on. The streets were especially alive in the summer, and he was allowed to stay up late and be part of it. His neighborhood was an American melting pot, full of Italians, Jews, Poles, Irish, and African-Americans. There was no trouble between the groups, though things could get wild: once, another kid dropped a brick out a third story window and hit him on the head. But he hadn't been trying to hurt anyone; as always, it was only in fun. Also, there weren't many chores for him in the tenement, but the move changed that. While their sisters cleaned and their mother washed and cooked, the boys fed chickens and cleaned their coop, cut wood for the furnace, weeded the garden, cut the grass with a reel (non-power) mower, and dug up the yard each spring for their large garden. Every few years they repainted the green picket fence, and the boys fought over who got to paint the outside, which was easier than the inside. They also quibbled over whose turn it was to work. Meanwhile, their friends were playing baseball without them. Most of the disagreements were between Sonny and his younger brother Harry. They argued a lot. Sonny didn't appreciate Harry always tagging along with his friends. He also resented Harry for being his parents' favorite.

Sonny got into plenty of mischief. Hooky was bad enough, but his parents would have been even more horrified if they'd known what else he was up to. One trick he and his friends played in New Haven was snitching donuts cooling on racks that hung out of the windows of the Elmer Brothers bakery, where their cousin worked the counter. They always risked being chased down the street by her husband, the baker. In West Haven, his substitute for donut snatching was raiding other people's fruit trees with his new friends. They also ran a couple of scams in New Haven. The first was harmless: placing an old wallet on the sidewalk right next to bushes, making sure the string they'd attached didn't show, and then hiding in the bushes. When someone came along and started to pick it up, they yanked the wallet back by the string. Another was quite offensive. They would put Sonny's younger brother on a stretcher and made him appear to be sick. Right next to him on the street was a carton for donations to a "fresh air fund" that would actually go into the young delinquents' own pockets.

One time they picked the wrong target. They sometimes acted as lookouts for older boys shooting dice in an alleyway between their apartment house and the next building. Because it involved betting, the game was illegal. The young boys, perched on the roof, could see police approaching and alert the players in time for them to scoop up their stuff and scatter. Once, when they knew there was a lot of money on the ground and the boys wouldn't have time to gather it all, they yelled, "Police!" Then they jumped off the roof to collect the loot. The older boys ran off at first but caught on when they saw there were no police in the area. They turned around and caught the little guys before they could get away.

Not everything Sonny did was felonious. He was actually quite industrious. Since his parents couldn't provide him with any pocket money, he worked for it. In New Haven, at age seven, he had his first job: shining shoes. Following in his older brothers' footsteps, he got a license from the "shoe shine club" and was assigned a street location. This territory was his alone, and nobody else was supposed to work it. He did well, earning enough to go roller skating every Saturday. Sonny's older brother Tony had an especially good corner spot—so good that he sometimes rented it out to others. But he didn't allow anyone to use it without permission; he beat up intruders and threw them off the corner. After the move to West Haven in 1941, Sonny tried setting up a shoeshine shop on the streets there. Everyone ignored him. Finally he guessed folks in West Haven "didn't care about getting their shoes shined" and gave up. Instead, he mowed lawns, shoveled snow, worked summers for his father, had a job in a florist's shop, and delivered groceries carried in a basket on his bike. He sometimes returned to New Haven for yet another way to pick up extra cash. When Yale University had Saturday football games, open-air trolleys transported fans to the Yale Bowl. Sonny and his friends ran alongside the open cars yelling,

"Scramble!" This was the signal for passengers to throw coins out of the trolley and watch the youngsters "scramble" for them.

Sonny didn't have many playthings, but he was resourceful. He made a scooter out of orange crates and old roller skate wheels, and made or refurbished ice skates and sidewalk skates. At a Jewish community center, he sometimes borrowed from the toy lending library. He and his friends got their winter thrills "sled riding" on hilly, snow-covered New Haven streets. After pulling their sleds into position in back of stopped cars, they held onto bumpers with one hand and their sleds with the other while being pulled downhill at breakneck speed.

As a little boy, Sonny's favorite thing to do with his friends was skipping school. As a teenager, it was hanging around the drugstore to listen to popular music on the juke box. In between, it was playing on the street: dodge ball, softball, ringalario. There was an open storage shed belonging to a factory at the end of their street that neighborhood kids used as a clubhouse, playing among drums and tanks of chemicals. They swam at favorite spots in New Haven, West Haven, and Milford. Walked to the country club in Orange trying, always unsuccessfully, to get caddy jobs. Went to the theater to see cowboy movies. And listened to their favorite radio shows: The Inner Sanctum, The Green Hornet, and The Shadow. And on summer evenings he played hide 'n' seek, softball, and football with his family.

He got into scrapes. Coming down a steep hill in West Haven with another boy riding on his handlebars, Sonny lost his brakes and hit the iron fence at a cemetery. The other child was unhurt, but Sonny broke his collarbone. Another time, he was at the Y playing "Frankenstein" in the locker room. In this game, someone would hide in a locker and jump out when the others came by. Then they all pretended to be scared as they screamed and ran. Once, Sonny got carried away and put his hand through a glass door. He needed stitches, which were put in without any anesthetic.

Sonny's parents were Catholic, and religion was important to them. They didn't go to church regularly, but the children were required to. After church there was a big Italian dinner. Sometimes on summer Sunday afternoons they went to Fort Hale Park for a picnic on the beach. These picnics, and occasional day trips to his mother's sister in Waterbury, were all the "vacation" they ever had. Summer was his father's busiest time and he couldn't afford to take time off. His parents sometimes got away by themselves, though. Every Wednesday—Dish Night—they went to the movies at the White Way Theater. And his father belonged to an Italian club off Legion Avenue that offered the pleasures of a bar, cards, and bocce.

Easter and Christmas were Sonny's favorite holidays. On Easter, they had lasagna, ham, and potatoes; on Christmas, ham, salads, macaroni, and meatballs. There were no presents on Christmas, but it was still a lot of fun. The kids had a treasure hunt for the pennies and candy Mr. Miconi had hidden all over the house.

As the only picky eater in the family, Sonny wasn't forced to eat anything, but he was scolded about it. The food he most disliked was cabbage. He usually ate toast for breakfast, and sometimes scrambled eggs. He didn't like milk and was allowed cocoa instead. Lunch was a bologna or ham sandwich. Supper was the biggest meal of the day: maybe ham slices or chicken; salad; tomatoes from their garden; an Italian dish with beans, macaroni, and pepperoni. This was followed by olives and cheese.

There was something Sonny disliked even more than cabbage: school. He didn't like to read, and school involved lots of that. But in high school he settled down, got serious about studying, and started getting good marks and enjoying school. He even chose to wear a tie and suit jacket. The older he got, the higher his grades got, and the only class he had difficulty with in high school was typing. But he had gotten off to a slow start as a young child. Sonny had started public preschool a month before he turned five and gone on to kindergarten and first grade. Halfway through first grade he was sent back to kindergarten— for fighting, as he remembers it. (One day his class was lined up for the bathroom, and another kid cut in line in front of him. Sonny didn't let him get away with it.) It's hard to believe that was the only reason for being sent back, but who knows? It happened over seventy years ago.

One incident with a terribly insensitive teacher stands out in Sonny's mind after all these years. In 1941, before he moved to West Haven midway through the school year, his teacher was a Miss Shoemaker. Sonny liked her, and he often stayed after school to help her care for her plants—watering, pulling off dead leaves. One day she called him to her desk and told him in front of everyone to go home and ask his mother to give him a bath and wash his hair. Embarrassed, he went home, and his mother did as requested. On his return, Miss Shoemaker made things even worse: she stood him in front of the class and asked, "Now, doesn't he look much better?" Sonny was totally humiliated. He remembers trying to regain his dignity by announcing, "Well, I don't care, because I'm moving to West Haven." He felt betrayed: she had publicly disgraced him after he had been so nice to her.

Student behavior was pretty good through the sixth grade. In seventh or eighth they had a science teacher, Mrs. Logan, who was too lenient, and of course the kids took advantage. Sonny became the class clown. A teacher he especially enjoyed in high school was Miss Dodd, sister of future U.S. Senator Thomas Dodd (who was the father of later U.S. Senator Christopher Dodd). He understood her style of teaching and got an A in her civics course while also helping his friends to learn the material.

Sonny had a pretty happy childhood. All he could remember ever wanting and not having were two things: a bicycle long before he got one; and milk and cookies at morning recess when he was little. He ate well at home, but there was no food or money left over for any kind of snacks. He graduated from West Haven High School in 1952, during the Korean War, and went right into the Army, where he served in the Signal Corps. On discharge, he worked as a laborer, helping build parts of Interstate 95 while some of his buddies were getting valuable career training on the G.I. Bill at the Connecticut School of Electronics. Sonny eventually joined them there, partly because his boss had lied about him, which had resulted in his being unjustly fired, but also because he had realized he didn't want to spend his whole life doing pick-and-shovel work.

Looking back at what he has learned in his long life, Sonny has only one regret. He learned how to dance after he met his wife, but he sure would have enjoyed knowing how earlier.

31

Shirl

HALLOWEEN WAS ALWAYS FUN for Shirl. But then, so were Christmas, Thanksgiving, and the Fourth of July. It was hard to pick a favorite. She liked the big parade on Memorial Day, too. The Fourth was especially fun, with a carnival at the Sacred Heart field, two special parades for children—one for bicycles, one for doll carriages—and neighborhood gatherings to set off fireworks. There was fun the rest of the year, too. On Saturdays she could see movies at the town hall. In the winter she could sled down Pettee's Hill and skate on Lake Massapoag or Mann's Pond. The town even sent a sidewalk snowplow to clear the ice. Sharon, Massachusetts was a good place for a kid to grow up.

Shirl enjoyed playing with her dolls and being with her friends. They jumped rope, played hopscotch, rode their bikes or scooters, roller skated, and went for walks. And played marbles. "Emmy Hassam lived on Billings Street, and she had a large front yard where we would play marbles—mostly girls but sometimes boys too," Shirl recounted. "We would make a hole in the dirt with the heel of our shoe and then smooth out its edges. Then we'd bend down or sit on the ground behind a line drawn with a stick. With our fingers we'd shoot or flip the marbles, one at a time, trying to get them into the hole." Or they joined neighborhood boys at large fields on Billings Street and Cottage Street to play group games like Capture the Flag and Red Rover. Dwight Derry, who was a few years younger than Shirl, flew gas-propelled model airplanes

Born *at Norwood Hospital, Norwood, Massachusetts in October 1928*

When I was your age, *I liked to daydream in school.*

What were your very favorite foods to eat? *I liked almost everything, but especially my mother's Swedish meatballs that she prepared in a pressure cooker.*

What did you like least? *I didn't like fish or liver.*

Did you or your friends ever eat out at restaurants or diners? *Yes, we did*

You were not required to attend church growing up. Is religion important to you now? *Yes, it is*

Did you ever address adults by their first names? *Generally not. Close friends of my parents I called "Aunt" Nellie, "Uncle" George, etc. Others were all called Miss, Mrs., or Mr.*

What did you call your parents? *Daddy and Mum*

What was your first job while you were still in school? *Summers, I worked at a snack shop owned by Cliff Jerauld, at the large lake near the center of town. Winters, I babysat.*

How old were you when you went on your first date, and where did you go? *There was an after-school dance for the sixth grade, and Elliot Aronson asked me to it. I didn't want to go with him, but my mother made me! Probably my first "real" date, though, was with Rus White when I was sixteen. I went—walked!—to the Sophomore Hop with him.*

How old were you when you got married? *I was 23, and Bob was 26.*

What was your first full-time job? *Receptionist for an advertising agency*

What was your occupation for most of your working life? *Church secretary*

Many things have been invented since you were a child. What has given you the most pleasure, or been the most valuable to you? *TV has both good points and bad. Other inventions I have found valuable are computers, calculators, dryers, freezers, and self-cleaning ovens.*

What do you think you would most enjoy about being a kid today? *I think that I would enjoy having so many opportunities to do things, have things.*

What would you most dislike? *Kids don't make their own fun as much as we did. Too much is planned for them.*

By *today's standards*, did you have a lot of "stuff" growing up? *No, not at all*

In general, today we have many more possessions than when you were a child. Do you think this has affected our happiness? *I think that people were happier when I was young. They spent more time together as families. Their values were more family-oriented.*

Today we hear that the lives of many American children are very stressful. Was yours stressful in any way? *No. Well, maybe school was a little stressful. I didn't like book reports!*

What is your name now? *Shirley Ann Schofield*

Did you eat beans and franks for Saturday night supper? *Yes*

with his friends at the Cottage Street field, where Shirl's parents had played baseball with neighborhood boys when they first moved to Sharon. In 1950 the Cottage Street School was built on the site.

Her parents had both been poor growing up. They told their children stories about sleeping three to a bed, and wearing socks with holes. Shirl's mother, Dora Mildred Clement, had picked blueberries that she sold for five cents a pail. Dora was a high school graduate who was born in North Walpole, New Hampshire, right across the Connecticut River from Bellows Falls, Vermont where she attended school. She also went to the Congregational Church in Bellows Falls as there were no Protestant churches in North Walpole. The town was almost entirely Catholic, and supposedly the Clements were the only Protestants. Dora's family was Yankee, with roots throughout New England. The Clements had come to Haverhill, Massachusetts from England in the 1600s, and her branch went from there to Bucksport and Ellsworth in Maine, before settling in New Hampshire. Dora's mother's ancestors, the Thomases, had settled in Marshfield, Massachusetts before relocating to Middleboro and later still to Vermont.

Frank Harris, Shirl's father, was a World War I veteran who had moved to Sharon to work at Plymouth Rubber Company in neighboring Canton. Although he had not graduated from high school, he climbed the ranks from General Manager to Vice President and Director. Frank, who was Jewish but not observant, was the son of Annie Bashner and Israel Harris. Israel's parents, Susan and Henry Harris, lived and died in eastern Europe, in what is now either Poland or Russia. Israel was a tailor, and he immigrated to the United States via Liverpool, England. It is not known how long he may have lived in England, but he sailed with his family for this country about 1880. His wife had died, leaving him with a daughter, and he had married a widow with a son. Six more children, five sons and one daughter, were born to them as a couple. Although both girls married Jewish men, five of the six boys married out of the faith, which was very unusual at the time. Only Shirl's Uncle Dave had a Jewish wife. When Shirl was growing up, her father sometimes went to David's home for meals during Jewish holidays.

Both parents were active members and volunteers in civic and municipal groups and clubs, and Frank was an air raid warden during the war. They enjoyed playing bridge, going to ball games and horse races, and playing sports and games with Shirl and her brother Buzzie, two years younger. Frank got two weeks of vacation, and by the time

Shirl was eight or ten they were renting a cottage every summer on New Silver Beach in Falmouth. Shirl also tried Girl Scout camp one summer at Camp Child in Plymouth. She signed up for three weeks and was enjoying herself until her parents came on visiting day after the first week. Seeing them made her homesick, and she left camp with them.

Neither Frank nor Dora attended any religious services, but both Shirl and Buzzie became involved at the Congregational Church. Shirl started going in high school because her friends went there. Around fourth grade, Buzzie wanted to join Amici Fellowship, a boys' group that did woodworking and other projects with the pastor, Mr. Jonas. Boys were supposed to be from the church, but after the pastor got to know Mr. Harris he allowed Buzzie to join. Frank ended up giving financial support to both the Congregational church and the United Jewish Appeal.

Shirl had a typical middle-class life: light chores like dishwashing and setting the table; quarrels over silly things with her brother; arguments with her parents about how late she was allowed to stay out; radio programs like The Shadow as a kid, and popular music in high school; movies and dances at the town hall and the high school gym; candlepin bowling at the Cloverleaf on Route 1 in Norwood; Raiders Restaurant on Route 1 with groups of high school friends after dances and basketball games; piano lessons. Sharon got a lot of snow, and every family member pitched in to shovel it.

Like some other children whose parents did not struggle to put food on the table, Shirl was not required to eat foods she didn't like, or to finish everything on her plate, although she usually did anyway. She was allowed to snack between meals, which for her meant bread with mayonnaise after school. There was often fish on Fridays; her father especially liked deep-fried haddock for Friday supper. They had the leftovers cold for Saturday lunch, with vinegar poured over them. During the war her mother often served chicken-in-a-can by Banquet—an entire cooked chicken squished into a tin can! Shirl remembers that it was moist and "very tasty." On Sunday there was a big meal at noon, often with guests. Ham on Easter. Beans and franks on Saturday night.

Elementary school students had an hour off at lunch. A big urn of soup was prepared so that those who lived too far away to get home could have a hot meal. Occasionally Mrs. Harris was away at noon and Shirl would buy the school lunch, but otherwise she walked home. Usually she had a sandwich and soup; however, she remembers having canned La Choy chicken chow mein on the day her class watched the Hindenburg come over Sharon. [For the details, see chapter 56.]

A couple of months before she turned six, Shirl started first grade. The school day ran from nine to three: six hours total, which was about four-and-a-half hours of instructional time plus two recesses and the hour for lunch. First-graders went to the School Street School, second- and third-graders to High Street, and fourth- and fifth graders to Pleasant Street. Grades six and up were at the high school. Shirl liked Abbie Matheson, her sixth-grade teacher, but didn't care for "Pop" Avery, her eighth-grade homeroom teacher. She learned a lot with Margaret Wells in cooking and sewing class in grades six through eight. A stuffed elephant, an apron, and a pillowcase were among the items she made. Her mother didn't make any of her clothing, but Shirl learned enough at school to later be able to make clothes for her own daughter. And when school was cancelled due to weather, the fire department blew a 7-3-3 signal on its whistle.

The Harris family was comfortable financially. They owned a car, and both Frank and Dora drove it; when Dora needed it for the day she drove her husband to work. They owned their home and had at least two radios. In the early 1940s they added an extension telephone, which they placed on the second floor at the top of the stairs. There was one bathroom, an oil furnace, a gas stove, and a refrigerator. Dora had an up-to-date laundry setup, but washing the clothes was still a lot of work. Shirl describes the process: "Mother had a round metal washing machine with a hand wringer attached. It sat on a platform in the basement, next to the set tubs—I think that is what they were called. There was a soapstone sink with two deep tubs and water faucets. She filled both those tubs with water. After items were washed in the machine, she put them through the wringer, and they dropped into tub #1. She swished them around to get soap off and then re-adjusted the wringer so that they dropped into tub #2 for a second rinse after another wringing. Then the wringers were moved once again so that the clean clothes from tub #2 landed in a laundry basket. Mother carried that via the bulkhead steps to the back yard, where she hung the laundry out to dry."

After graduating from Sharon High School in 1946, Shirl went to Dean Junior College for two years to study fashion illustration. After Dean, she studied for a year at the Vesper George School of Art in Boston before taking a job as a receptionist for an advertising agency. She met Bob Schofield while traveling daily to Boston on the train. Bob had served in the army in both World War II and Korea and had fought with the 41st Armored Infantry in Europe in the Battle of the Bulge. They married and raised three children in Sharon. After they were all in school Shirl went back to work as the church secretary for First Congregational. Bob passed away in 2013, and Shirl continues to live in Sharon. She is the chief archivist for the Sharon Historical Society and is active in the Congregational Church.

32

Bella

BELLA IS NOW an athletic-looking ninety-four-year old widow who could pass for twenty years younger. Named for an aunt, she was the fifth of ten children in a family with eight girls and two boys. Both of her parents were born in Scotland: her father in Dundee and her mother in Edinburgh. Some of their siblings came to America, but their parents stayed in Scotland, and Bella knew nothing about them except that they were "hardworking folks." Neither her mother nor her father would talk about the lives they'd left behind. Not at all. In fact, they even refused to answer any questions about Scotland. They subscribed to a Scottish newspaper, however, which Bella thinks was published in Boston.

John Stuart Monroe, Bella's father, was an excellent soccer player. "Discovered" in Scotland, he was recruited by Smith & Dove, a linen manufacturer on the Shawsheen River, and brought to Andover, Massachusetts to work for the company and be the goaltender on its soccer team. After the mill closed in 1927 he stayed in Andover, finding work at the Tyer Rubber factory in the press room, making hockey pucks. His future wife was already in this country: Jessie Cairnie had moved here at fifteen to live with her brother. At least one sister also came to America.

Bella led a carefree life, working hard but with plenty of time to play. She and her sisters did all the housecleaning, including scrubbing down the stairs with wooden brushes, and they sometimes helped

Born *at home in Andover, Massachusetts in October 1919*

When I was your age, *I enjoyed life*

When I was your age, *I worked hard and learned that you can't get everything for free.*

What was your very favorite food to eat? *Lyonnaise potatoes in a cheese white sauce.*

Did you or your friends ever eat out at restaurants or diners? *No*

You were required to attend church growing up. Is religion important to you now? *Yes. And I still go to the Free Christian Church.*

Did you ever address adults by their first names? *No*

What did you call your parents? *Papa or Dad, and Mum*

What was considered a respectable age to start dating? *About 17. My mother thought I should be 25. My father didn't care. I just had to be home by 9:00.*

How old were you when you went on your first date, and where did you go? *I was about 16, and we went candlepin bowling.*

their mother with the cooking. When Bella was older she worked part-time after school, first babysitting, and then, from fourteen on, at Tyer Rubber. And the boys? According to her, they were "the pets" who had "little to do." She does admit that they shoveled the snow. And took care of the garden. The kids bickered and fought sometimes, often with the girls blaming things on the boys and vice versa. But usually they didn't dare sass their parents or talk back to them. That would get them "the back of the hand."

How old were you when you got married? *I was 17, and he was 21.*

What was your occupation for most of your working life? *Stay-at-home mother*

Many things have been invented since you were a child. What has given you the most pleasure or been the most valuable to you? *Television, and appliances like the vacuum and dishwasher*

Is there anything you wish had never been invented? *No*

What do you think you would most enjoy about being a kid today? *Being able to play sports*

What would you most dislike? *Life is moving too fast, and the kids aren't enjoying it.*

What is your name now? *Isabella Hutchings*

Did you eat beans and franks for Saturday night supper? *Yes, and so did all the neighbors, including the Irish and French families.*

On Saturday mornings Bella did housework or traveled with her mother on the trolley to Lawrence, where they bought meat, vegetables, and other goods in the markets for better prices than in Andover. In the afternoon she might go to the youth center or to the movies. "If we'd been good," Bella says, "we'd get ten cents to go; if we'd been bad, we wouldn't. Sometimes I was fresh and didn't get to go."

On Sundays they attended morning and evening services at Free Christian Church. In between, there was a big dinner with relatives in attendance. Mondays it was back to school, as Bella put on long stockings and a dress that hung below her knees. In her neighborhood, mothers dyed old flour sacks and made them into dresses. The girls wore these or hand-me-downs, and nobody thought anything of it at the nearby Indian Ridge School. But starting in seventh grade they had to walk up to the center of Andover and go to class with more affluent students who were much better dressed. They snubbed Bella and her friends, the mill workers' children who lived, literally, on the "other side of the tracks."

Bella started first grade at six. At Indian Ridge there were two grades to a room and about ten per grade, or twenty students to a class. Miss Brown, from Vermont, was her teacher for grades one and two; Miss Pearl for three and four; and Miss Hilton for five and six. Sometimes boys misbehaved and "got the ruler" across their knuckles. The Monroes went home for lunch, and when they arrived one child was sent over to the factory with their father's meal. In addition to sandwiches there was always soup made from leftovers, kept simmering all day in a big pot on the kitchen's wood stove. After school, Bella changed into an old dress or dungarees. Sometimes she and her friends headed for Andover's youth center on Brook Street, where Miss Davis was in charge. There were crafts, two bowling alleys, and a gym where kids could play ball. They had a lot of fun there, but just as often they played games in their own neighborhood: releevio, hide-and-seek, tag, kick the can, run-my-good-sheep-run. Or the girls got together for hopscotch or jump rope, or to play dolls. Summers they walked two miles to Pomps Pond to swim.

Bella and her friends may not have dressed as well as some, and her family never got to go away on vacations, but in some ways Bella had an idyllic childhood we might envy today. They didn't have a car but were able to get everywhere they needed to go. They never had a phone and didn't have a radio until she was ten. But they owned a four-bedroom house in a safe, friendly neighborhood. The large fenced yard had a pear tree with a swing on it, and plenty of room to garden, raise chickens, and play. Inside, there was running cold water which could be heated on the stove for dishes, laundry, and baths. Clothes were washed in the bathtub using a scrub board. At first, the kitchen stove was the only source of heat, with grates in the ceiling to allow some warmth to reach the second floor. Later they added a furnace. They kept their food cool in an icebox, putting a sign on the front door on delivery days to let the ice man know how many cakes of ice they would like. They had a piano, too, but no money for lessons. They all fooled around on it, however, and one of the girls learned to play by ear. They even had a Victrola, the most popular record player of the day. The children received only one gift on Christmas, but it was still Bella's favorite holiday. She would have loved a doll carriage and a bicycle, but she did get sidewalk skates. They all shared a sled.

One Christmas afternoon was especially exciting. Bella's friend Mary, who lived up behind her, had gotten a toboggan that morning. It was small and could hold only two passengers, but the girls could hardly wait to try it out. They boarded it behind Mary's house and whizzed down the slope. However, they entered Bella's yard going faster than they had expected and were picking up speed every second. They flew right over the roof of the chicken coop and kept going, sailing airborne all the way to the Shawsheen before landing on the river. Too bad the ice was so thin. The flight ended with the girls soaked and the brand-new toboggan swallowed up by the river. It was never seen again.

Bella's family ate well. Her mother could reach stores by trolley or on foot and also had the convenience of regular visits from fish and fruit sellers, and daily visits from a bakery. Nothing was wasted. Leftovers that weren't put into the soup pot were baked, sliced, and served with syrup for breakfast, along with a big pot of hot cereal. Most nights they ate a supper of meat, potatoes, and vegetables, and on special occasions they had a chicken from their back yard flock. Their frugal ways left them well off enough to afford fruit for the kids' snacks when they were hungry, and money for the movies—when they had been good.

Bella went on to Andover's public high school, Punchard High, about a mile's walk from Baker Lane, but she never really cared for school. One day, instead of going to class she met up with a young man she had been dating for a while. He was a few years older than she and had a good job at General Electric (G.E.). They had recently decided to get married right away instead of waiting for Bella to graduate. That evening they had a big surprise for everyone: they had eloped! Her parents were not thrilled, but they accepted the marriage. There was no money for a big wedding anyway. It was a good marriage, and Bella's parents grew to like him very much. He was a turbine engineer, first at G.E. and then in the Navy, where he rose to the rank of Chief Petty Officer. He spent twelve years in the service before returning to G.E., and during WWII he was on the U.S.S. Massachusetts when it was hit by enemy fire. Apart from eighteen years in North Carolina, he and Bella spent their married life in the Andover area, where she still lives today. As she looks back on her childhood, Bella says it was a happy time, full of "lots of good laughs and fun." Her advice, after ninety-four years on the earth? "Be happy and enjoy things."

33

Eating, Treating

PAID VACATION TIME was a relatively new concept when we were growing up. More than half of us came from homes where our fathers had no paid time off, but things were starting to change. **Butch** was one of the youngest of us. His father was a factory worker who had no paid vacation. But after his death when Butch was fourteen, his mother went into factory work and did receive vacation pay. **Walt** was the youngest of all. His father had no paid vacation as an elevator operator but did after he switched to a job at a soap factory. Even those fortunate enough to have vacation time usually used it for staying home, traveling to visit family, or going to inexpensive cottages with extended family. At least in our group, even among the middle class, there were no vacations at hotels or resorts.

Christmas was the favorite holiday for most of us. Thanksgiving came in second and the Fourth of July third. Some holidays and other special occasions were celebrated by our communities with parades and other festivities. A lot of us remembered parades on Memorial Day, the Fourth of July, and Veterans Day. (One who did not get Veterans Day off from school recalled that it was marked by a period of silence at 11:11 a.m., to commemorate the official ending of World War I at 11:00 a.m. on 11/11/18.) Several communities had Christmas-themed parades. Boston had a schoolboy parade in the spring, and at least once the American Legion held a large parade.

Lowell had a fireman's parade, and Fall River had a Santo Christo parade. Others were held on Columbus Day, Easter, Thanksgiving, and St. Patrick's Day.

We ate almost all of our meals at home, as most of us walked home for lunch until high school. Only six of us said that we ever ate out at restaurants. Some of our favorite foods are still popular with children today: spaghetti, corn on the cob, hamburgers, hot dogs, pizza, ice cream, donuts, and Popsicles. Others are a little more "serious" but familiar: steak, lobster, seafood, chicken, turkey, pot roast, ham, roast pork, fish, roast beef, fresh vegetables, baked beans, potatoes, Swedish meatballs, Wheaties, and baked desserts. Plus homemade bread, and homemade applesauce, which are rarities today. Favorites that are now on the unusual side were chicken feet, codfish cakes, and tomato sandwiches.

Half of us remembered liking everything we were served or couldn't think of anything being our least favorite food. The other half had clear memories of individual dislikes: anything with fat on it, liver, under-cooked dumplings, fish—especially fish with lots of tiny bones, clams, rice, squash, cabbage, sweet potatoes, beets, green beans, or just vegetables in general.

We were also divided by whether or not we had to eat things we didn't like. Some of us had to eat whatever was served, and some did not; some had to finish everything on their plates, and some did not; others couldn't remember. Some families had a compromise system: **Pumpie** did not have to put food she didn't like on her plate, but she did have to finish everything she took.

We ate a lot of home-raised food. Over half of us were from families that kept a flock of chickens at one time or another, and over half ate fresh produce from their vegetable gardens.

We didn't eat much "junk food." In fact, half of us were never allowed to snack between meals. The other half's snacking was very limited: one of us was allowed only fruit, one had a coffee bun every day after school, several could eat if there was anything available (but there usually wasn't), and the rest snacked only occasionally or seldom, even if allowed to. It hadn't yet become a national habit. Homemade cookies or an occasional Popsicle were the closest our snacks came to empty-calorie junk food.

A bowl of hot cereal was the most frequently mentioned breakfast food, with cold cereal coming in a strong second. We tended to eat our evening meal pretty early. About half sat down to supper by five o'clock each night. For many, the noon meal was the heaviest of the day, and schools and workplaces were often close enough that students and parents came home. All but five went home for lunch through at least elementary school; all but one had a midday break of at least one hour, and a few had an hour-and-a-half or longer. In two families a child spent part of that break delivering a hot home-cooked meal to a father at work.

For the lighter meal, whether at noon or night, the most common menu items were soup or sandwich. The heavier meal usually consisted of meat, potato, and vegetables. Although some of us came from immigrant families that served traditional ethnic foods on holidays and other special occasions, **Lucy** and **Sonny**, whose parents were from Portugal and Italy, were the only two whose everyday dinners differed significantly from the norm.

The heaviest meal of the week, for most of us, was at midday on Sunday, when we had "fancier" and/or more expensive food. And a full eighty percent ate "beans and franks," or at least beans, every single Saturday night. Several mentioned that they lived in ethnically diverse neighborhoods where everyone followed this Yankee custom for a cheap, nutritious meal.

Then there was Thanksgiving dinner. For the majority, but not all, that meant a turkey dinner. Here are menus as we remember them.

For **Rozzy**, there was no feast on Thanksgiving, and no turkey. Her mother tried to make it special with whatever she could save or scrounge. **Lucy** didn't have a turkey, either; there was just a regular "Sunday" meal. **Sonny** had a blended feast: America's turkey, nuts, and apple, squash, and pumpkin pies along with traditional Italian salad, macaroni, other meats, dessert, cake, and coffee. **Okie**'s family always cooked a rooster, and **Beena**'s ate roast pork and gravy, squash, potatoes, and apple and squash pies.

Charlotte, Claire, and **Walt** each had turkey dinners. **Helen** ate turkey or chicken meat donated by the restaurant where her father sometimes worked. **Louise**'s family ate either turkey or chicken with stuffing, potatoes, gravy, squash, and turnip, followed by apple, mince, and pumpkin pies. Three of us usually had a chicken from the family's flock: **Vicki**, who also remembers mince, apple, and squash pies; **Shirley**, who also had vegetables, and pumpkin and apple pies; and **Stillman**, who had butternut squash and pies—mince, which he did not like, and apple, squash, and pumpkin, which he *did* like.

The remainder had traditional Thanksgiving meals of turkey, stuffing, gravy, mashed potato, and vegetables, in addition to a variety of pies and other remembered items. **Adrianne**'s family added squash, carrots, turnips, and a green vegetable, with apple, mince, and pumpkin pies. **Rosanna** had turnip-with-carrots and apple, pumpkin, and pineapple pies. **Bella** had "a feast" of squash, peas, and carrots from the garden, and apple and blueberry pies. **Butch**'s family deviated from tradition only on potatoes, which were sweet rather than white. They also served corn, rolls, his mother's pumpkin pie, and his grandmother's apple pie. **Pumpie**'s had sweet potato *pie,* spinach or peas, pearl onions, and apple pie. **Elaine**'s mother served *canned* peas, but the apple pies were made with fruit from their own trees. **Tom** had beets and was emphatic that there were *no turnips.* There were lots of pies—mince, custard, apple, squash, and pumpkin. Usually **Nancy**'s family hosted relatives for the occasion. They had squash, onions, and homemade mincemeat pie. **Ellie** had carrots, onions, turnips, squash, and plain celery stalks, followed by apple or squash pie. There was only milk to drink—no cider. **Shirl** ate squash, parsnips, boiled onions, rolls, cider, and pies—apple, mince, and pumpkin. **Ellen's** bread stuffing was made with Bell's seasoning. She also had turnip, squash, and celery sticks. For dessert, there was sometimes Indian pudding, and always pie—apple, squash, and her father's favorite, mince (which Ellen didn't like, but later learned to serve with applesauce to make it palatable). Finally, **Edith** remembered the whole menu: in addition to the turkey, stuffing, gravy, and mashed potato, there were turnips, peas, creamed onions, celery, olives, rolls and butter, canned cranberry sauce, fresh fruit cup, and pumpkin and mince pies. Although her mother often baked her own pies, on Thanksgiving she was too busy and they were bought at the Federal Bakery.

34

Meeting

SUNDAY MORNINGS FOR MOST of us kids meant going to Sunday school, a church service, or both. Some of us went with our families, some of us were sent alone while our parents stayed home, and others had parents who attended Saturday or Sunday services without requiring that we do the same. Only seven did not have to attend religious services or training, but four of those decided to anyway, on their own. Just three didn't regularly attend any type of religious observances. And all but two of us say today that religion or spirituality of some kind is important to us, including seven of the eight who had parents for whom religion was not very important.

Almost half our parents participated in community organizations. They were involved in church life by holding offices, serving on committees, or belonging to clubs; and in civic affairs by sitting on municipal boards and committees or serving as volunteers. Nine families had someone who belonged to social, ethnic, or service clubs such as the Grange, Masonic Lodge, or American Legion. We mirrored our parents in this area. We got involved in social and service groups such as scouting, youth groups, and junior versions of our parents' organizations.

When our parents were not working or volunteering, most of them had at least a small amount of leisure time to spend as they wished; five of us remembered, though, that our mothers or fathers were so busy or tired that they had no time at all for themselves. Parents who went to the movies regularly usually did so partly because of a brilliant giveaway incentive offered by theaters across the country: Dish Night. One weeknight, usually Wednesday, was designated for this program, which was heavily promoted by local theaters. Paying patrons were each given one free piece—same item for all customers—from a china dinner service. If they returned often enough they could accumulate an entire set of matching tableware including sugar and creamer, gravy boat, salt and pepper shaker, cups, saucers, plates, bowls, and platters.

35

Beena

VERENA ANDERSON—still Beena to most—had a very happy childhood. However, she also claims she was spoiled. Odd thing for an oldest child to say. We often think of the youngest in a family as being spoiled, with the overworked and over-disciplined eldest pointing an accusing finger at the baby. She didn't really explain how she was spoiled; she had chores and learned to work hard. True, she refused to help her grandmother one summer when she was running the Village Inn and really needed Beena to pitch in. She . . . just didn't want to do it. So her mother went in her place. But Beena took over all her mother's work in running their home that summer. She also liked to play "Sink" and leave her father to find his dory and get it back to shore. And she was allowed to be a picky eater. *Really* picky. She hated vegetables. Still does. Wouldn't drink milk. Still won't (and no, she's not allergic; she just prefers to get dairy via ice cream). Didn't have to eat what was served, and didn't have to finish everything on her plate. And she's embarrassed to remember a time from early in ninth grade when she had a sleepover at the home of a brand-new friend. She declined the hash and vegetables on the supper table, so her friend's kindly mother cooked some macaroni just for her. But her spoiled childhood doesn't seem to have done any lasting harm. She raised three sons while working in a sardine factory and helping her husband renovate their home from top to bottom, and today she is a delightful lady with

Born *at home in Port Clyde, Maine in October 1919*

When I was your age, I *. . . Hmm. I don't really know. But kids nowadays drive me nuts!*

What was your very favorite food to eat? *Roast pork*

Did you or your friends ever eat out at restaurants or diners? *No*

Your aunt brought you to church when you were a child. Is religion important to you now? *Yes. And I taught Sunday school in Port Clyde for fifty years.*

Did you ever address adults by their first names? *No*

What did you call your parents? *Daddy and Mama*

What was considered a respectable age to start dating? *About 13. We would sit on the dock with a boy, or go to a high school dance.*

How old were you when you went on your first date, and where did you go? *I was about 14, and I think we went to church together.*

How old were you when you when you got married? *I was 18, and he was 19.*

a wonderful sense of humor, still living in the house they transformed from an overgrown shack into a comfortable home. And in spite of her lifelong picky-eater diet, she is strong and sharp at the age of ninety-four. Perhaps her secret of healthy longevity lies in the two bowls of Breyer's coffee ice cream she consumes every day.

Beena lives in Port Clyde, in mid-coast Maine, in the house where she was born. You might think she has lived there all her life, but she has not. When she was born her parents were renting one side of

What was your first full-time job? *My first job was working in a sardine factory.*

What was your occupation for most of your working life? *I worked in a sardine factory for twenty years.*

Many things have been invented since you were a child. What has given you the most pleasure, or been the most valuable to you? *Everything, especially the dishwasher. I hated to wash dishes.*

What do you think you would most enjoy about being a kid today? *Nothing. I wouldn't want to be a kid today.*

What would you most dislike? *Drugs, and the great increase in drinking*

By today's standards, did you have a lot of "stuff" growing up? *No. I might get a doll for Christmas. We had very few toys.*

Today we hear that the lives of many American children are very stressful. Was yours stressful in any way? *No*

What is your name now? *Verena Anderson*

Did you eat beans and franks for Saturday night supper? *Just beans—no franks. We probably had them with biscuits and pickles my mother had made.*

what is now her home. Five years later they bought a house very close by, where she grew up. The first house was eventually converted to a one-family, and Beena and her husband bought it for only $700 in the 1940s. It came complete with one cold-water faucet and one outhouse. She has lived there ever since.

Forrest Lee Davis, Beena's father, was a Yankee fisherman and lobsterman like his father, Ellsworth. He sometimes traveled ten miles north to Thomaston, where he peddled his haddock, hake, cod, and lobsters from a wheelbarrow. Forrest was born in nearby Pleasant Point, one peninsula to the west of Port Clyde, and went to school through the sixth grade. Ellsworth died when Forrest was only fifteen. He had been taken to a hospital with appendicitis, but his appendix ruptured before it could be removed. Forrest's mother, Lilian Hussey, came from East Friendship, one peninsula to the west of Pleasant Point. After Ellsworth's death she married John Coffin, who was the captain of a private yacht. She supplemented their income by running a snack shop for local fishermen out of her home in Port Clyde, with a little counter and stools in her kitchen where she served homemade cupcakes, pies, and cakes. Later she ran the Village Inn.

Fannie Helen Munro, Beena's mother, finished the eighth grade in school. When she married in 1918 she was twenty-nine years old, nine years older than Forrest. Her ancestors were mostly English Yankees. Fannie was born in Friendship, but her family moved around the area quite a bit, living in Round Pond and New Harbor before settling in Port Clyde. As a teen she worked at the Pemaquid Point Hotel in New Harbor, and in Port Clyde she worked at a sardine factory. Her parents were Charles Munro and Rose Cushman. He was a fisherman who, according to Beena, "wasn't very ambitious" and eventually was unable to support himself and his wife. He ended up "on the town"—in other words, on welfare. The town put him to work in a gravel pit, but while he was working the pit caved in and he lost a leg. The town bought Charles a new leg.

Forrest and Fannie had four children, and they all lived to adulthood. Verena was born in 1919, followed about three years later by Agnes Bell. Kenneth Lee came in 1925, and Chester Marshall in 1929. Between Agnes and Kenneth in age was a double cousin, Gladdie May, who lived with them off and on until joining them permanently when Beena was thirteen.

Beena's second home was a big step up. Downstairs was a living room, dining room, and kitchen. The black iron sink had a cold-water faucet. A stove had been converted from wood or coal to oil and had a copper boiler to heat water. They bought oil by the bottle for fuel. Usually it was the only heat for the house, but a wood stove in the dining room was sometimes lit if the children had scrounged enough driftwood to burn in it. Upstairs were two bedrooms and a toilet, but no bathtub, so the family continued to take sponge baths. A washtub and scrub board were used for laundry. The girls shared one of the bedrooms, and a curtain partitioned the other into two sections: one for the two boys, and one for the parents. For at least six years they had no ice box, but there was a small shed built onto the back of the house where Beena's father hung the half a pig he purchased every fall. It stayed frozen all winter, and he cut off chunks to cook throughout the season. When Verena was eleven, in 1931 or 1932, the house got electricity.

Like most others in the village, Beena's family was poor. They never went hungry, however. Her father had to pay some bills late, but he always got to everything eventually. In winter, when his fishing income was limited, he ran a tab at the local store, and in the spring, when fishing picked up, he was able to pay it off. But Verena's mother felt their poverty keenly in one area. She sent her children to church and Sunday school at the Advent Christian Church but never went herself, although she wanted to. She was very conscious of having nothing "nice" to wear and would have been embarrassed to show up in her everyday clothes.

Things got better when Verena was in high school. Her father was able to buy a Model A Ford and a radio. For a time, many years earlier when Beena was only a few years old, they had had a battery-operated radio that required headphones. She remembers her parents tuning in Santa Claus on it one Christmas. The new radio was a Crossley table version. The very first thing her mother heard on it after it was set up was "Happy Days Are Here Again," a popular Depression-era song. They also got party-line telephone service. Like most who had phones in those days, they had to ring up the operator in order to make calls. After Verena married, things started going even better for her father. Someone advised him to switch to fishing for sardines; he did, and he started getting far higher prices for a day's catch. He and his wife both started attending Advent Christian and became very involved there.

Agnes and Beena were responsible for a few chores. On Saturdays they washed windows and dusted. They also had to do the dishes. They were supposed to alternate between washing and drying, but Beena hated washing and often bribed her sister to switch by promising she could borrow her clothes. Unlike Beena, Agnes enjoyed house-work and was very good at it, and she didn't mind scrubbing pots and pans. Interestingly, the family still called their frying pans "spiders"—a throwback to the name given to the "ancestors" of these items. This extinct cookware had legs and was designed to sit inside fireplaces rather than on kitchen stoves. Somehow Beena's family and/or community had kept the original terminology long after the piece itself had disappeared from American life.

A few times a year Forrest shot sea ducks, which are similar to mal-lards, in the Port Clyde harbor. Some he sold to neighbors, and others he kept for the family to eat. They needed a lot of preparation before cooking, and all the children helped in this process. Mr. Davis would set the box of dead birds on the living room floor so everyone could work together. First, they plucked feathers, which Beena's mother would later use to stuff pillows. This was "hard work and really tough on the fingers." Then the birds were impaled on sticks and singed in a fire to burn off the downy fuzz. After this they were scrubbed clean with Fels Naptha soap. Finally, they were soaked overnight in soda water to rid the bodies of soap odors.

Every November, Forrest went off to a rented cabin for a week with some other village men for a hunting trip. He also owned foxhounds, and he hunted locally for fox and sold their furs. Most evenings he joined the other village men at the general store, where they gathered around the pot-bellied stove to socialize. He often brought an ice cream bar home for Beena. Fannie, however, had no similar social outlets. She pretty much was always at home, always working hard. Occasion-ally she and her husband played cards with another couple. They also enjoyed card games with their children. "Sixty-three" was everyone's favorite. Their church was "against almost everything, it seemed." This included drinking, dancing, smoking, and playing cards. Beena played cards at home, which she didn't think was wrong because she wasn't gambling. She didn't drink or smoke until she was married, but she did go to school dances as a teen.

The Davis kids had few real toys but used everyday objects cre-atively. They played store with Fannie's clothespins that doubled as pretend money or goods, on a table leaf that served as a counter.

(This leaf also served as their mother's ironing board.) Another game was played with fallen chestnuts in a grove of chestnut trees. A third involved sitting on the grass, pretending to go for a drive in a car, with the driver holding a stick for a steering wheel. They also enjoyed the radio. Beena liked Amos 'n' Andy and The Lone Ranger, but not The Shadow, which was too scary for her. Christmas, their favorite holiday, brought a few gifts. She occasionally got a doll, but more often homemade doll clothes from her mother, or mittens her grandmother had knitted.

All of Beena's clothing was homemade except for her heavy cotton stockings. Forrest's sister helped Fannie make the children's coats out of worn-out men's overcoats. They were turned inside out, cut down to size, and re-sewn to fit. Beena didn't get a store-bought coat until she was a teenager.

The children spent a lot of time outdoors. Forrest installed swings on their big porch so they could be outside even on rainy days. Mostly, Beena says, her playground was the ocean. She rowed, played in her father's dories, and swam. "Sink" was a favorite activity. They also played tag and baseball on a large open area near her home, and alley-over, which they pronounced as "halley-over," in which they tossed a ball back and forth over housetops. An aunt in Massachusetts provided second-hand skates and skis, but they had brand-new sleds. There was a lot of snow in those days, and roads in the village went unplowed because there were so few cars. They were able to slide all the way from the top of a hill outside town, down through the village, and right down to the harbor. The fun changed a little when Beena was a teen. She and the other young people liked to gather on the porch of an empty building owned by a wealthy summer resident, sitting on its wide railing to chat. Soon after, the owner provided the villagers with a community room and a library inside the building.

Beena shared a talent and love for music with her mother. They sang together at home, and Beena sang her first public solo at four, in the Advent Christian Church. They also owned an old pump organ and later a piano, and Fannie taught her what little she knew from the few lessons she had had. Beena went on to become a very good self-taught organist and pianist. As a teen, she earned a guitar as a sales reward through a Signet Club and learned three basic chords, enough to let her accompany simple songs. She passed on this sparse knowledge to a granddaughter, who built on it to became an accomplished guitarist.

The Davis family ate lots of fish and lobster. They also had meat, some of it from their half-a-pig and some from a "meat truck" that came around a couple of times a week. Beena especially loved meals of roast pork, or stripped fish and potatoes. She liked dried fish even better than candy. For breakfast they had hot cereal and coffee. Beena didn't care for coffee and still does not, although she enjoys coffee ice cream. In Port Clyde the noon meal was termed dinner, and it was the heaviest of the day. Everyone came home—fishermen, workers, children—all except high school students, who were too far away. Supper was light, often soup such as beef vegetable. Beena usually brought either a bologna sandwich or a fried pork chop sandwich for her high school lunch. She could snack between meals on her mother's cookies.

Beena started at the village schoolhouse when she was five. Its downstairs room housed grades one through four, and the upstairs six through eight, with fifth-graders spending part of the day in each room. There were about six or seven children per grade. Two outhouses in back of the building were the toilet facilities. The day started at 8:30 and ended at 3:30, with two recesses and an hour off for lunch. Her youngest brother was born in September of 1929, right at the beginning of her fifth-grade school year. Because whooping cough and measles were going around, her mother kept her and Agnes out of school, not wanting the infant exposed to germs the girls might bring home. But when they finally returned to school Beena caught whooping cough right away. She didn't get back again until January and by then was hopelessly behind, especially in math. It was actually her favorite subject, but she had missed all the new instruction in fractions and was unable to catch up in time to move on with the others in her grade.

For high school, students from all the villages in the town of St. George were brought together in Tenants Harbor, and Beena caught the school bus in the village center for the five-mile ride. St. George High School offered both college preparatory and general courses, and Beena enrolled in the general track. She didn't like French, and although she was required to take two years of it she talked her way out of having to do the second year. Beena graduated in 1938 at the age of eighteen, in a class of sixteen, and her father borrowed $25 so she could be properly outfitted for baccalaureate and graduation ceremonies with a cap, gown, new dress, new shoes, and new hat. Several weeks later, in a small ceremony at the home of a pastor, she married nineteen-year old Douglas Edwin Anderson, whom she had been dating for two years. Doug and Beena raised three sons together and were still married when he passed away at the age of ninety-five.

36

Helen

HELEN WAS THE OLDEST of her parents' thirteen children, all born at home. Three died at birth. Of the ten who lived, eight were girls. Four of her sisters were developmentally disabled to some degree, and one of them was also born with a cleft palate. Their home in Sandwich, Massachusetts, on Cape Cod, had no electricity. Ice for their icebox was delivered twice a week. Two stoves, one in the kitchen and the other in the living room, provided heat, burning wood and occasionally coal. A hand pump in the kitchen supplied water. Once a week a tub was carried into the kitchen for baths in water heated on the stove. Toilet facilities were in an outhouse. At first Mrs. Sanford washed clothes in that bathtub on a scrub board and wrung out the water with a small wringer; later she had a laundry tub with an attached hand wringer. After clothes were dried outside on a line they were pressed with flat irons that were kept on the stove to absorb heat. When an iron became too cool to smooth cloth it was put back on the stove and a hot one taken off to continue the work.

Hubert Hall Sanford, Helen's father, was born in Mashpee. Dark complexioned, he was part Wampanoag, part English, and possibly part Irish. When Helen was very young, Hubert had a Model A Ford and a good job at a shop in Sagamore that made Ford auto parts. When the shop closed in the Depression he lost the job. After that, he worked only on and off, in part because he had become an alcoholic. Sometimes

Born *at home in Sandwich, Massachusetts in November 1924*

When I was your age, *I was scrubbing floors, changing diapers, feeding babies, and doing drudge work. My entertainment was the library and my own fantasy world, and school was my escape.*

When I was your age, *I was interested in my dolls and my books.*

What were your very favorite foods to eat? *Fresh tomatoes from my grandfather's garden, and my mother's home-baked bread and donuts*

Did you or your friends ever eat out at restaurants or diners? *No*

You were not required to attend church growing up. Is religion important to you now? *Organized religion is not, but spirituality is*

Did you ever address adults by their first names? *Never*

What did you call your parents? *Daddy and Ma*

What was your first job while you were still in school? *Babysitting*

How old were you when you went on your first date? *I was 20, and a student at Bridgewater.*

How old were you when you got married? *I was 45, and my husband was 35.*

What was your first full-time job? *5th grade teacher*

What was your occupation for most of your working life? *High school English teacher*

Many things have been invented since you were a child. What has given you the most pleasure, or been the most valuable to you? *CD players, microwaves, refrigerators*

Is there anything you wish had never been invented? *Perhaps cell phones and computers*

What do you think you would most enjoy about being a kid today? *I would not want to be a kid today. There is too much to be afraid of, there is too much to have to want, and there are too many temptations at school, such as drugs.*

By *today's standards*, did you have a lot of "stuff" growing up? *No!*

In general, today we have many more possessions than when you were a child. Do you think this has affected our happiness? *Yes. We are less happy, because people don't value anything. We have to possess a whole lot of things, but we don't care about them. And we always want more.*

What is your name now? *Helen McGarry*

Did you eat beans and franks for Saturday night supper? *Yes*

Hubert was employed by the town of Sandwich. He also went clamming, selling some of the clams he dug from the local tidal flats and keeping the rest for his family. He brought home such a steady supply that Helen got thoroughly sick of clams and clam chowder. Another fairly steady part-time job was as a cook at a restaurant, The Yankee Clipper, which was owned by Helen's godfather. This work provided additional food for his family, as Hubert was given leftover chicken and turkey carcasses and meat, and the bones could be boiled for soup broth. His father lived right across the street and worked as a caretaker on various farms in Mashpee. He cultivated a big garden behind his son's house, and Helen was very close to him. When he died, he was "laid out" in his living room, an old custom still common among those who couldn't afford to send their dead to a funeral home.

Christina Chase, Helen's mother, was part Yankee and part German and was from the Sagamore section of Bourne. Her parents were opposed to her marriage to Hubert and totally ostracized him. He was not welcome, ever, in their home. Helen later recognized this attitude as cruel racism and withdrew herself from her grandparents, but while she was young she was close to them. Her grandfather operated the old drawbridge over the Cape Cod Canal, and she enjoyed watching him work. Her grandmother made wonderful cakes and pies, and Helen loved to visit her. After one visit, her sister was pedaling their boy's-style bicycle with Helen riding on the crossbar. They had just come off the bridge and were on a horseshoe turn on the road leading down to the canal, when they skidded on the pebbly road. Helen was thrown over the handlebars and landed in the road. She still has scars, and the remains of some pebbles, in her elbows and knees.

Helen started school at six. In a time when some rural towns still maintained one- or two-room schools in different areas, Sandwich brought everybody to one school building in the center of town, where there was a separate room for each grade. It was a modern building, with a gymnasium. Grades one through six were on the first floor, seven through twelve on the second. There were about thirty in Helen's elementary classes, and about twenty stayed on through high school. The school was about two miles from her home by road, but Helen took shortcuts across the fields, cutting the distance to only a mile. Either way, her feet got soaked if it rained or snowed, as she had no boots. Some teachers handled discipline better than others, and some students behaved better than others. One of Helen's cousins on her mother's side was caught smoking outside in the bushes. She was suspended for a week.

There was one very kind teacher she particularly admired. Esther Thorley, who taught seventh grade, was a "perfect lady" and the kind of teacher who made you want to learn. Helen wanted to be just like her. Later Miss Thorley married their high school principal, Mr. Kiernan. Owen B. Kiernan would later become the Commissioner of Education for Massachusetts and education advisor to seven U.S. presidents. He was instrumental in enabling Helen to go to college, encouraging her and finding scholarship money. There were others who were not so kind. At the end of eighth grade, when she told her teacher she wanted to sign up for the college track in high school she was told she could never do it, could never get to college. Not because of any problems with her academic work, but because of her family. They were poor, and from the "other side of the tracks" socially. They received town aid, the welfare of the day, and the children weren't expected to amount to anything. Fortunately, Helen had people in her life to encourage her, not only Mr. Kiernan but also another very special couple, a minister and his wife.

Helen's family did not attend church regularly, but she herself went to the Federated Church in the town center, a combination Congregational/Methodist church whose current minister, Alexander Chandler, was a Congregationalist. He and his wife, Frances, became very significant influences in her life. They first hired her as a nanny when Frances was pregnant with twins, and she worked for them after school, summers, and vacations all the way through college and remained "part of the family" for life. By both word and example, the Chandlers taught her a lot about life in general, and gave her the stability of a good family life. They urged her to go on to college in spite of family opposition.

Life at home wasn't always pleasant. While they never actually went hungry, sometimes there wasn't enough food to fill their stomachs. Children were never told they had to eat everything on their plate, because if they didn't, a brother or sister would be glad to. Money that should have gone for food was spent on alcohol. Although she usually got along well with her father, she once got very, very angry with him for hitting her mother when he was drunk. Another unfortunate consequence of their situation was that the family needed welfare help. To receive it, you needed to go to Town Hall. Her father had a car at times, but usually not. So he would send Helen on the two-mile walk, pushing their empty baby carriage. At Town Hall she would approach a man behind a high counter who would hand her a voucher good for a certain amount on clothing and food. Then she would shop, and push the goods home in the carriage. She hated the feeling she got from these experiences. It was as if she personally had done something wrong, something to be ashamed of.

There were good times, too. In the summer she might take her brothers and sisters to the beach, an hour's walk away, or to band concerts in the gazebo in the town center. At home there were board games, and balls, and a sled, too, although the Cape didn't receive much snow. When her father made fudge, there was a saucepan to lick out. She had some dolls, and sidewalk skates that went over her shoes and were tightened with a big key. She had a bicycle in high school, which she needed for the paper route she shared with her sister Doris. She had woods to escape to, where she read her books or picked wild blueberries. She had a town library she went to as often as she could. She even had a friend who understood: Vivian lived close by, and her father was also an alcoholic. She and Helen read and studied together.

She worked hard. Since they had no electricity, Helen went to bed early and got up early. Besides having a paper route, at fifteen she also started taking long-term babysitting and nanny jobs. Most people were not kind to them, but Helen remembers fondly some who were, all on her paper route: a family who owned a dairy; a German family; and Mrs. Barton, who allowed her to earn some money helping her with housekeeping.

Mrs. Sanford was constantly busy caring for her large family, cooking, washing, and ironing endlessly, but she was resourceful and always looking for ways to bring in more money. Sometimes she baked cookies and had the children bring them around to the neighbors to sell. She arranged to get day-old soured milk from the kind family with the dairy, which she used to make chocolate cake. And she cared about her children. For Helen's senior prom, she somehow managed to buy her a beautiful midnight blue satin gown with black lace overlay.

When Hyannis State closed after her sophomore year, Helen transferred to Bridgewater State Teachers College, which is now Bridgewater State University. Her first job after graduating in 1946 was teaching fifth grade in Northborough, Massachusetts, with *fifty students* in her class! After two years she moved to Dartmouth High School to teach English and in 1961 to Sharon High. She picked up a master's degree from Northeastern University along the way.

Helen married later in life, at 45. After retiring from teaching, she became a counselor at a substance abuse program for alcohol and drug addiction. At the time of her interview, she was still volunteering in the office five days a week.

She had very little growing up, and yet Helen never wished for anything more—nothing that money could buy, anyway. She cannot say that her childhood was a happy one. The cause was not her family's poverty, but the stress that her father's alcoholism brought. She tried to escape it by staying in the woods, reading until her mother called her back to help. Even when very young she knew that things weren't right at home. She wouldn't want to go through it again.

In the end, says Helen, now an energetic and active eighty-nine-year old, she learned that she had to be true to herself; that if she wanted something, she needed to work for it, and that she could do anything if she worked hard enough. She was able to help her family more by leaving home than she ever could have by staying. Because of her education she was able to earn enough to provide them some comforts after she started teaching, paying for the installation of a telephone and electricity. Even so, she says, money is the least important thing in life; what matters the most is people.

37

Butch

AND BUTCH GOT AWAY with it! His parents let him stay at the public school instead of making him go back to St. Francis.

Butch Corbett didn't seem a likely candidate to have his likeness appear in almost every American home, on the cover of the country's most popular magazine, drawn by its most famous and most beloved illustrator. Yet it happened. He was a model for a cover of *The Saturday Evening Post* by New England artist Norman Rockwell. And it probably never would have come about if he hadn't stayed back in school. Twice.

Butch was born in Bennington, Vermont, where he was still living when interviewed at the age of eighty-two. Apart from his time in the army he has spent his entire life in the town. Butch was the oldest of four siblings, with sisters three and thirteen years younger and a brother eight years younger. An older sister had died before he was born. The family rented houses owned by other family members, and at one point they all lived with his grandmother on his mother's side. After his father, Frederick, died of cancer in the 1940s when Butch was fourteen, they moved in with one of his mother's sisters so that his mother, Barbara, could return to work and support them.

When Butch was small, Frederick Corbett worked in a paper mill making wax paper and later, wrapping paper. In his last few years of life, during the war, he worked for Union Carbide, making batteries.

Born *in a hospital in Bennington, Vermont in June 1931*

When I was your age, *we played on people's lawns until we were kicked off.*

When I was your age, *we didn't have TV or cell phones. We made our own fun.*

What were your very favorite foods to eat? *Pizza and steak*

Did you or your friends ever eat out at restaurants or diners? *No*

You were required to attend church growing up. Is religion important to you now? *Yes*

Did you ever address adults by their first names? *Occasionally*

What did you call your parents? *Dad or Fred, Mom or Barbara*

What was your first job while you were still in school? *I delivered maple products and baskets for a wholesaler. I drove a truck, delivering to businesses and roadside stands.*

How old were you when you went on your first date, and where did you go? *I was 14 or 15, and we went to the movies.*

How old were you when you got married? *I was 23, and she was 22.*

Frederick's ancestors had been here for several generations on each side. His father, a "railroad man," was Irish on one side. Frederick's mother's ancestors were German.

Although Butch grew up knowing his mother's relatives well and lived for periods with her mother or sister, he has no idea at all what her ancestry was. Her maiden name was Mathers, and she grew up

What was your first full-time job? *I worked in the Union Carbide factory.*

What was your occupation for most of your working life? *I had a wide variety of jobs: factory worker, soldier in the U.S. army, part-time policeman, volunteer fireman, carpenter's helper, school custodian, bartender.*

Many things have been invented since you were a child. What has given you the most pleasure, or been the most valuable to you? *Television*

Is there anything you wish had never been invented? *War. People want too much power.*

Do you think you would enjoy being a kid today? *No. There are no free ball fields. Every sport is organized. There's nothing for kids to do.*

By *today's standards*, did you have a lot of "stuff" growing up? *No*

In general, today we have many more possessions than when you were a child. Do you think this has affected our happiness? *We're less happy now. We used to get out and do things more.*

Did you eat beans and franks for Saturday night supper? *No*

in Bennington, but that is all he knows. Barbara worked at Ben-Mont Paper Company after Frederick died. Interestingly, Butch sometimes called his parents by their first names. He used Dad or Mom interchangeably with Fred or Barbara.

Bennington got lots of snow, and there was plenty of snow-clearing equipment, including special plows to clear the sidewalks. Plows had no engines, however: they were pulled by horses! But even in well-pre-pared Bennington school was sometimes canceled because of snow.

The area didn't really feel the Depression until about 1933. Even then, local mills kept running. There were cloth and paper mills, and a woolen mill, and most of the population could find work. After the war, following a general pattern throughout New England, the mills moved to the South for cheaper labor. But the town had other challenges. The buildings were old, wooden, and prone to fire. Butch says that "most of Main Street burned down over the years." In 1938, a ferocious hurricane roared through New England. Hurricanes usually damage only coastlines, but this one went inland as well, right through Vermont and on into Canada. Main Street was flooded.

The family went through a tough time financially when Frederick was sick with cancer and his mother had a newborn and three other children to care for. But they were always in decent housing because of their extended family. They had a telephone. It was on an old-fashioned exchange, so you had to go through an operator to make a call. There was a big floor model radio, a Victrola record player, and a Model A Ford with rumble seat, which both parents drove. They had indoor plumbing, a gas stove, coal furnace, and a washing machine. The refrigerator was modern for its time, with the motor up on top.

Butch never lived more than a mile from school and always came home for lunch, even during high school. Pizza and steak were Butch's favorite foods, and squash his least favorite. During the war oleo was substituted for butter, and it was "awful." He didn't have to finish everything on his plate, but sometimes he did have to eat foods he didn't like. He was allowed to have snacks between meals if there were any available.

There was no paid vacation at Frederick's job. Barbara did get vacation, but perhaps that was because benefits for workers were starting to improve by the time she went to Ben-Mont. They never did go away for a vacation, but once the family drove all the way to Erie, Pennsylvania, to visit one of his mother's sisters. This was before modern highways, so it took "a long, long time." His parents enjoyed getting together with friends on Friday nights to play cards, until Mr. Corbett became too ill to play.

School started when he was five, with kindergarten at St. Francis. Butch missed a lot because he came down with both measles and mumps, and he repeated the year. He also stayed back once more, in seventh grade, again because he had missed too much school. That time, though, it wasn't because he was sick. It was because he skipped a lot. To go fishing. Butch wasn't a great fan of school. (One random fact he remembers is that Mrs. Welch, an English teacher at the high school, drove a 1936 Chevy.) An interesting memory concerns his winter galoshes. They were high-cut boots, with a pocket near the top designed for a boy to store his jackknife. It was perfectly acceptable to bring these knives to school. They were viewed as tools, not as weapons.

When he was ten, America entered World War II. Frederick became a neighborhood air raid warden, and Butch helped him out by being his "runner." When his father found a home in violation of black-out conditions, he sent Butch up to the door to tell the occupants. They carried only "teeny" flashlights to help them find their way around.

Helping his father during air raid drills—being allowed out on the streets when everyone else had to be inside—was much more exciting than Butch's regular chores. He was supposed to do dishes, shovel snow, mow the lawn, and take care of the vegetable garden. They raised chickens, but his father was the only one to tend them. Butch also had part-time jobs while he was in school.

Butch sums up his childhood as, "I enjoyed myself." He spent it mostly with his friends, who all lived within a couple of blocks, but when he was at home he liked to listen to radio programs, especially The Lone Ranger and The Shadow. He only read when he had to and didn't play much with his siblings. Christmas was Butch's favorite holiday. He says that during the war most toys were made of cardboard. They had previously been metal, but huge amounts of that were now needed to manufacture airplanes, tanks, and weapons. There were lots of kids around. Usually the boys played baseball or football, or basketball at the Y in bad weather. Occasionally girls joined them for baseball. Butch had a bicycle, ice skates, sidewalk skates that could be tied to his shoes, a toboggan, and a red wagon with wooden sides. On Saturdays he played in the morning and went to the movies in the afternoon. In the summer he swam in the Branch River. Many streets in his neighborhood ended at the river, and at the end of each one, neighborhood kids would dam up an area to use as a swimming hole. (Environmental regulations have probably ended that practice.)

Because Butch was very athletic, older boys allowed him to play with them. When he was ten or eleven, they were all hanging around a lumberyard when the others decided to have some fun with him. They lifted him onto the top of a board and hung him from it by his clothing, so that only the tops of his shoes touched the ground. Then they stuck around nearby, where they could see him. After ten or fifteen minutes they'd had enough fun and let him down.

In high school, Butch played varsity football, basketball, and base-ball and was selected for All-State in both football and basketball. In September 1950, during his senior year, Butch's football coach was asked to recommend someone to pose for Norman Rockwell, who was living close to Bennington at the time. Rockwell was planning an illus-tration featuring a coin spinning in the air, the referee who had just flipped it, and two football players with their eyes on it. Butch posed two or three times, and he remembers Rockwell as "a nice guy." On October 21, the painting appeared on the cover of *The Saturday Eve-ning Post.* Its official name is "The Referee" but it is often referred to as "The Coin Toss." Butch is the player on the left, wearing a blue jersey. And if he hadn't stayed back in both kindergarten and seventh grade, he would already have graduated from high school and the coach would have found someone else for a model.

If Butch has one big regret in life, it's that he did not go to col-lege. After graduating from Bennington High School in 1951 he was supposed to attend Siena College in New York on an athletic scholar-ship, but knee trouble took away that opportunity. Instead, he stayed home and went to work for the carbon company, the locals' name for Union Carbide. Over his working life he held a variety of jobs, paid and unpaid: factory worker; Army soldier; carpenter's helper; custodian; bartender; basketball coach; semi-pro ball player in basketball, base-ball, and softball; basketball referee; part-time policeman; and volun-teer fireman. One of his police duties was to ring the "curfew bell"—a bell in one of the town's churches—signaling all kids under fifteen to get off the streets. If he saw any youths still out, he shooed them home. (He says that Bennington's curfew ended by 1953 or 1954.) He had a good life but feels he could have gone further with more education. Both of his children graduated from college.

Butch is glad he was born when he was. He can't imagine having every sport organized by adults and his free time replaced by "activities." If his friends decided to play ball, they could always find a field to use. Now that all field use in Bennington is booked in advance by organized groups, those casual games are gone.

38

Ellen

ELLEN NEVER DID get to ride a school bus. The house on the country road in North Dana, Massachusetts burned down, and her family moved into the village center, consisting of a general store, two-room schoolhouse, and a few occupied houses. The grove is gone, too. The four Swift River valley towns of Dana, Greenwich, Prescott, and Enfield were all forcibly abandoned by the end of the decade. The land sits in what is now the Quabbin Reservoir.

The fire was in the spring of 1933, when Ellen was five. She had gone on errands with her parents, Flavel and Doris Gifford, while her brother and sister, eight and ten years old, had instructions to buy milk from a farmer half a mile down the road. Apart from a "hermit" who lived across from them, a reclusive man Ellen never even caught a glimpse of, the farmer was their nearest neighbor. She recalls, "On our way home, I was sitting in the back seat of our Ford when I heard Mother's frantic voice cry, 'Flavel! That smoke is coming from either our house or the neighbor's!' Dad pushed the pedal all the way down and away we went." Ellen had the wildest, bounciest ride of her life as they raced home over the bumpy roads. They arrived to see the house in flames. William and Dorothy had returned with the milk, and William was helping the volunteer firemen remove their furniture and belongings. Flavel joined them, but Ellen was ordered to stay in the car. They concentrated on emptying the structure rather than trying to save

Born *at Cooley-Dickinson Hospital in Northampton, Massachu-setts in January, 1928*

When I was your age, *we played outside.*

When I was your age, *almost all the cars on the road were black.*

When I was your age, *you could get a lot of pieces of candy for one penny.*

When I was your age, *Hoodsie cup tops had pictures of movie stars on the underside.*

What were your very favorite foods? *I loved hot dogs, corn on the cob, and Popsicles.*

What did you like the least? *Liver & onions; and my mother's chicken dumplings, because she undercooked the dough.*

Did you ever eat out at restaurants or diners? *Never, except on two vacation trips we took. I always ordered a grilled cheese sandwich.*

You were required to attend church growing up. Is religion important to you now? *Only somewhat. It's always there, but it's in the background.*

Did you ever address adults by their first names? *No. That would have been considered very rude.*

What did you call your parents? *Mother and Dad*

What was your first job while you were still in school? *I started babysitting in my early teens to earn money for the clothes I wanted, and at about fifteen I got my first department store job. I earned thirty-three cents an hour working at the Star Store's soda fountain at sixteen.*

How old were you when you went on your first date, and where did you go? *When I was eleven years old, ten-year old Billy Clark, who was in the group of kids I played softball with, told my best friend, Norma Duckworth, to tell me that "B.C. likes you." Soon afterward he invited me to his dancing school party as his date. Afterward, he bought me a hot fudge sundae at the drugstore. We "went together" for about a year, with a standing date every Saturday night, usually at my house but sometimes at his. We played board games like Easy Money on a card table in the living room, and I would serve refreshments. Also we went to the movies together almost every Saturday, along with other friends. We were very innocent, but serious. Billy once showed me the family silver and said, "Some day this will be ours," meaning, of course, that we would be married to each other.*

What were the strangest things that ever happened to you? *When I was five, I was injured when I fell out of a moving car. When I was twelve, my friend and I got locked inside the electric company building for several hours, with no way to tell anyone where we were.*

How old were you when you got married? *I was 20, and he was 21.*

What was your first full-time job? *Secretary*

What was your occupation for most of your working life? *Executive secretary*

it, as it was to be demolished for the flooding in a few years anyway. Because the fire burned extremely slowly, they were able to get almost all the contents out. The cause was never determined, but the house was owned by the state, which was buying up properties so the inhabitants could relocate. Once the flames were out, a grateful Doris went

Many things have been invented since you were a child. What has given you the most pleasure, or been the most valuable to you? *Clothes washers with spin cycles that replaced wringers, and clothes dryers*

Is there anything you wish had never been invented? *Communication methods that are replacing intimate connections, such as Facebook and texting*

What do you think you is the biggest difference between your generation, and today's kids? *Today's generation is more spoiled, so it's harder for them to learn wrong from right.*

By *today's standards*, did you have a lot of "stuff" growing up? *No*

In general, today we have many more possessions than when you were a child. Do you think this has affected our happiness? *We have become greedy and wasteful. We have a lot more clothes now, for instance. But possessions don't really affect happiness, which depends on relationships in your family, how you get along.*

Today we hear that the lives of many American children are very stressful. Was yours stressful in any way? *No. Mine was pretty carefree until my brother was badly wounded in the war.*

What is your name now? *Ellen Mayhew Downing*

Did you eat beans and franks for Saturday night supper? *Yes*

to the cellar and retrieved a stash of orange soda to give the workers. That night they stayed with friends and the next day moved to one of the empty state-owned houses in the village center. Ellen remembers feeling very strange that first night after the fire, climbing the stairs up to bed in someone else's home because hers was gone forever.

The Giffords were not from the valley. Ellen was born when her family lived in Hatfield, the only one of their four children (the oldest, George, had died at only six months) to be delivered in a hospital. The summer after her birth they moved to Maynard, where her father had been appointed high school principal. Two years later he became the superintendent of schools in the four Swift River valley towns of Dana, Prescott, Greenwich, and New Salem, three of which were scheduled to be flooded in the Quabbin Reservoir project. After four years they moved to Holliston when he took on the superintendency of the Holliston-Medway-Sherborn schools. In another five years Flavel made his final career move to be superintendent in Fairhaven and Mattapoisett.

After the valley was flooded, Flavel and Doris joined an association of former residents and returned yearly for its reunions. There was much bitterness, some of it over country-versus-city water usage. Doris recalled one woman lamenting, "If the people in Boston didn't take so many baths, we could have kept our town."

Ellen's parents were from Martha's Vineyard, and a great many of their ancestors had lived on the island for centuries. Flavel Mayhew Gifford was from West Tisbury, where his father, George, owned a general store and his mother, Georgene, operated a seasonal ice cream parlor. Before marriage she had worked in a hat factory in Foxboro, off-island. Georgene was the daughter of David William Mayhew, a "49er" who crossed the isthmus of Panama during the Gold Rush and become a cattle trader in Sacramento, California. After the Civil War he returned to the island to visit his mother but ended up marrying and raising a family there.

Because of the large incidence of hereditary deafness on the Vineyard at the time, especially in the up-island towns of West Tisbury and Chilmark, Flavel's family learned to converse in what was later termed Martha's Vineyard Sign Language. Although not deaf themselves, they sometimes needed it for communicating with classmates and customers. This signing system was a major contributor to what later became standardized as American Sign Language.

Flavel could claim both Mayflower and Wampanoag ancestry (though very little of the latter). He graduated from Massachusetts Agricultural College (now the University of Massachusetts) in Amherst with a degree in economics, but his college years were interrupted by World War I as he served for two years with the army in France. After college he married Doris Allen Cottle and briefly taught high school mathematics and French in Holderness, New Hampshire before getting his first high school principalship. In 1930 he was hired as superintendent for the doomed valley communities after earning a master's degree in education from Harvard University.

Doris was born in 1894 and was a Mayflower descendant through her father. Her mother, Eleanor Simpson, was not an island native; she was born in England and came to this country at the age of ten and to the island after marriage. Doris was born at her father's parents' home in Chilmark and lived in Vineyard Haven through her early elementary years, on Nantucket through the ninth grade, and in New Bedford for the remainder of high school. Her father, Zadoc, the son of whaling captain Francis Cottle, was a marine engineer on the steamship line. Doris graduated from Bridgewater State Normal School (now Bridgewater University) and taught school for a few years before marriage.

Flavel and Doris were active in the Congregational church, community clubs, and civic groups. Doris also led Ellen's 4-H club in Holliston and taught sewing basics to the girls. After mastering basting and hemming they made bureau scarves and then progressed to cotton slips and skirts from patterns. (Girls always wore slips under dresses and skirts.)

In the evenings, Doris sometimes sat down at the piano to play and sing, and she and Flavel liked doing acrostics and crossword puzzles together. Flavel always listened to Lowell Thomas give the news on the radio before heading out to evening civic, church, or school meetings. He had little free time, as each town in his multi-town districts had its own school committee meetings for him to attend, but several times a week he could play a quick game of Peggity with Ellen. Before she was old enough for school, she sometimes went with him to daytime meetings, either waiting alone in the car or amusing herself quietly indoors with coloring books and paper dolls.

Before the fire forced a move from her remote, rural area, Ellen had no playmates and spent most of her days alone with Polly. After the move she played with the little boy her age across the street, from the large, "desperately poor" Baxter family. In Holliston she had many girlfriends nearby. They liked to roller skate, play hopscotch, and jump rope on the sidewalk. Many of them also had bicycles, ice skates, and skis, as did Ellen's brother and sister. She wanted these things, too, and quietly hoped she would get them as gifts. Her parents, on the other hand, assumed she had no desire for them because she didn't ask! But she did have a sled and roller skates. On cold or rainy days she and her friends played dolls, or card games like Go Fish. Then there was marbles, which they also called aggies. They played on the parlor rug, aiming for the center of a pattern; they might play for "funsies" one day but "keepsies" the next, keeping their opponents' captured marbles. When left to herself, Ellen's favorite pastime was playing with paper dolls. She also liked to read, fill in her coloring books, walk to the library, read the comics in the daily paper—her favorite was the strip *Etta Kett*—or play with her dog. Polly was so well-behaved that Ellen could take her along on errands and right into stores. At the meat counter the butcher would give Polly a bone. On Saturdays, she and her friends often went to a matinee at the Town Hall, where they could see a "grade B" movie for ten cents. A few times her parents took her to a real movie theater in Framingham, usually for a Shirley Temple film. But on one memorable occasion she saw Disney's *Snow White and the Seven Dwarfs*. Ellen still vividly remembers the wicked stepmother, the happy dwarfs, and the beautiful Snow White, brought to life so amazingly in that first color film she had ever seen. For a couple of summers Ellen attended a two-week session of Girl Scout camp, where she slept in a platform tent, had swimming lessons (which she enjoyed) and did crafts (which she did not enjoy). Campers were required to bring their own mosquito netting to cover themselves with at night, and an orange crate which, turned on its end, served as a cot-side storage unit.

In Fairhaven, Ellen's new neighborhood had very few children, so she joined a group of kids living several blocks away who played a lot of softball on a vacant lot, along with kick-the-can and other games. Girls wore dresses to play, even on Saturdays. One of the neighborhood leaders was a boy a year older than she, Everett Downing, whose father was the high school principal. They started to date each other in their late teens and married a few years later. When Everett passed away in 2008 he and Ellen had been married two months shy of sixty years.

When she was a child, her radio taste ran to kids' programs like The Lone Ranger and The Shadow, and her very favorite, Little Orphan Annie. As a teen, she tuned in to Lux Radio Theatre and the weekly Hit Parade, and she bought sheet music for all the hits and played them on the piano.

The Giffords were not wealthy, but they did have more than most others, and they lived in the "nicest" sections. Ellen always had friends who had less, and friends who had more, and it never made any difference to anyone, except for one sad time. On her first day of school in Fairhaven, Ellen stood by herself on the playground at recess, knowing nobody, until a girl named Dorothy Maciel befriended her. They played together, and Ellen invited her to come over after school. Dorothy had to go home first to tell her mother, and meanwhile Ellen got some games and toys ready. She waited all afternoon, but Dorothy never came. It turned out that she lived in the very poorest section of Fairhaven, and when her mother learned Ellen's address she didn't allow her to visit; she told Dorothy that she didn't "belong" in Ellen's part of town. Ellen felt she might have been trying to protect her from being rejected by rich snobs, something which would not have happened.

Ellen's family always had a car, which her father needed for work. But they were less up-to-date in other areas. Both of their homes in North Dana were old-fashioned: ice box, outhouse, wood stove, and a hand pump in the kitchen for water. For heat, there was a wood stove in the living room. Upstairs was "just freezing. In the morning we grabbed our clothes and ran downstairs to dress by the stove." In 1934 they moved to Holliston, to a more modern rental on Washington Street. This home had a gas stove, indoor bathroom, sleeping porch for hot summer nights, and even a play house in the yard. After several years they replaced the ice box with a refrigerator, but Doris still did the laundry in the kitchen sink. A card placed in the living room window let the ice man know how much to deliver, and children picked up ice chips that fell from his wagon. Sometimes a "rag man" came down the street in his wagon, calling out, "Rags! rags!" in the hope that housewives would emerge with items beyond repair. In 1939 they moved again, to 51 Green Street in Fairhaven, which sported a bath-and-a-half and the convenience of a washing machine. When that house went up for sale in 1944 Flavel decided not to buy. They moved to 82 Fort Street. Doris went back to scrubbing clothes by hand in the kitchen sink, but she did have a view of New Bedford Harbor while she worked. Whether washing by machine or by hand, she followed the old practice of laundering only the bottom sheet each week. When remaking the bed, the top sheet was brought down to the bottom and replaced by a fresh top sheet. (These were the days before the invention of fitted sheets; they were interchangeable because they were all flat. Ellen continued this practice for many years herself, as a housewife.) The only items Doris didn't launder were her husband's shirts, which she sent to a laundry to be washed, starched, and ironed.

One of the highlights of the year was the Fourth of July. In Holliston, Ellen played bugle with the Girl Scouts' drum and bugle corps in the morning parade. Everyone in the troop was required to play in the corps. Her favorite part of the Fourth was evening, when everybody set off fireworks, even right on the sidewalks. They were sold legally everywhere, and everyone had a stash. Ellen especially loved doing sparklers, and she saved up her allowance to buy them.

Ellen had a few chores to do, but not as many as some of her friends who were less well-off or lived in larger families. She and her sister always did the dishes. She liked to wash and her sister liked to dry, but if either were mad at the other, that girl would spitefully insist on switching jobs. Her father and brother took care of the coal furnace, shoveling and feeding it daily. William did the lawn with a mechanical reel mower, and shoveled snow, and when he entered the army Ellen took over his jobs. She wished she had learned more about housework, as she entered marriage knowing little about cooking or cleaning. Her mother worked fast and preferred to do everything herself. She usually got all her housework done in the morning, leaving her free to be out of the house almost every afternoon at various club meetings, all of which she could reach on foot or by bus. She followed the common schedule of the era: wash on Monday, iron on Tuesday. Ellen had one unusual chore in Holliston: "phone duty" on mornings when it looked like school might be canceled for snow. Many residents who lived beyond the range of the fire whistle that signaled "no school" were in the habit of calling the superintendent to find out whether there would be school or not. Ellen's job was to sit next to the telephone and field the endless calls.

Snacking on cookies was allowed between meals, as long as it wasn't too close to supper. Doris baked delicious cakes, pies, and cookies. But her greatest strength as an everyday cook was speed rather than care: she undercooked the dough for dumplings, flavored jello with leftover coffee, and served lumpy pudding and sandy spinach. She was very fond of canned goods, the "convenience foods" of the day: canned vegetables, canned Franco-American spaghetti or canned vegetable soup at lunch, canned beans with their franks on Saturday night. Suppers were often meatloaf, hamburg, roast chicken or beef, or corned beef and cabbage, accompanied by boiled potatoes and a vegetable. This was usually canned, but Doris also cooked fresh beets, carrots, and asparagus.

Ellen started school in the downstairs room of the North Dana school when she was five years old. There were about five students to a grade. Each of the four grades sat in a row: Ellen, as a first grader, was by the door, and her brother, in fourth grade, was by the window. Dorothy was upstairs with grades five through eight. Miss Doane, Ellen's teacher, worked with one grade at a time while the others did seatwork. At the end of that school year the family moved to Holliston, where there was usually only one grade to a room. She recalls that there were "lots of playground fist fights" among the boys, sometimes even over national politics, but that students usually behaved well enough in class. After sixth grade they moved again, to Fairhaven, for Ellen's final year of elementary school.

Eighth grade on was spent at Fairhaven High School. Students were separated by gender in the cafeteria, where they could purchase milk, grapefruit juice, or a hot meal. Ellen especially liked several of her teachers: Miss Hoyle brought Shakespeare alive; Miss Hastings was dynamic and held her attention in eighth-grade history; Mr. Lawton was a very good math teacher.

During high school Ellen volunteered as a "coastal spotter" with her mother, climbing a ladder to a high tower to scan the sky and sea for enemy craft. Fortunately, none ever appeared. The summer before she started college she briefly joined the war effort at Cornell Dubilier, a manufacturer of critical electrical components, starting on the assembly line and moving to clerical work.

After graduating from high school in 1945, Ellen spent a year at Massachusetts State College (now the University of Massachusetts) in Amherst. But she decided she wanted a more practical education, and instead of returning for her sophomore year she switched to the Katharine Gibbs School in Providence for a secretarial course, boarding with her aunt just outside the city. An old-fashioned dress code required them to arrive at school wearing hat and white gloves, and Ellen felt quite conspicuous on the city bus. After finishing Gibbs she got a job back at the University of Massachusetts, where Everett, who had been in the army for two years, was now studying. They married in 1948. Ellen stopped working in 1950, when the first of their three children was born, and re-entered the workforce when their youngest entered high school.

39

Rosanna

TODAY, AT THE AGE of ninety-two, Sister Rosanna has absolutely no regrets about entering that convent. She had wanted to be a nun since she was ten years old, so much so that her mother had helped her to make a nun's habit to play in and use for a Halloween costume. The coif—a white covering over the forehead of her realistic outfit—was made from pieces of corrugated cardboard from Royal Lunch cracker boxes. When she played school with her friends, using old orange crates as desks, she got to be the teacher, since she looked the most like a real one. (All the teachers at their Catholic school were nuns.)

Soon after entering the convent, Rosanna was sent to Mt. St. Mary's, a "normal" (teacher training) school in Hooksett, New Hampshire run by her order, the Sisters of Mercy. She taught elementary school subjects and French for nine years, often to extremely large groups; she once had fifty-six students in her class! Then she was a nanny in a private home for another nine years. After that, she was finally assigned to a job she had requested all along: cook, which she kept for the rest of her official working years. Today she still works and serves almost full-time in different capacities for the Sisters at their retirement home in Windham, New Hampshire.

Rosanna was born at home in Troy, New Hampshire in 1920 and moved to Keene when she was nine. Her parents were French-Canadian, both from St. Leonard, Quebec, near Montreal. Times

Born *at home in Troy, New Hampshire in December 1920*

When I was your age, *I wanted to be a nun.*

When I was your age, *I grew up fast. I had to take responsibility for the cooking and the ironing.*

When I was your age, *Father insisted on Camay soap for the girls, and Palmolive for the boys.*

When I was your age, *we listened for the fire department whistle to signal school cancellations. It would blow twice for a delay, and three times for a cancellation.*

What was your very favorite food to eat? *Spaghetti. I loved to go to my Italian friend's house and eat it there. My mother didn't cook it.*

Did you or your friends ever eat out at restaurants or diners? *My father took us out once. I don't remember the occasion.*

You were required to attend church growing up. Is religion important to you now? *Yes*

Did you ever address adults by their first names? *No*

What did you call your parents? *Ma and Pa*

What was your first job while you were still in school? *I babysat in high school and starting at 16 I also worked every Saturday for my father cuffing pants. He paid me five dollars a week.*

How old were you when you went on your first date? *I was about fourteen, and I went on a double date with two brothers.*

were hard in Quebec, and her parents had very, very little growing up, far less than their own children would have someday. They couldn't anticipate how comparatively "rich" they would become, couldn't even

What was your first full-time job? *I was a teacher with the Sisters of Mercy order.*

What was your occupation for your working life? *I was a nun. Through my order, I was a teacher for nine years, then a nanny for another nine, and finally a cook.*

Many things have been invented since you were a child. What has given you the most pleasure, or been the most valuable to you? *It's not an invention, but what gave me the most pleasure was learning to drive. I got my license when I was thirty.*

What do you think you would enjoy most about being a kid today? *I would enjoy having more freedom to do what you want to do.*

By today's standards, did you have a lot of "stuff" growing up? *No*

In general, today we have many more possessions than when you were a child. Do you think this has affected our happiness? *It's nice to have things, but we don't need them. We made our own fun, accepted what came, never questioned why things were as they were.*

What is your name now? *Rosanna Descoteaux, Sister DeChantal, or Sister Rosanna!*

Did you eat beans and franks for Saturday night supper? *Yes*

conceive of the difference there would be. They just knew there was more opportunity for them in the United States. In 1905 they left Canada and settled in Hinsdale, New Hampshire. Sister Rosanna's father was Joseph Benjamin Descoteaux, known as Ben. He was a tailor for several women's and men's clothing stores, and later for his son's dry-cleaning business. Rosanna was named for her mother, Rosanna Cecile Metivier, who died in 1935 at the age of fifty-one. Several of her brothers also came to the U.S. Ernest and Henry lived nearby in Keene. Oliver arrived in 1905 in Manchester, New Hampshire, where he worked as a baker. Another brother settled in Lowell, Massachusetts. A sister, as well as several brothers who were furriers, remained in Quebec.

There were fifteen children born to the couple—ten of them boys, including twins. One of the twins died at six months of whooping cough, but his brother lived to be ninety-three. Rosanna's oldest brother had tuberculosis as a young man but was treated successfully and lived to be eight-eight. Rosanna was the second youngest of the five girls. Her older sisters were Antoinette, who lived to be one hundred one, Lucille, and Pauline; and her younger sister was Mary.

All the children helped with chores. Even the youngest could make beds or dry dishes. Mr. Descoteaux was very strict not only about his children's attendance at Mass at St. Bernard's, but also about their appearance. On Saturdays they were expected to get their Sunday clothing prepared for church and to shine their shoes. When the three oldest girls had fulltime office jobs, Rosanna and Mary were responsible for all of the housecleaning and laundry. After their mother died when Rosanna was fifteen and Mary thirteen, they also took on all the cooking.

Because Ben was self-employed and worked alone, he never took time off for vacations; nobody could cover for him at the stores he serviced. His only workday leisure consisted of reading the paper when he came home for supper. Afterwards he usually went back to his shop to continue working. His wife enjoyed listening to the radio, especially to Bishop Sheen's broadcasts, but that was her only leisure activity. On most Sundays there was a family get-together, either at their home or in Troy, with all the Descoteaux children and grandchildren. They relaxed in the house playing whist or poker or enjoyed badminton and croquet in the yard. There was also a pool table in their basement for more fun.

Thanksgiving was Rosanna's favorite holiday, with its big meal and her mother's special dressing recipe that called for chopped onion, sage, cloves, cinnamon, chopped-up Royal Lunch crackers, and ground beef. Christmas was a little hard, because her parents couldn't afford presents. Although Ben worked long hours and was a successful tailor, and the family grew vegetables in their large garden, there were seventeen mouths to feed and a big house to heat and maintain. Rosanna's mother was able to make the Christmas season a little more special by baking pork pies for Christmas and New Year's mornings.

The Descoteaux family kept their food cool in an icebox that was later replaced by a refrigerator. There was one radio, which was placed in the corner of the living room. They had no phone until Rosanna was in high school. Their first home in Keene, on Church Street, was a rental that was heated by stoves. They cooked on a stove fueled by oil that they bought by the bottle, and they scrubbed laundry in a large washtub. In 1935, just before her mother's death, they moved to a more comfortable place on Winchester Street. This fourteen-room house featured a furnace in the basement, radiators in each room, a laundry room with an electric washing machine and hand-cranked wringer, and a pantry off the kitchen for additional cool storage. However, it had only one bathroom to serve the entire family! They could have crowded into a smaller place, but her parents preferred to have their children's friends come to play in their large house and big yard instead of letting their children be scattered all over town at others' homes. Rosanna liked to jump rope and play hopscotch and marbles with her sisters and friends. As a teen she listened to big bands on the radio, especially Tommy Dorsey, Sammy Kaye, and Benny Goodman.

Every day except Sunday the milkman delivered between fifteen and twenty quarts of milk. Mrs. Descoteaux skimmed the cream off each bottle (as milk wasn't homogenized in those days, so the cream rose to the top) and saved it to make whipped cream for Sunday dinner's strawberry shortcake. She made very good cakes, especially white cake with chocolate frosting; and light, flaky pie crusts.

Everyone was home for supper at 5:00. As there wasn't enough room at the table for everyone to be together, the adults and older children ate in the dining room and the younger children in the kitchen.

As older siblings left home and places opened up in the dining room, others moved in from the kitchen. They ate everything served to them, and finished everything on their plates. There was no extra food left over to snack on later. After his wife died, Mr. Descoteaux got up early every morning to cook oatmeal in a double boiler. His children couldn't choose between hot or cold cereal on arriving at the breakfast table, though; he prepared only enough hot cereal for those who had signed up for oatmeal the evening before.

Rosanna started school at the age of six. She walked five minutes to St. Joseph School for grades one through eight, and later to the public high school, ten or fifteen minutes away. She doesn't remember exactly how many were in her classes, just that there were "too many—probably forty-five or fifty." Rosanna usually brought a fig square or a Mr. Goodbar candy bar to eat at morning recess. Teachers had a "switch" to use on students' hands for punishment, and children were punished not only for misbehavior, but also for academic failures. Rosanna was never hit, but her brother was punished regularly for getting his spelling words wrong. Once he moved his hands at the last minute, causing the teaching Sister to hit her own legs. But the discipline was not supposed to be completely uncontrolled. On another occasion this brother came home with his hands bleeding. His parents complained, and the teacher was recalled to headquarters in Manchester, and replaced. And it wasn't only St. Joseph teachers who were less than exemplary. Rosanna remembers her ninth grade English teacher, Mr. Ewing, well. Not only was he extremely sarcastic, but he also made it plain that he didn't like "St. Joe's kids."

There was no pressure on them as children to have fashionable clothes, or to wear their hair in certain styles, but in high school Rosanna and her sisters were more conscious of fashion. They bought their own clothing from their small earnings and wore high heels and nice outfits to school. They each owned two or three outfits and were all a similar size, so they traded clothes with each other regularly for more variety. They didn't have a separate set of casual clothes, so they put on aprons when working around the house to keep their good clothing clean.

Rosanna had a happy childhood and is glad she had the opportunity to make her own fun. One of the most important things in life, she says, is to accept what you can't change. If you do what you think is right, and it turns out you were wrong, you can't blame yourself, and you can't change anything. You shouldn't try to accomplish the impossible. Don't let anything overwhelm you. Just take one day at a time.

40

Responsibility and Respect

CHILDREN IN OUR GENERATION almost never addressed adults by their first names. If we used a first name for extremely close family friends, a respectful "Aunt" or "Uncle" preceded it. Elder status of even younger adult cousins was often acknowledged by calling them "Cousin Jane" or "Cousin Tom." But there was one exception among us: **Butch** often called his parents by their first names.

In the "chores" department, there were no exceptions: every last one of us helped out at home. Some had pretty light duty; we did the supper dishes and occasional yard work, shopping, or cleaning. A couple of us had such significant duties that there was little time for play; we were burdened with all or most of the responsibility for keeping house and caring for younger siblings. But most of us fell in the middle; we tended gardens, milked cows, cared for livestock, scrubbed floors, ironed clothes, watched the younger children, canned fruits and vegetables, shoveled snow, and mowed lawns while still having plenty of time for ourselves.

Some people seem to think that kids in our generation behaved like either angels or robots both at school and at home and that our parents were either all kind and wise, or harsh villains. Believe us: that wasn't true. Every family and every person was different. Even those of us who felt we were in happy families—which was most of us—argued with sisters over the dishes and with parents over curfews, or got annoyed with little brothers for tagging along, squabbled over petty things, overheard our parents fighting. Sometimes we found our friends' parents to be quite unpleasant. Occasionally we witnessed abuse or experienced it ourselves.

At school, our behavior tended to vary with different teachers. In general, we didn't respect teachers who couldn't keep order, tending to like the better disciplinarians but bitterly resenting those who were unnecessarily harsh or unfair. We agreed that most students were fairly well behaved and that teachers had an easier time controlling their classes than they do today, but that there were always at least a few "clowns" or troublemakers in every class. Our teachers had one tool in their box that has since vanished: corporal punishment, which was legal in all six New England states. Some school systems used it much more than others, so some of us don't remember anyone being punished in that way.

Rosanna, who later became a teacher herself, made the interesting observation that "windy, stormy weather" made it harder to control the kids. She felt that outdoor recess was crucial for good classroom discipline, and that while some teachers were better than others at keeping control, all had more trouble when bad weather resulted in the loss of outdoor play time; students needed the opportunity to "run around and burn up energy." Given that most of us enjoyed three recesses per day, it may not be surprising that today's students have so much trouble sitting still and focusing on their work; most schools now have only one short recess, and some none at all.

41

Carefree Liberty
or Neglect?

WITH FEW EXCEPTIONS, we got ourselves to school, friends' homes, movies, and everywhere else, on our own. We walked, rode our bicycles or scooters, or took public transportation. Only about half of us lived in families owning a car *or* truck—never more than one vehicle. Fathers needed them for work, so they weren't often available to cart us around after school. And though our mothers were usually home, most of them couldn't have given us rides anyway, since only six of them had driver's licenses.

Since most of us went home for lunch until high school, we got in at least four walks a day. Our schools were as close as a few buildings away, and as far as five miles. Those who lived two miles away didn't come home at lunch, but still walked to and from school. Some school systems provided school buses or bus vouchers, but we must have been "too close" at two miles to qualify. Only two of us, Ellie and Okie, rode school buses; Okie's was a horse-drawn wagon, and Ellie's did double duty daily as a farmer's cattle truck. But they lived quite far from school, in rural areas with no public transportation.

Although not many of us could remember how old we were when we were first allowed to play outside alone, some could. They remembered that they could be in the yard at two or three years of age, and in their own neighborhood at three or four. Others simply recalled that they were "very young." The oldest age anyone remembered for this was five or six.

Negotiating the neighborhood at four and walking alone to school at five are no longer activities kids with "good" parents engage in; that behavior might trigger allegations of neglect, followed by social service investigations. But there is some controversy over whether our neighborhoods and towns are truly more dangerous now than in our day. We may simply have incorrect perceptions, created by media that inform us of every attempted abduction in the entire country and fed by a twenty-four-hour news cycle. Then again, those fears may be justified. Either way, our grandchildren and great-grandchildren do not have the freedom we and our own children took for granted in our childhoods, or the satisfaction we gained from learning how to navigate our world independently.

42

Ellie

ELLIE WAS BORN on her family's farm in South Westport, Massachusetts. Her father, James Smith, came to this country from Laurencekirk, Scotland as a young teenager with his parents, siblings, and extended family including his Smith grandfather and great-grandfather. They started farming in Westport, and by the time Ellie was born her father and his brother John had established adjoining properties on Horseneck Road. James, the family's youngest son, had seven or eight cows, three working horses, chickens, hens, and a pony, along with cash crops of beans, corn, squash, tomatoes, peppers, and turnips—Macombers, the local Westport specialty variety. He grew raspberries, winter pears, and apples as well, but only for family use. Just to the north of James's property was his brother John's Long Acres Farm, which has since gone out of the family and is now called Westport River Vineyards.

Lula Wilkins, Ellie's mother, was born in Stoneham, Massachusetts. She was the daughter of Elvira Lucretia Smith from New Hampshire (no relation to James) and Peter Hay Wilkins, both Yankees. Peter worked for the Boston and Maine Railroad as a crossing tender. Lula attended Normal School to become a teacher. She taught for a while, then did clerical work in Boston before returning to teaching with a post at the South Westport School, which was located on Pine Hill Road at the time. Lula boarded with local families: the Entwhistles,

Born *at home in Westport, Massachusetts in June 1914*

When I was your age, *I had to work.*

When I was your age, *my family always said, "Use it up, wear it out, make it do, or do without."*

What was your very favorite food to eat? *Baked beans*

Anything you didn't like? *Beets*

Did you or your friends ever eat out at restaurants or diners? *No*

You were not required to attend church growing up. Is religion important to you now? *Yes*

Did you ever address adults by their first names? *No*

What did you call your parents? *Pa and Ma*

What was the most valuable lesson you learned in school? *I learned to keep my mouth shut!*

What was your first job while you were still in school? *I helped on the family farm.*

Where did you go on your first date? *We took a car ride over toward Fairhaven.*

What was your first full-time job? *Bookkeeper*

What was your occupation for most of your working life? *I was a bookkeeper.*

Many things have been either invented or come into wider use since you were a child. What has given you the most pleasure, or been the most valuable to you? *Plenty! Washers, dryers, telephones, electricity, plumbing.*

What do you think you would most enjoy about being a kid today? *There is more freedom now to do more things.*

What would you most dislike? *Hearing all the bad news. It would be depressing.*

By today's standards, did you have a lot of "stuff" growing up? *We did have a lot of stuff, but it was the accumulation of past generations and it was mostly kept in the attic. I recently donated much of it to the Westport Historical Society.*

In general, today we have many more possessions than when you were a child. Do you think this has affected our happiness? *We are less content. We have much too much.*

Today we hear that the lives of many American children are very stressful. Was yours stressful in any way? *I had a peaceful childhood. I may have been stressed at the time, but looking back on it now it doesn't seem that way.*

Did you eat beans and franks for Saturday night supper? *We had baked beans with salt pork.*

the Lawtons, and finally the Smiths, where she got to know the young man who would become her husband.

James and Lula had only two children: Elvira, or Ellie; and Esther, two years younger. The farm's relative isolation meant that the girls usually had only each other to play with. In general, Esther helped her mother indoors with cooking and cleaning, and Ellie helped her father with the outside chores. At harvest time he employed hired help, but the rest of the year he and his daughter handled everything themselves. It was hard work, especially in the hot summer, yet Ellie remembers helping her father as the highlight of her childhood. They cut grass with a scythe, then carted the clippings to the barn and unloaded them. Ellie fed the chickens and gathered eggs, but her father cleaned the henhouse. She closed the barnyard gates at night and stashed loose hay in the barn during the summer. She also watered the large animals, bringing first the horses and then the cows down to the brook and giving them about five minutes to drink. Then she drove them back, keeping them going and not permitting them to stop and graze on the way.

In the evenings, after chores were done, the family might listen to their battery-powered radio or play games together. Mr. Smith did not approve of playing cards, but they had dominoes and several board games which they often played by their own house rules. Sunday was a whole day off to rest, a chance to take a break from heavy farm work and housework. In the morning they usually attended services at Second Congregational Church in South Westport. In the afternoon the girls played quietly while James enjoyed a nap and Lula read.

Occasionally Lula took the girls to visit their grandparents and cousins back in Stoneham. James drove them in his hand-cranked pickup truck to Lincoln Park, where they caught the trolley to Fall River. From there they took a train to Boston, and from Boston another trolley to Stoneham. James normally stayed behind to tend the farm, but for Thanksgiving he made the trip with them. Peter Wilkins bought their holiday turkey at Faneuil Hall in Boston.

Ellie enjoyed working on the farm after school and all summer, or playing alone or with her sister, although she also felt isolated and lonely at times. Her favorite holiday treat was "getting gifts at Christmas." Ellie's toys were mostly dolls, but she had just as much fun with her "real" toys, the farm's cats and dogs. She also enjoyed playing her violin and ukulele. She and her sister played hand games like Pease Porridge Hot. Jumped rope. Sledded where their land sloped down to the east branch of the Westport River. Played hide 'n' seek. Picked wild strawberries, blueberries, checkerberries, and wineberries. Swung on the rope swing in the yard and the wooden swing set with two facing seats. Ellie never did go fishing. Not interested. She did like to explore, and once she found a still in the woods near the historic Handy House. (A still is used to produce liquor. This was during Prohibition, so it was probably in active use.)

At mealtimes Ellie had to eat what was served and finish everything, and there was no snacking in between. Mr. Smith was the first up in the morning, and he started breakfast—hot cereal cooked in a double boiler—and then went out to milk the cows. Ellie never wanted to eat in the morning, but her mother made her. "She had to stuff it in," she says. If she was carrying lunch to school she made a sandwich filled with whatever was handy, usually sardines, tuna fish, or egg salad. Supper was after the last milking, at five or six depending on whether standard or daylight time was in effect. Occasionally her father would cook liver and onions for their supper.

The Smiths had neither electricity nor a telephone but did own a pickup, and Ellie got a license to drive it at sixteen. They also used a horse-drawn wagon or sleigh and had a pony cart to haul lumber and other small loads. The "fish man" came through on his rounds once a week, blowing his horn to announce his presence.

Toilet facilities were outside. There were two water pumps: one outdoors, used for watering the animals; and one at the kitchen sink. Water for baths was heated on the kitchen stove and poured into a tub that was brought into the kitchen every Saturday night. Laundry was washed in a big tub. Food was kept cool not in a refrigerator or even an icebox but in a "spring house." This little structure was built right over a spring whose flowing waters kept the temperature low enough to slow food spoilage. The kitchen stove was fueled by wood and later switched to coal. The only other heat in the house was from a coal stove in the living room that was removed every summer and re-installed in the fall.

Ellie didn't start school until she was seven. She went right into the second grade, as her mother had already taught her to read at home. The one-room South Westport School served grades one through five and was located directly opposite the end of their very long farm lane on Horseneck Road. It took Ellie five or ten minutes to walk there. After fifth grade she caught the school bus at this same building to take her to the upper grades in other Westport villages. Grade six students went to the Head of Westport, seventh graders to Westport Factory, and eight through twelve to Westport High School in Central Village. The bus was actually a farmer's delivery truck fitted with dark green fold-down benches along the sides. After its morning run the vehicle was used to transport cattle for the next several hours. Then it was hosed down before reverting to bus duty. At school, "the ruler" was used to enforce discipline, but there were still always two or three "clowns" in Ellie's class. She learned to remain quiet, but not happily. She enjoyed talking with her classmates, but talkers were reprimanded in front of everyone so she settled for socializing at recess. One of the favorite South Westport recess games was alley-over, in which kids threw a ball back and forth over the school roof from the girls' to the boys' side and back again.

Ellie retains a few random memories of her school days. One is of her seventh-grade teacher, Gladys Kirby, who was "very strict, but very good." Another is of a time when a high school boy, Jonathan Potter, was judged to have been a tattletale. Some of the other boys punished him for this by at least partially stripping him, and then spanking him. Norman Gifford was their high school principal. The students nick-named him "Pussy Foot."

Unfortunately for Ellie, who wanted to take clerical courses in high school, the town got rid of the commercial track just as she entered. She graduated second in a class of seventeen or eighteen in 1932 and as the salutatorian she was required to deliver a graduation speech. Ellie had always been shy in front of audiences and was scared to death, but she overcame her fear and did it. She went on to a four-month course at a commercial school and then entered the workforce as a bookkeeper—and bought a 1930 Chevy to commute in. Ellie worked first for a wholesale fruit and produce distributor, E.L. Fisher. After it dissolved, she got a job at a moving and storage company in Fall River for eighteen dollars a week and worked there for forty-nine years before retiring.

After James died in 1936 or 1937, Lula sold the farm and moved with Ellie just over the town line to Dartmouth, where they had a small house built for them. Ellie still lives there, going strong at the age of ninety-nine. Until a few years ago she was still able to get up on her garage roof to replace shingles. Second Congregational has been gone for many decades, but she attends Pacific Union Congregational Church at the Head. She has a wonderful sense of humor. And she does online brain exercises her doctor has recommended, using her brand-new computer!

43

Rozzy

WHEN ROZZY WAS BORN, she already had three siblings—Connie, five; Philip, four; and Marion, two. When she was three, another brother, Frank, was born. Their father was Raymond Frank Hutchinson, and their mother, Evelyn Knowles.

Evelyn was born in Salem, Massachusetts to a Yankee father and a Yankee/Irish mother, Jeanne Crawford Morrison. She was a high school graduate who worked as a private secretary in Peabody or Salem before marrying. One of her four brothers always met her at the office and escorted her home, a walk of a mile or two, because in that time and place it wasn't considered proper for a young lady to be on the street alone. Rozzy remembers her telling them how spoiled she was as a child. She was both the only girl and a "change of life baby" who was eighteen years younger than her closest brother. She didn't like to share with other children. If she knew any were coming to the house, she would put all her toys into her big toy box and then, to make certain they wouldn't play with anything, sit on it. For the entire visit. Evelyn's father died before Rozzy was born, but her brothers seemed like grandfathers to her. Her Uncle Bill was a fireman in Salem, and Uncle Chester owned a drugstore.

Ray Hutchinson was from Lynn and of Yankee ancestry. He had served in the army during World War I. Ray was a barber, and he owned his own barbershop in Randolph. Rozzy remembers going to work with

Born *at home in Randolph, Massachusetts in November 1925*

When I was your age, *there was more expected of us, especially in terms of minding, and behaving well.*

When I was your age, *I walked two miles to school by myself, but in some ways we had less freedom.*

What was your very favorite food to eat? *The custard my mother made from the cream skimmed off the top of our bottled milk. She served it in small custard cups.*

Did you ever eat out at restaurants or diners? *Later in childhood I did, but only because my oldest sister, who had a good secretarial job, enjoyed taking us out almost every week to a little Italian place nearby.*

You were required to attend church growing up. Is religion important to you now? *Yes*

Did you ever address adults by their first names? *No*

What did you call your parents? *Mum and Dad. After I married, I started calling my father "Ray" because he really had abdicated his position as my father.*

How did you wear your hair? *My mother was very good at doing our hair. I wore braids when I was young and switched to a pageboy cut at twelve or thirteen.*

What was your first job while you were still in school? *I sold shoes in a department store, T.W. Rogers, starting at sixteen.*

How old were you when you went on your first date, and where did you go? *When I was about fourteen I went to the movies with a neighbor boy who was deaf and had a crush on me. But soon afterward I met Ben, my husband-to-be, and we started dating.*

How old were you when you got married? *I was 17, and he was 21.*

What was your first full-time job? *After graduation I went full-time at T.W. Rogers.*

What was your occupation for most of your working life? *I was a housewife while my children were growing up. I also cared for foster children. Later I became a small business owner.*

Many things have been invented or improved since you were a child. What has given you the most pleasure, or been the most valuable to you? *The vacuum cleaner*

By *today's standards*, did you have a lot of "stuff" growing up? *No*

In general, today we have many more possessions than when you were a child. Do you think this has affected our happiness? *It certainly has changed how children use their time. Because they have much more interesting stuff available inside, they are content to remain in the house. We went out to play.*

Today we hear that the lives of many American children are very stressful. Was yours stressful in any way? *I had many worries and uncertainties because my father was gone. Otherwise it was not stressful.*

What is your name now? *Rosamond Knapp Kinsman*

Did you eat beans and franks for Saturday night supper? *Yes. And when I was little, my father cooked the beans.*

him when she was very young and sitting in the sun in the shop's big front window. However, Ray lost his business during the Depression, and when Rozzy was five the family returned to Lynn, where Ray found work as a barber. His mother, Fanny, still lived in the city, although

Rozzy met her only once. Possibly because he didn't cope well with the loss of his shop, he started drinking heavily and gambling, spending a lot on those habits and on flashy clothes and jewelry. Sometimes he gave up alcohol for long periods, but eventually he always returned to it. He would come home drunk; once, Evelyn sent Philip to rescue him because he had fallen into a snow bank while dead drunk and couldn't get out. Evelyn always covered for him and protected him, putting him to bed and telling the children, "Your father is sick. You need to be quiet." Rozzy believed her until Connie eventually revealed the truth. He was often away from home, and he left for good when Rozzy was thirteen. After that she saw him about once a year.

Evelyn died in her early fifties when Rozzy was eighteen, after losing a battle against stomach cancer. She loved her husband to the end. They never divorced, and she always spoke well of him. Rozzy found out years later that he had stayed in frequent contact with her, visiting during the day when the children were out. He especially wished to avoid Connie, his eldest, who had never gotten along well with him. She had witnessed things the younger ones hadn't, seen him abuse and hurt their mother, and she had no respect for him. She refused to call him anything but Ray and fought with him constantly. He considered her "uppity" and used her attitude as an excuse for leaving home. By that time Connie had graduated from high school and had a good job as a secretary at General Electric. She was glad he was gone, and she happily took over his job of supporting the family.

Their first home in Lynn was the second and third floors of a two-family on Red Rock Street, near the beach. When Rozzy was ten or eleven they moved to a first-floor apartment with six very small rooms on nearby Stone Place. Their final move was to five large rooms on Chatham Street in East Lynn, near Flax Pond. Most of their apartments were relatively modern and had coal furnaces. The fuel slid from a truck into the basement coal bin via a chute. Sometimes between deliveries in the winter the coal ran out, and the children were sent to buy it in bags to haul home by sled. There was indoor plumbing, and a kitchen stove which burned both wood and coal. They owned their own electric washer with an electric wringer. In the summer, an "ice man" came by in a horse-drawn cart; in the winter, he arrived in a sleigh. Customers who wanted ice placed a card in a front-facing window indicating how large a piece he should bring inside. The Hutchinsons generally bought ice every three to four days for their ice box, which was kept in an unheated hallway.

Mrs. Hutchinson was a member of the Christian Science church. She took the children to services every week, but her husband never attended. She did not follow every tenet of her religion strictly: her children were rarely sick, but she took them to doctors if she thought it was necessary. She did so when four-year old Frank was hit by a truck in the street after he followed Marion to the store without her knowledge, resulting in a head injury. He recovered fully and developed into "the brightest of all of us," according to Rozzy. Evelyn was also not upset when her children switched to orthodox Christian denominations. She was close to the Lord, says Rozzy, and always reading her Bible and other religious material. As a teen, Rozzy joined her sister Marion at the Congregational church.

The Hutchinson children all helped with chores. The boys shoveled the snow, took care of the garbage and trash, and ran errands for their mother. The girls took turns doing the dishes, and they brought clothes in from the line when dry. They did not hang them out, however. Evelyn liked it done a certain way and preferred to do it herself. She was also the only one to handle the coal furnace; even when Ray was home that job was hers. The older children banked the coals at night, but furnaces were finicky and took a lot of fussing over to run properly.

Life as a single mother was difficult in many ways for Evelyn. She loved her children and they loved her, and they never sassed her or argued with her. But although the children played together, they also fought among themselves, which distressed her, and she tried in vain to stop it. The girls argued over who was supposed to wash or dry the dishes. Marion and Rozzy wore Connie's clothing in spite of constantly being told not to. (Connie had very nice outfits because she was working, and in spite of her sisters' efforts to avoid her knowing, she could always tell and was very annoyed. "Who's been wearing my clothes again?" she'd shout.) Their mother usually responded to any trouble by calling out, "Hark! hark!" which meant, basically, "Cut it out!" But the children ignored her. "We kids controlled our mother," Rozzy says. "She wasn't firm enough; she didn't follow through. Her 'discipline' consisted mainly of "Hark!"

There wasn't much money in the household, and Connie supplied almost all of it. But Christmas was still fun, and birthdays always brought a special surprise. There were no big presents—just one very small gift that Evelyn wrapped in waxed paper and baked inside the cake. Another holiday that was fun for them was the Fourth of July, when they watched the parade and set off firecrackers.

Because money was so tight, the children were expected to finish everything on their plates. Evelyn was very interested in nutrition and was always reading up on it. She worked hard at making meals as nutritious as possible. There were usually no snacks between meals, but Mrs. Hutchinson did occasionally bake cookies. When Rozzy's father was still with them he sometimes made wonderful donuts that the kids could smell baking from outside. Rozzy often had hot cereal for breakfast and a lunch of hash made from the previous day's leftovers. From fourth grade on she brought a sandwich to eat at school, which was two miles from home.

Grandmother Knowles was skilled at making hats, and when Rozzy was still very young she taught her how to design and sew hats and clothes for her dolls. After that, Rozzy spent a lot of time playing with her dolls and making new clothes and beautifully lined hats for them. The dolls were the only toys she owned, but there was also a player piano she fooled around on and an old harp that Evelyn kept under her bed. When Rozzy was about twelve they got a radio. She liked listening to classical music, and programs like Amos 'n' Andy. As a teen she added popular music.

Rozzy spent a lot of time playing outdoors, especially on her scooter, sled, ice skates, and roller skates. She planted a flower garden in her yard (and her brothers kept a big vegetable garden and grew tomatoes, carrots, potatoes, and onions). They all had firecrackers, but they were strictly for July 4. Even then her brother Philip wasn't allowed to use them without permission, because he had been careless once, throwing a firecracker backwards by mistake instead of forwards. It narrowly missed Rozzy, going off right by her ear; she was deaf in it for quite a while afterwards. Sometimes Rozzy went to the movies on a Saturday afternoon, bringing five cents for a ticket and five cents for a treat. In the winter she skated on Flax Pond, and in the summer she swam there. There weren't many other children in the neighborhood. If she wanted to play with school friends she had to walk a couple of miles to see them.

At the age of five Rozzy started first grade at the Lewis School. She liked her teacher, who "held me on her lap often." She stayed there until the fourth grade, when she went on to grammar school. At recess she enjoyed jumping rope and playing marbles and jackstones. She liked school, but she learned that she shouldn't speak out. In the fourth grade she "got the ruler" on the palm of her hand from the principal: another girl had cheated in their jackstones game at recess, and Rozzy had complained about her to her teacher—one that she didn't like, and who, likewise, did not like her. The teacher told her to stop complaining. When she didn't, she sent her to the principal.

A particularly frightening episode stands out in her mind today. Her mother's childless friends, Olive and Fred, were extremely fond of Rozzy. She spent a lot of time with them, and when she was six she spent an entire summer at their house. When she returned home in the fall, Rozzy overheard them asking her mother if she would let them adopt her. She wept hysterically at the prospect. Although she loved Olive and Fred, she loved her mother more and was afraid of losing her. (At the time it was not unheard of—though rare—for financially-strapped parents to allow their children to be adopted and given a "better chance" in life.) Fortunately, Evelyn said no, and Olive and Fred found two sisters to adopt instead.

One somewhat silly scene also stands out. In its small way, it says that no matter how much the world changes around us, human nature itself never does. On this occasion, Rozzy's younger brother kept asking her something—the same question, over and over and over. She answered the first few times but finally got annoyed and stopped. Even then he just kept it up, asking and asking.

Rozzy graduated from Lynn English High School during World War II and immediately switched from part-time to full-time work in a department store. Her brother Philip was no longer at home, having joined the Navy as soon as the war started. At seventeen, Rozzy married Benjamin Kinsman. He signed up with the Marines soon afterward, and she became pregnant with their first child right before he shipped overseas. After the war they had two more children and also welcomed many foster children into their home.

Childhood for Rozzy was a mixture of stressful uncertainty and worry, brought on by her father's absence; and of peace and contentment, made possible by a mother who always remained calm and never let anything get her down. But overall, she says, it was a happy time.

44

Tom

TOM'S PARENTS HAD NEVER left him before, and he sure didn't want them to that night. They had thought he was a little more grown up than he actually was, and old enough to take charge of his sisters—Meg, four; and Fran, two—for the evening. Probably he would have managed just fine, but he was shocked and frightened at the prospect. He was only five years old, and he didn't want any part of the plan.

Thomas Bernard McGarr, Tom's father, was born in Lowell, Massachusetts near the end of the nineteenth century, the youngest of three boys. His parents, of English and Irish ancestry, died in an epidemic when he was seventeen. Thomas went to live for a while with his Aunt Lizzie and then joined the navy. During World War I he survived the sinking of two different ships he was serving on. After the war he returned to Lowell and learned the plastering trade on the side while working in a textile factory as a "bobbin boy." There he met his wife, Etta, who was the daughter of an overseer at the mill. After marriage Thomas worked as a plasterer until the effects of the Depression dried up the work. He joined the W.P.A. and got a job digging ditches, but Etta kept at him to take the Civil Service exam to be a fireman. He finally did, and in 1933 he joined the Lowell Fire Department.

Etta Frances Walworth was thirty-nine years old, nine years older than Thomas, when they married. She enjoyed telling her children stories about her childhood and mill-working years. Etta had worked in

Born *in a hospital in Lowell, Massachusetts in February 1927*

When I was *your age*? *I still am your age. I never grew up!*

When I was your age, *I knew what hard work was, what it was like to get up early every morning and milk cows.*

What was your very favorite food to eat? *Probably ham* **Your least favorite?** *Rice*

Did you ever eat out at restaurants or diners? *I never remember doing so*

You were required to attend church growing up. Is religion important to you now? *Yes, very*

Did you ever address adults by their first names? *No*

What did you call your parents? *Ma and Pop*

What was your first job while you were still in school? *I had a summer job working on a dairy farm when I was twelve.*

What was considered a respectable age to start dating? *Around freshman year in high school*

How old were you when you went on your first date, and where did you go? *I was fourteen, and we went ice-skating.*

How old were you when you got married? *I was about 25, and she was about 23.*

What was your first full-time job? *High school teacher*

What was your occupation for most of your working life? *Education: teaching and administration*

Many things have been invented since you were a child. What has given you the most pleasure, or been the most valuable to you? *Power drills. I have two of them. They're very handy; make a lot of jobs much easier.*

What would you think about being a kid today? *I would probably be on the computer a lot. I don't use one, although I would like to. I took a computer course, but using the keyboard was just too difficult because I had never learned to type.*

By *today's standards*, did you have a lot of "stuff" growing up? *No*

In general, today we have many more possessions than when you were a child. Do you think this has affected our happiness? *People have a lot now, but it hasn't seemed to have made them any happier. They have too much. The more they get, the more they want.*

Today we hear that the lives of many American children are very stressful. Was yours stressful in any way? *No.*

Did you eat beans and franks for Saturday night supper? *Yes.*

the mills for well over half her life sewing buttons on long underwear, garments that have almost completely disappeared from the American wardrobe but were worn by millions at the time. In wintertime, woolen underwear with long sleeves and full leggings provided protection from the cold, and there were lighter weight versions for the warmer months. Etta "ruled the roost" when Tom was young. It didn't seem to bother Thomas that his wife was the boss. Tom says that "her management style worked, and Pop was happy with the situation. It was a happy house. There was no yelling. You were better off if you didn't argue with Ma." (But one of Tom's sisters did, anyway.)

Meg and Fran had indoor chores. Cooking was not one of them; that was Etta's domain, because she loved to cook. She also was the only person to tend the coal furnace, which could be tricky. Her husband had a very long work week, including twenty-four-hour shifts, and it made sense for the person who was always home to know how to handle it. But Thomas alone tended his small vegetable garden. He also kept chickens, and sometimes turkeys, on their large city lot. Tom cleaned the henhouse, fed the flock, and collected eggs, but his father killed, plucked, and dressed the birds.

Etta and Thomas were serious Catholics, and they attended Mass with their children, walking about a mile to church every week. In his free time, Thomas enjoyed fishing. Etta belonged to a school organization that was the equivalent of the P.T.A., but her main loves were taking care of her home and spending time in the kitchen. They rented, and later bought, a little "camp"—primitive summer cottage—on Cobbett's Pond in Windham, New Hampshire, twelve miles from home, and spent much of the summer there. Thomas, who bought a car in 1937, commuted from the pond to work. He also got annual vacation time which he spent at the pond. For the Fourth of July, the camp association collected funds from everyone to set fireworks off over the pond. Tom also enjoyed the carnivals and parades in Lowell on both the Fourth and Memorial Day, and Thomas often marched with the fire department.

When Tom was twelve he got his first summer job, working on a dairy farm near the family's camp belonging to a Mr. Parker. He helped pour milk into bottles and made all the deliveries to the camps on the pond, working from 7:30 until 3:30 or 4 and getting paid twenty-five cents a day. [To put his wage into perspective, the quarts of milk he sold were ten cents a bottle. He was paid less than a gallon of milk per day!] But he gained experience and a good reference. At fourteen, he got a year-round job milking cows by hand in Dracut, about a twenty-minute walk from home.

Tom played with his sisters at home, but other than that he did not play with girls. Their neighborhood had a lot of children, and playtime was strictly segregated: girls with girls, boys with boys. Tom and his friends played basketball at a hoop attached to a telephone pole, sandlot baseball, and football, and took long, multi-mile walks. Tom loved being outside, skating, sledding, or playing ball. He also liked finding work to do in his yard; he made sideboards for his wagon so he could move dirt around, as he didn't have a wheelbarrow. He was allowed to leave the yard alone when quite young, but like all the others in the neighborhood he was restricted to staying within "calling range." He knew not to use "I didn't hear you" as an excuse for not coming home when called, because it would mean he had left neighborhood bounds without permission. There wasn't much Tom liked to do inside. He didn't listen to the radio much, and he didn't like to read. About the only toy he owned was a small fire truck. Etta made all three children take piano lessons. Tom took for three years but never became a good player, nor did his sisters.

The McGarrs owned their own six-room home: three bedrooms upstairs, and parlor, kitchen with pantry, dining room, and their one bathroom, downstairs. In the kitchen were an ice box and an old Glenwood stove that had originally burned wood but had been converted to coal/coke on its "heater" side and city gas on its cooking side. Hot water came off the coils in the coal-fired furnace that furnished steam heat. Etta had an electric washer with a hand wringer. When Tom was young they had neither car, telephone, nor radio. In first grade the family got a radio; in third grade, a phone, and around fifth, a car. The farthest he remembers riding was to Arlington for the occasional visit to an uncle and his five children.

The family ate all meals together until Tom went to high school. For breakfast they had either eggs from their own chickens, or hot cereal. Tom liked peanut butter or homemade-jelly sandwiches for lunch, but not both together. If Mr. McGarr was on duty, one of the children brought his lunch to the firehouse; for a twenty-four shift, Etta included enough food for two meals. Supper was at five, always with potatoes, whatever meat was reasonably priced, and vegetables, sometimes from their garden. There was no snacking, but for special occasions Tom's mother baked pies, and other treats like banana bread. Thomas especially liked her mince pie.

At five-and-a-half, Tom entered public school. He switched to parochial school for grades six through eight and went on to a Catholic high school, Keith Academy. This school was two miles across town, so Tom bought a bicycle for fifteen dollars and rode it there unless the streets were snow-covered. The all-male school was run by the Xaverian Brothers and was academically challenging. Tom hadn't tried very hard to do well in school prior to ninth grade, but because he wanted to go to college he buckled down and really started to work. He had some excellent teachers. One was his Latin teacher, who taught him on his own time how to run a wood lathe that he owned. They stayed in touch for many years.

Tom graduated in 1944, during World War II. He joined the Navy in 1945, got sent to the Pacific, and was on Okinawa when the war ended. Then he entered the University of Massachusetts on the G.I. bill, where he majored in animal science and played on the football team. He was hoping to become a farmer or to work in some other way with large animals, but after the dean talked him into trying out some education courses he decided on teaching. He was an "animal sciences shop teacher" in Templeton, Massachusetts for two years before switching to Westport High School in 1952. At that time Westport ranked second in Massachusetts in its number of dairy farms; only neighboring Dartmouth had more than Westport's sixty-five. [Today there are only four.] Tom stayed in Westport for ten years, including a sabbatical year off in 1960 to earn a master's degree from Cornell University. The rest of his career was spent in vocational education administration, at UMass Amherst, Norfolk County Agricultural High School in Walpole, and Diman Regional Technical Vocational High School in Fall River. He and his wife, Jean, had three sons. He retired to Westport and still lives there.

Sitting at his dining room table in 2014, Tom says he had a stroke two years ago. Nobody would have guessed. And he seems ten years younger than his age of eighty-six. But there are things he no longer does because of the stroke—no more using power tools, for instance. The key to his happy childhood, he insists, is this: he learned early that his mother was the boss.

45

Edith

EDWARD DOUGLAS RINGWALL, Edith's father, was born in Birmingham (now Derby), Connecticut and moved to the coastal community of West Haven when he was young. He served in the Army in World War I and was gassed during combat in France but recovered. In 1925 he married Marion Kathleen Eiter, who had grown up in the Columbus Circle area of Manhattan. After graduating from high school she had worked as a secretary for the magazine *Collier's*. She and Edward met at a vacation boardinghouse in South Woodstock that was popular with the Swedish community. Edward supported his wife and children as a salesman for construction supplies for the Howard Company in New Haven.

Edward's father, also Edward—Edward Emmanuel Ringwall—was born about 1870 in Sweden, one of ten children. He was a cabinetmaker who came to this country as a young man at some point before 1892 and settled in Milford, Connecticut. His wife—Edward Douglas Ringwall's mother—was Mathilda Börg. She was twelve years older than her husband and had worked as a domestic. Mathilda came from Sweden as a young woman during a time of severe famine which many Scandinavians were fleeing. They first met on the green in Milford on the Fourth of July. The Ringwalls attended the Swedish Baptist Church in New Haven. They had three children: Edward; Elvira, who died of diphtheria at four; and Violet, who had Down syndrome and

Born *at Grace Hospital in New Haven, Connecticut in July 1928*

When I was your age, *I lived in a whole different world. It was friendlier. Children had better manners and more respect for each other.*

When I was your age, *families were different. Everyone in my neighborhood had both a mother and a father at home.*

When I was your age, *clothes were different. Music was different. Priorities were different. Transportation was different.*

When I was your age, *I won a bottle of cod liver oil in a contest.*

When I was your age, *our culture was much less crude.*

What were your very favorite foods to eat? *There were so many! Turkey, mashed potato, pot roast, pineapple upside down cake.*

What did you like least? *Shad, a fish hard to come by now. It had about a million little fine bones. Codfish was also a problem. Now we can buy them de-boned, but we couldn't then. Mother made a cream sauce and served the fish with the sauce already poured over it, making it even harder to pick out the bones.*

Did you or your friends ever eat out at restaurants or diners? *No*

You were required to attend church growing up. Is religion important to you now? *Yes.*

Did you ever address adults by their first names? *Only one, and only because she insisted on it*

What did you call your parents? *Daddy and Mother*

What was your first job while you were still in school? *I babysat some but found it boring. In high school I worked at Feinson's Department Store. My boss called me "Miss R." During college summers I was a playground counselor through the Community House and later at Painter Park.*

How old were you when you went on your first date, and where did you go? *I went to a semi-formal dance at the Masonic Temple with Wade Bowden when I was about fourteen, arranged by our mothers. Wade arrived at my house on his bicycle, and my father drove us to the dance. Other friends took the trolley, even though they had on long gowns. Most of us walked home afterwards.*

How old were you when you got married? *I was 23, and he was 22.*

What was your first full-time job? *Fourth grade teacher*

What was your occupation for most of your working life? *I was a stay-at-home mother until the youngest of my three children entered first grade. Then I returned to teaching.*

Many things have been invented since you were a child. What has given you the most pleasure, or been the most valuable to you? *Televisions, dishwashers, dryers, bread makers, air conditioning in cars, and other things that make life more comfortable. My husband's favorites are his snow blower and power mower.*

What do you think you would most enjoy about being a kid today? *I would enjoy watching television and would like the increased opportunities to travel.*

What would you most dislike? *The stress of trying to "keep up"*

By today's standards, did you have a lot of "stuff" growing up? *No. We had fewer clothes and toys. And we kept items like family games on shelves in the attic, so our home was pretty uncluttered.*

In general, today we have many more possessions than when you were a child. Do you think this has affected our happiness? *People don't realize that we can get along very nicely without a lot of what we have, since marketers have convinced us otherwise.*

Today we hear that the lives of many American children are very stressful. Was yours stressful in any way? *Only in trying to complete my homework thoroughly in high school.*

What is your name now? *Edith Lucille Warner*

Did you eat beans and franks for Saturday night supper? *No*

died at fifty-four after living at home for most of her life. Violet was institutionalized only after her family could no longer care for her, but they continued to visit her regularly.

Marion was the daughter of yet another Edward - Edward Joseph Eiter, who was born in Newburgh, New York and grew up around Saugerties. He did "graining" of wood in doors and woodwork in his clients' Madison Avenue offices. Edward was a highly skilled artisan who utilized unusual and diverse aids such as combs and even beer to make patterns in wood grain. His parents, Joseph Eiter and Jacobine Müller, had come from a section of Germany near the Swiss border. Joseph fought in the Civil War and died at Walter Reed Hospital from battle wounds. Marion's mother was Margaret O'Connor, who was born in Dublin while her parents were visiting Ireland but spent most of her childhood in England. She also lived for a while in France while her artist father, Bernard O'Connor, retouched and restored paintings in the Louvre. Margaret died of pneumonia when Marion was only four.

Edith herself grew up on North Street in West Haven only a block from New Haven Harbor, in a middle-class neighborhood that was about twenty-five percent Swedish. The others were of English,

German, and Irish backgrounds, a mix of Catholics and Protestants. They were close-knit and friendly; folks sat on their porches and chatted with passing neighbors. When there was a death, neighborhood children went from house to house collecting money for a gift of flowers or cash for the grieving family. The Ringwall family was Protestant. Edward was a Methodist and his wife an Episcopalian, and Edith was baptized in an Episcopal church. However, the Methodist church was closer, so they decided to make this their family church.

Three children were born to Edward and Marion: in 1926, Edward Douglas, who was born a month past his due date and died three days later from a forceps injury; in 1928, Edith; and in 1933, Douglas Edward. They rented half of a two-family house from Edward's father; after his death in 1946 they became the owners. There was a coal furnace for heat and a gas/coal four-burner kitchen stove. A coal pail was kept next to the stove for ashes, which they used to fertilize the yard and garden. The family had an ice box until it was replaced with a refrigerator, and they placed a sign in their front window to let the delivery man know how big a block of ice to bring in. Children followed his truck, picking up ice chips from the street to suck on. The Ringwalls lived at generally the same level as their neighbors, with one telephone, and two radios—a small portable in the kitchen, and a large floor model in the living room. But they came out on top in the laundry department by owning an Ironrite mangle, an automatic ironing machine which was not a common item. And although they had no clothes dryer—and neither did anyone else around them—they did have a modern washer, a Bendix, which was the first automatic on the market. Mr. Ringwall used a company car to get to work, and his father owned a car that they sometimes took on drives on Sunday after church and a big dinner.

Douglas and Edith both had plenty of chores. Edith scrubbed the kitchen floor on her hands and knees, washed windows, hung laundry, and did dishes. (She didn't enjoy drying silverware, though, and if Marion wasn't looking Edith sometimes put it away wet.) Her mother taught her to use their Ironrite, which required a good bit of coordination in guiding fabric while operating the roller with a knee. Edith also helped her mother can hundred of jars of jams, jellies, juices, and vegetables from their huge "victory garden" on an extra lot they owned in another section of town and which she occasionally helped her father and brother tend. They grew corn, potatoes, tomatoes, string beans, carrots, celery, beets, cucumbers, yellow squash, and other vegetables.

Edward and his wife enjoyed listening to the radio, reading books and the daily newspaper, and occasionally seeing a movie. Marion belonged to a bridge club and took Red Cross courses in first aid during the war. She also served on church committees and organizations, as did her husband. She was a member of the Eastern Star, and her husband was a Mason. At home, they played board games and card games with their children, although Marion disliked playing Parcheesi with them because the children argued too much during it.

Christmas was Edith's favorite holiday, though she received many fewer presents than is typical today. Christmas Eve started with a traditional Swedish smorgasbord dinner, and then, following Swedish custom, all the adults opened their gifts. In a nod to newer American customs, Edith and her brother opened only one gift and saved the rest for the morning. Stockings were opened at 6 a.m., followed by a Christmas service at church at about 6:30.

Holidays featuring parades were also fun. On Memorial Day Edith marched with the Girl Scouts and her father with the World War I veterans. After the parade the family visited relatives' graves and laid fresh flowers on them. There was a huge victory parade at the end of World War II after Japan surrendered, and all the high school classes marched. Schools were closed for the day.

When Edith was with the neighborhood kids or her friends from school they roller skated; played outdoor games of hopscotch, hide and seek, kick the can, red light, and giant steps; played card games like pinochle or Go Fish; made up guessing games such as *Here are the initials: what movie star am I thinking of*; played school; formed clubs; had birthday parties (that did *not* include sleeping over); and met at each others' houses to just talk. Most of them lived within four or five blocks from her, but occasionally her father drove her to visit others living farther away. Within the neighborhood, boys and girls played outside games together. As a teen, Edith sometimes went sledding down Shingle Hill with friends from the Methodist Youth Fellowship after the

Sunday evening meeting. They slid right on the street in the dark, all the way from the top to Lake Phipps. Fortunately there was very little traffic, as the area was still undeveloped and there were no houses on the street.

When alone, Edith mostly liked to read library books, especially series books like Nancy Drew or the Bobbsey Twins. She had dolls, including a Dionne Quintuplet doll, and her mother made some clothes for them. Her favorite radio shows were Uncle Don, The Shadow, Grand Central Station, One Man's Family, I Love a Mystery, and Jack Armstrong. She didn't listen much to music on the radio, but she bought sheet music of the current hits to play on the piano. Edith took piano lessons for eleven years, and organ lessons some summers. She had a bicycle which she rode to her lessons. She also had sidewalk skates, which fitted over her shoes, white ice skates, and a red skating skirt with a green satin lining.

On Saturdays, Edith helped around the house in the morning and occasionally went to a movie in the afternoon. Other times her father took the children to the woods, bringing a wildflower guide to help them identify plants they found. Or they might have an afternoon picnic in their back yard, at a picnic table her father had built for them.

Edith's mother served lots of Swedish foods along with standard American favorites: meatballs, coffee bread, coffee cake, poached fish, and macaroni and cheese. She sometimes served spaghetti, but with canned sauce; she never made her own. Occasionally they had char-broiled steaks cooked in a distinctive manner: laid on the grate of their coal furnace. Unlike many of the others interviewed for this book, they never had beans and franks on Saturday nights. Edith thought that that was "maybe more of a Massachusetts thing." She didn't have to finish everything on her plate, but she usually did. After school, Edith had a snack, usually a Swedish coffee bun. She had no soda, or junk food like potato chips. And she has no idea why, but they never, ever had peanut butter.

When Edith was five years old she started kindergarten and walked alone the seven or eight blocks to the school and back every day. Classes often had up to forty students to a room, and in eighth grade there were forty-two. Boys and girls entered the building through separate doors on opposite sides of the building. The day started with teachers reading verses from the Bible and leading their classes in the Lord's Prayer, the Pledge of Allegiance, and the Star-Spangled Banner. There was a morning snack break, with milk available to buy. There were no school-wide outdoor recesses, however, and there was no playground equipment. Each teacher scheduled a time to bring her own students outside, where she kept them together as a group and led them in an activity. From fifth grade on they also had one or two daily sessions of exercise by their desks for about ten minutes. All students went home for an hour-and-a-half lunch break. In high school, classes were on double sessions: the three upper grades went from 7:45 a.m. until 1:00 p.m., and the ninth grade from 1:00–5:15 p.m.

Florence Felicity Fogarty, Edith's sixth grade teacher, was one of her favorites. When school ended for the year she got married and invited the entire class to the wedding (but not to the reception). For the occasion, the class took up a collection and bought a lamp as a wedding gift. Edith helped Miss Fogarty clear out her things from the classroom and was given some "real" teacher things for her effort. This made her games of school with her friends even more realistic. Edith liked to be the teacher when they played, using a blackboard on an easel her father had made for her.

Edith once had an exciting adventure on a fishing trip with her father and her cousin Bob in a rowboat on Long Island Sound. She was nine or ten, and Bob about thirteen. A thunderstorm blew in very suddenly, so her father rowed to a nearby sandbar, pulled the boat onto the sand, turned it upside down, then tipped it up to form a lean-to, using the two oars to keep it propped in place. Bob thought this was great fun, but Edith was frightened and cried a lot despite her father's soothing words. Things seemed a little better when he brought out their lunch, and Edith remembers peeling an orange from it. Meanwhile, her mother saw the storm and was frantic. She phoned a retired sea captain who lived nearby, right on the waterfront, and kept a telescope on his front porch. Captain Bornman soon located them with it and called back to report that they were marooned but seemed safe.

Edith was also about nine when she won a prize in a drawing contest sponsored by a radio show. She liked to draw, and she had plenty of time to take great care and do an especially good job on her entry, as she was out of school with chicken pox. After she sent in her drawing of Mickey Mouse she forgot about the contest until someone who worked with her father heard her name announced over the radio. The prize for first place was a Mickey Mouse watch, but Edith's drawing earned second place, winning her a bottle of mint-flavored cod liver oil! As unappealing as that sounds now, it was actually a very nice prize. Many mothers forced a spoonful of foul-tasting cod liver oil on their children every day, as it was loaded with vitamins and seemed to have many health benefits, which studies later confirmed. The mint flavoring greatly improved the taste, and children welcomed it.

One thing Edith especially disliked was going to the dentist. When she was in high school she successfully avoided an appointment after school by actually hiding in a dark bedroom closet in the attic. Her father arrived home to drive her, but he couldn't find her even after searching the house, including the attic room where she was hiding. If he had looked in its *closet* he might have seen her, but he didn't even open the door (and she can only speculate on the reason for this omission). After he gave up and returned to work Edith came out and went downstairs to face her mother. "I don't remember any repercussions," she says now. "I'm sure my mother had something to say! But I wasn't made to suffer very much."

At fourteen or fifteen, Edith and a thirteen-year old neighbor went alone to New York City for the day, obeying strict orders to take only buses and *not* the subway. She and her friend went to attractions like Macy's and Stouffer's but also did something very unusual and special: they saw a live television show. Television had been invented many years before, but its development had come to a halt with World War II. Programming was very limited, and the government banned all commercial programming for the duration of the war. This had almost no effect on the population, as few people had even heard of television, let alone owned a set.

Edith graduated from West Haven High School with honors in 1946 and went on to New Haven State Teachers College (which is now Southern Connecticut State University). She lived at home and commuted to campus via trolley. One major difference between

teacher training in her day and now is the instruction in special education; Edith had virtually none and always felt it would have been help-
ful to have had more. After graduation she taught fourth grade at the
Colonial Park School in West Haven, which was on double sessions.
Her class met in the afternoon, so her students didn't get out of school
until after dark for much of the year. After teaching for three-and-a-
half years, Edith took a long break to start a family. She stayed home
until her youngest child was six years old.

46

Charlotte

THERE WAS ANOTHER STORY Charlotte's mother liked to tell her
daughter, one which was all true. Her parents had had a bed-and-
breakfast type of business in Poland. On one occasion their overnight
customers were a man and his young employee. The next morning Sarah's mother asked her, "How did you like that young man who just
stayed here? I signed a contract with him last night." Sarah Bendremer,
who was 21, was now officially engaged to 17-year old Benjamin Cohen!
They had met only briefly and had never had a real conversation.

Several years and three children later, Benjamin sailed to America, sponsored by a brother who sold fruits and vegetables off a street
wagon in Lawrence, Massachusetts. He found work with a Jewish
butcher and began saving up to bring his family over. After seven years
of hard work, sleeping in the cellar of the butcher shop every night,
he had enough money. His wife, daughter, and two sons joined him
in Lawrence and moved into a tenement on Valley Street across from
the shop. They soon added another son and, two years later, their
final child, Charlotte. At some point Benjamin was able to leave his
employer and open his own shop on Park Street. Neither Sarah nor
Benjamin ever learned English well. They lived in a neighborhood
where they could conduct all business in Yiddish.

The children born in Poland were much older than Charlotte and
left home before she got to know them well. As the only daughter at

Delivered *at home in Lawrence, Massachusetts by a midwife in December 1915*

When I was your age, *I wanted to be a physical education teacher. I was good at all sports. One of my sons did become a phys, ed. teacher.*

What were your very favorite foods to eat? *Whole wheat bread, roast beef, and gefilte (stuffed) fish*

You were not required to attend services growing up. Is religion important to you now? *Yes*

Did you ever address adults by their first names? *No*

What did you call your parents? *Pa and Ma*

How old were you when you went on your first date, and where did you go? *I was 16 or 17, and I went to my prom.*

How old were you when you got married? *I was 28 or 29, and he was 27 or 28.*

What was your first full-time job? *I was a clerk in the candy department of a department store.*

What was your occupation for most of your working life? *I was a stay-at-home mother and an "Avon Lady" who sold door-to-door. I became a top seller.*

What do you think you would most enjoy about being a kid today? *There's so much more available to do that I would like, including going to beaches.*

What is your name now? *Charlotte (Cohen) Blood*

In general, today we have many more possessions than when you were a child. Do you think this has affected our happiness? *No.*

home Charlotte had many chores; by the age of seven or eight she was already responsible for cleaning and scrubbing all the floors. But when she was about nine her mother had a terrible accident, falling as she descended the outside steps to their building and badly injuring her legs. Sarah was left a semi-invalid. She never recovered enough to walk without holding on to furniture and rarely left the apartment. While Sarah was able to continue to cook, Charlotte had to take over almost everything else, including all the cleaning and shopping. She also bathed and helped care for her mother. She felt no resentment—only a very strong love for her. She did, however, blame her father for refusing to get her any medical help. It might not have made any difference, but then, it might have.

The Cohens had less than their neighbors, and other mothers could do more for their children. But Charlotte was happy. She didn't mind that she had extra duties or that her few clothes weren't as good. She "didn't know the difference between a $5 dress and a $50 dress." If she was invited to a party but had no nice dress to wear, she went anyway, and had a good time. And they weren't desperately poor. They had a radio and a telephone, and cold running water. The kitchen stove that burned both wood and coal provided most of their heat. There was also a small stove in the living room that was used only for company and special occasions. Ice was delivered three times a week, and a sign in a bedroom window indicated how much they wanted that day. They washed laundry in the bathtub on a scrub board. When Charlotte started second grade the family moved to the grounds of a summer camp in Boxford. Benjamin slept at the shop during the week and made the very long walk home every weekend. They moved back to the city at the end of that school year.

There was enough to eat, and Charlotte especially enjoyed gefilte fish, roast beef, and fresh whole wheat bread from the Jewish bakery. She wasn't forced to eat everything on her plate, but she says that she would have been hungry if she hadn't! Her mother prepared traditional foods for Jewish holidays: corned beef and cabbage, potato pancakes, and big roasts with mounds of carrots.

The Cohens were not particularly religious. They observed the holidays, and her father occasionally went to synagogue but his wife and children usually did not. The other Jewish kids in her neighborhood all attended after school classes they called "Jewish school" to learn about their religion, but Charlotte did not. She spent a lot of her time helping her mother. She didn't have many toys besides a doll she won in a contest, or much time to herself, but she was content. She sometimes went with friends to the Young Women's Hebrew Association or to the movies. If the girls didn't have money for tickets they could stand in the alleyway and catch glimpses of the screen. They also played baseball, sledded, and had fun on their homemade stilts. These they made by piercing empty food cans and threading strong string through the jagged holes. Then they walked on the cans, pulling the strings tight to hold them to their feet.

Lawrence had four theaters in Charlotte's day, offering both movies and vaudeville acts. When the Victoria announced a talent show with a pony for first prize, Charlotte entered. Wearing a costume she'd made all by herself—black oilcloth vest, black cap, and black britches—she did a rendition of a Cossack dance. The winner was to be decided by who got the most applause, so her brother brought his friends to clap and stomp for her. They also brought pieces of wood that they thumped on the floor to make the applause seem even louder. It worked. Charlotte won the pony and named him Peanuts. Of course her father couldn't afford to keep and feed a pony only for Charlotte's pleasure, so he bought a cart and harness, and hitched Peanuts up. The pony cart was just wonderful for making deliveries.

On the very first day of first grade many parents walked to school with their children and went inside to get them settled. Charlotte's parents did not. They were both illiterate and felt awkward and uncomfortable in that unfamiliar world. Five-and-a-half-year-old Charlotte walked the three blocks all by herself. She felt so alone and frightened that first day that she wet her pants, adding shame to her misery. Soon, though, she came to love school and everything about it.

Teachers and principals were very strict. Disruptive students were punished with a whack from a ruler or made to stand in the corner wearing a "dunce cap." Charlotte was well-behaved and never received either punishment. She graduated from Lawrence High School in 1933 and is now its oldest living graduate.

Charlotte wanted desperately to go to college to become a physical education teacher, but with no idea how to go about it, and certainly no idea where she could find the money for it, she went right into the work force instead. While working as a clerk in a department store Charlotte met her future husband. Albert Blood was her supervisor, but eventually they started going out despite Albert's being Catholic. Her parents were aware of the situation, and Sarah was supportive; Benjamin was unhappy but didn't stop her. After they had been dating for five years, America entered World War II. Albert enlisted in the Navy, but before he left they became secretly engaged. After he survived his ship being torpedoed Albert was granted a short leave. During the leave the couple eloped, married by a Justice of the Peace. They told nobody about the marriage except Charlotte's mother, who loaned them her wedding ring for the ceremony.

After the war they told all the parents. At the time it was very rare to marry outside one's faith, and Charlotte was worried about her father's reaction. However, Benjamin Cohen accepted Albert immediately and all was well. The couple had four children and remained happily married until Albert's death.

Today Charlotte is ninety-seven years old and has had the great sorrow of outliving both of her sons. She feels our society is no happier for having so many more possessions than previous generations, and that academic competition and emphasis on high marks is making life stressful for children. The most important things in life, she says, are your children, what you do to help others, and the faith you should have in yourself—because you can do more than you think you can.

47

Learning, Yearning

WE ALL WENT OFF to school when we were old enough, which for about half of us meant entering first grade at age five, and half at age six. School systems used a wide variety of cutoff ages for entrance, but the most common policy seemed to be six years old by the end of the calendar year in which a child started first grade. Some systems took them extremely young. One was Fairhaven, where **Nancy** had just turned five the summer before she began school. **Ellen** missed a cutoff by about a month but got slipped in anyway by her father (playing superintendent's privilege). When she moved to Holliston a year later she was young for her grade, but five years later, in Fairhaven, she was right in the middle of the class age-wise. **Walt** turned six a couple of months into first grade in Boston, but his family had just returned to the city from a few years in Florida. Due to his fall birthday, if they had stayed in Boston he could have entered kindergarten at only three, and first grade at four. Public kindergarten, though, was still a rarity. Only three of us lived in places where it had been established: **Walt, Sonny,** and **Butch**. Significantly, these three were also the youngest of us, all born in the early 1930s.

At least two of us—**Lucy** and **Charlotte**—spoke no English until we entered school, but we became fluent quickly. Four others had parents who were immigrants from non-English-speaking countries but who did speak English at least part of the time at home. Both **Claire** and **Rosanna** studied French, their parents' native language, in their parochial elementary schools. Claire received half of her instruction each school day in French, and half in English.

Almost half of us spent at least one school year in a classroom containing more than one grade; about half of these were two-grade rooms, and the rest held four, five, or even six grades. **Beena** went to a two-room village school through the eighth grade; **Okie, Ellie,** and **Shirley** attended one-room schools through fifth or sixth grade, and **Ellen** and **Charlotte** each spent one year in a four-grade classroom.

Recesses were a time to stretch our legs and give our minds a break. Only **Rosanna** and **Claire**, who both attended parochial schools, had relatively limited recess time. Rosanna had one morning recess and only a one-half hour lunch break; Claire had no recesses but did have an hour off at lunch. Almost everyone else had two scheduled outdoor breaks a day, one in the morning and another in the afternoon. This was in addition to at least an hour at midday, giving an additional chance after lunch to burn up energy playing in the schoolyard or walking home and back. A few of us had an hour-and-a-half or longer.

We weren't overly burdened with homework. Well over half of us didn't start bringing home assignments until fifth, sixth, or seventh grade; and over a quarter didn't get any homework until eighth or ninth. Only three of us remembered receiving homework before fifth grade, and even that wasn't until third or fourth. Nobody had homework in the first or second grade.

We didn't like everything about school. (Well, actually, three of us claimed that we did.) Some objected to particular subjects. **Nancy** liked everything except math. **Lucy** didn't like geography but did like history. **Shirl** didn't like to write book reports. Neither **Helen** nor **Edith** liked gym class, and Edith also mentioned not liking the gym suits they had to wear. **Beena** didn't like French, and **Louise** didn't like Latin. **Tom**'s school required *both* of those languages, and he found them difficult. Since he wanted to do well, he voluntarily stayed after school for extra help, which he didn't enjoy very much. **Pumpie** said that it was tough to be assigned to the slow group, and **Louise** found it hard to follow on the heels of a brilliant sister who was the high school valedictorian. **Ellen** didn't like homework and considered it "a big waste of time that didn't do any good." **Ellie** wanted to be allowed to talk with those around her but knew she'd be reprimanded in front of everyone if she did. **Butch** thought that school was "too long." **Vicki** didn't mind school itself, but she hated getting up early in the morning for it. **Shirl** didn't like having to listen, because she preferred to daydream. When she was a student, **Rosanna**, who would later become a teacher, thought school was a waste of her time. She wanted to be going places, or dancing—not sitting down and reading. And probably nobody liked staying back, which several of us had to do—some *twice!* But that's how many schools operated then: learn it now, or try again next year.

Asked what we wished we had learned in school, **Lucy** answered by saying that whenever she wanted to know something she hadn't learned, she simply found a book on it. **Rosanna** later wished she had applied herself more. **Butch** regretted not going on to college. **Ellie** wished there had been clerical courses available at her high school, and **Tom** was unhappy that his parochial middle school didn't offer shop, which was available in the public schools. **Pumpie** wished she had learned how to cook and sew, and **Nancy** wished she could have learned more in her cooking and sewing classes. She also wished she had acquired better math skills. **Shirl** wished she had picked up better study skills. **Tom** wished he'd been taught to read better. **Ellen** wished she had learned more science.

For all our complaints, though, there were many aspects of school we were grateful for. **Lucy** and **Shirl** appreciated the cooking and sewing skills they gained. **Rosanna, Vicki, Ellen,** and **Louise** mentioned learning how to listen and pay attention. **Butch** says he learned to behave himself, and **Claire** said that school helped her grow up in general. Two referenced compassion: **Edith** learned to treat others as she would like to be treated, and **Charlotte** became aware of others who had even less than she did and looked for opportunities to help them. Others mentioned learning to be respectful, honest, obedient, and/or punctual. **Rozzy** and **Ellie** learned, reluctantly, how to keep quiet. **Lucy** commented that she "learned English very fast" and that *everything* she learned in school was valuable.

Did we have happy childhoods? Asked to reach back and honestly assess whether we had felt happy and content at the time, two of us had to admit that, no, we had not. Two more answered that they sometimes had, and sometimes had not. Another two "usually" had. The rest of us said that we definitely had felt happy and content.

Asked what we wished we had had, exactly half of us responded firmly, "Nothing!" And three of those added spontaneously that they were satisfied with what their parents could provide. The other eight mentioned a variety of things. **Ellen** wanted ice skates and skis but hadn't realized she needed to ask for them; **Beena** wished for more books because she had no access to a library; **Louise** wanted a store-bought coat (which she finally earned enough money for in high school) and a car, and **Sonny** longed for money to buy snack at school when he was very young. **Nancy** wished she could have had a Shirley Temple doll, and **Pumpie** wanted more toys in general but says that she "got over" it, knowing it wasn't possible. There was one common comment on the wish list. **Bella, Beena, Ellen,** and **Louise** all wished for the same thing, something Sonny wished he could have gotten a lot earlier than he did: a bicycle.

We all grew up with a lot fewer possessions in our homes than most people in this country have today. Nineteen of us responded to a question about whether or not that increase had led to more happiness in our society, and nobody said that, yes, it had. We mentioned being pleased to have nice things, especially dependable cars and labor-saving appliances, but we were clear that being more comfortable doesn't actually make us happier; that happiness is dependent on good relationships with others. We also mentioned a dark side to having so much: many of us thought that society is much less happy for it. We—even some who were very poor—felt we had had enough growing up, even though we sometimes longed for a little more. Now we see the results all around of having so much more. One is the effect on children, who have a lot more toys, most of which are designed for indoor use. We said, We made our own fun; We used to get outside and do things more; It has changed the way children use their time; We went out to play; I feel sorry for today's babies. Another result is the effect on our attitudes ["we" referring to society in general]: We don't appreciate what we have; We have to possess a whole lot of things, but we don't care about them, don't value them; Our possessions have overwhelmed us; It's not beneficial to always get what we want right away: delayed satisfaction is a GOOD thing; We always want more; We have become greedy and wasteful. Two of us said, The more we get, the more we want. Five of us came up with exactly the same four-word response: "We have too much." And a few of us blamed this on the advertising industry. According to Edith, "People don't realize that we can get along very nicely without a lot of what we have, because marketers have convinced us otherwise."

48

Times of Earning

ALL OF US WORKED at least occasionally by the time we were in our teens, either at paying jobs or helping with the family farm or home. A lot of the girls started with babysitting before moving on to work in retail stores.

We tended to end up with more education than our parents had had, and we went on to more-rewarding jobs. All but three of us graduated from high school, and about two thirds went on to further training or college. Three of the boys and thirteen of the girls—about sixty percent of each group—greatly surpassed their parents in both education and job status. The men had careers in education, electronics, manufacturing, and the military. Some of the women were career housewives or farm wives. Others had jobs in factories; helped their husbands in family businesses or ran their own; taught school; worked as secretaries, bookkeepers, or nurses. Almost all of the sixteen women who became mothers left their jobs to stay home and care for their children. Most of those who later returned to the work force waited until all of them were old enough to be left alone.

49

Here's a Look at What We Wore

CLOTHING WAS MUCH MORE expensive than it is today, and we had much less of it. Most of us had several outfits for school; for footwear, there was one pair of shoes for school, one for church or dress-up, and sneakers or sandals—not both—for the summer. Elaine and Rozzy had more—Elaine because her family was pretty well off, and Rozzy because her aunt was a housekeeper for a wealthy family and was routinely given boxes of beautiful hand-me-downs. Pumpie's mother was also a housekeeper and received nice hand-me-downs, but with eight children she had a larger family to outfit than Rozzy's. A few of us had very little. Helen, who was extremely poor, had only one skirt, one blouse, and one dress. But even Ellen, whose family was relatively well off, usually owned only two dresses for school and one for Sunday, plus a few shorts and tops for summer, until she started working in high school and buying her own clothes.

For well over half of us, either all or some of our wardrobe was made at home—usually by our mothers, although some girls also sewed some of their clothes themselves. One father was involved: **Rosanna**'s, who was a tailor, made her brothers' clothing himself. Several mentioned that their mothers made dresses and other items out of colorful flour sacks. These sack dresses were just fine, because as children we didn't pay much attention to fashion trends, or to how others dressed or wore their hair. When asked about this, some of us responded that we noticed clothes "very rarely," or "only if something was really unusual, really dirty, very shabby, or extremely expensive." There weren't generally any kiddie advertising appeals or other pressures for us to try to dress in more expensive clothes than our families could afford. One exception to this was noted by **Bella**, who grew up relatively poor. The school in her neighborhood went through the sixth grade; in seventh, students had to walk to a more affluent part of town and mingle with others who were better dressed. The richer kids snubbed them, and Bella felt that this was due at least in part to the obvious difference in their dress.

In high school, we started to pay more attention to appearance. Most of us said that teenagers dressed differently than younger children, although seven of us—from a variety of backgrounds and a wide span of ages—disagreed. (Perhaps communities differed, or maybe some of us simply remembered more accurately than others.) Tom and Walt encountered dress codes requiring neckties for the boys; and in an outward show of an inner conviction, Sonny started wearing a tie, completely of his own accord, as he got more serious about school. Nine of the girls said that dress conventions in their schools changed as students hit their teen years. They "took on a more grown-up appearance in dress" or just "became more particular" or "wanted to look nice." In Rozzy's community, seventh-grade girls switched from dresses with sashes, ties, and bows to two-piece outfits. In Beena's, girls started curling their hair. Fads took hold, some long-term and others short-lived: high school girls wore ankle or bobby sox with either loafers or saddle shoes; plaid wool skirts were popular at Ellen's school, and flared circular ones at Louise's. Cardigan sweaters were definitely "in." But Edith's classmates wore them backwards, and Ellen's wore "sloppy Joes"—sweaters several sizes too big. Finally, there was the makeup issue. In an absolute dividing line between childhood and young adulthood, according to Edith, grade school girls did not wear it, and high school girls did. On the first day of high school, in a rite of passage, Edith put on lipstick before leaving home.

Almost all of us walked to school every day, and we were well prepared with appropriate outerwear for trudging through any kind of weather. We wore rubbers and carried umbrellas for rain; had heavy coats, extra sweaters, gloves or mittens, hats, and scarves for the cold; wore boots to protect our feet from snow and slush. Sometimes we added leggings or long underwear for extra warmth. Girls who wore snow or ski pants in the cold or snow put them underneath their skirts to avoid the bulges they would have had from skirts tucked into the pants. Helen and Lucy, however, too poor for warm or protective gear, suffered as they trekked through bad weather, getting frozen or soaked.

Until their parents allowed them to switch to long pants, boys wore knickers or short pants. Knickers, shorter than pants but longer than shorts, came in varying lengths, buckled either above or below the knee, and were usually worn with knee-length socks or stockings held up with garters. Because they could be buckled up at different lengths, they were an economical alternative for growing boys. During the years of World War II, however, they fell out of favor with the public; after the war, they virtually disappeared.

Of the four of us who attended parochial schools, only one—Claire—wore a uniform. Otherwise, the dress code for just about all girls was skirts or dresses for school. (One exception was the high school attended by Nancy and Ellen, which allowed girls to wear slacks on cold days. This was considered so unusual that the New Bedford newspaper sent a photographer to get a picture of the slacks-wearers, which happened to include Ellen that day. To leave no doubt as to how they felt about the Fairhaven girls' garb, they ran the photo right next to one of properly-clad New Bedford High girls.) After school, most of us girls stayed in our dresses or changed to old "play" dresses, but a few, like Bella, changed into dungarees. Ellie, the oldest of us all, put on dungarees for her farm work. But few of the rest owned even one pair of pants or slacks, although we might have shorts for the summer. Pumpie was married before she ever wore pants.

50

Louise

EVERY MORNING WAS THE SAME. Louise claimed to be dressed, then actually *got* dressed and raced downstairs. She had breakfast with her mother and three sisters; her father, too, if he hadn't left for work yet. If it was summertime, then Grammy, her father's mother, would be there as well.

Louise was born in South Paris, Maine, in the north bedroom of the farmhouse on Grammy Hammond's Farm. The second of four children, she was fifteen months younger than Carolyn, two-and-a-half years older than Barbara, and six years older than Mildred. A few years later the property went out of the family. Grammy had taken out a mortgage to pay college tuition for her sons, and when the Depression hit she was unable to make payments and lost the farm. The family had to move but remained in South Paris, living in two different rentals until 1944, when Louise's father was able to buy a home.

Charles Henry Hammond, Louise's father, was a Yankee and the descendant of some of Paris's first white settlers. He was too young for World War I and too old for World War II, but he served in the National Guard. Charles had a two-year agricultural education from the University of Maine, but with the loss of the farm he took on non-agricultural employment. He worked for many years at Paris Manufacturing, which made sleds and skis, and then spent twenty-two years as a deputy sheriff. Charles was also a Mason and a volunteer fireman. In retirement

Born *at home in Paris, Maine in October 1926*

When I was your age, *I practically lived outdoors. There was no computer or television.*

When I was your age, *I had a very enjoyable, enchanted life, with freedom to roam the town.*

What was your very favorite food to eat? *My mother's homemade bread*

Did you or your friends ever eat out at restaurants or diners? *Very seldom*

You attended church growing up. Is religion important to you now? *Yes, it is*

Did you ever address adults by their first names? *No*

What did most people call you? *Either Louise or Hammy*

What did you call your parents? *Dad and Mom*

What was your first job while you were still in school? *I started getting babysitting and housework jobs when I was twelve.*

How old were you when you went on your first date, and where did you go? *In the eighth grade a boy walked me home from Pilgrim Fellowship and then kissed me on the cheek. He was in around tenth grade. I never let him walk me home again!*

When did you see television for the first time? *I was working in Boston in the late 1940s. One day I was walking by a bar and happened to look in. There was a T.V. playing.*

How old were you when you got married? *We were both twenty years old.*

What was your first full-time job? *I was an R.N. at Massachusetts Memorial Hospital for two years. It is now part of Boston Medical Center.*

What was your occupation for most of your working life? *R.N.*

Many things have been invented since you were a child. What has given you the most pleasure, or been the most valuable to you? *I like the proliferation of cars and planes. I love to travel.*

What do you think you would most enjoy about being a kid today? *Not computers!*

What would you most dislike? *I wouldn't enjoy being in the house so much instead of being outside playing and learning about nature.*

By today's standards, did you have a lot of "stuff" growing up? *No, but some lovely things had been passed down to me.*

In general, today we have many more possessions than when you were a child. Do you think this has affected our happiness? *Yes. We have too much.*

What is your name now? *Louise Hammond Bailey*

Did you eat beans and franks for Saturday night supper? *Yes, I did. We had beans and franks with brown bread.*

he followed in the footsteps of his father and grandfather by serving in the state legislature, which met in the capital for only a couple of months each year. Legislators stayed in Augusta during that period and received a small stipend and transportation expenses.

Louise's mother, Pauline Estella Hammond, was also a Maine Yankee. She was born in Nobleboro, graduated from the local high school, Lincoln Academy, and met her husband at a county fair when her family moved to his area. Marrying someone with the same last name meant a lifetime of explanations whenever anyone in the family had to fill out forms. *Yes, Hammond was my mother's maiden name as well as my father's last name. Yes, I'm positive about that.* During Louise's childhood she worked a few summers canning corn and beans at a local plant, but mostly she was a thrifty homemaker who canned, sewed, cooked, and made do with very little. She belonged to a mothers group, giving her an evening out every month to socialize, and also to the Firemen's Auxiliary.

At midday they came together for dinner, the main meal of the day. Mrs. Hammond had a big meal ready when her husband arrived from work at 12:05 and the girls from school at 12:10. Supper, at 5:30, was lighter, with soup, leftovers, or a one-pot dish such as macaroni and cheese. Some of their food came from their garden and fruit trees, and when Louise was young they kept chickens. Every fall the Hammonds bought half a pig and a quarter of beef to keep them supplied with meat and lard. The girls had to eat whatever was served and finish everything on their plates, but Mrs. Hammond was a very good cook. Their friends enjoyed her fresh bread, homemade jam, and hot cocoa when they visited. On holidays they had a roast of beef, chicken, or pork. On one—and only one—Thanksgiving there was a goose. After that they stuck to chicken or turkey.

There were no between-meal snacks except on Friday afternoons, when the girls visited their mother's mother who lived nearby. However, this grandmother was known more for the quantity than the quality of her cooking. The sisters took the cookies or gingerbread she served them out to the yard, where they pretended it was chewing tobacco. After wadding it up in their mouths they'd see how far they could spit it!

The Hammonds got alone fine without a car. Occasionally they hired someone to drive them somewhere, and they could ride the trolley line to Norway, a town two miles away. But mostly they walked everywhere—work, school, church, shopping, friends' homes, and meetings. Housewives got regular visits from salesmen and delivery men. The ice man came once a week, and a sign placed in a front window let him know what size ice block to bring into the house. A meat peddler also came weekly. The fish man appeared every Friday. A rag man came every year to buy rags for the Armstrong Rug Company in

New York, which turned wool rags into braided rugs, and cloth rags into "rag" rugs. Entertainment even made its way to the town: every summer, a traveling Italian organ grinder and his monkey showed up. The portable street organ churned out pre-recorded songs at tempos determined by how fast the operator, or "grinder," cranked the handle. Passersby were supposed to drop money into a tin cup his small monkey held out.

The family's standard of living rose during Louise's childhood in spite of the Depression, as newer technologies became more affordable. The Hammonds got a telephone when she was around twelve. They used an ice box and other cold storage methods until she was in high school, when a refrigerator replaced them. An electric wringer took the place of the hand wringer attached to their wash tub. And the second rented house, on Brook Street, brought them indoor toilet facilities when Louise was eight. Wood, coal, and oil stoves and/or furnaces were used for cooking and heating.

The girls all helped with the chores: dishes, cleaning, hanging clothes out to dry, stacking wood for the stove, keeping their bedrooms clean, darning their own socks, and, for the older ones, caring for younger sisters. They also shoveled paths to the shed and the clothesline using wooden scoop shovels. Grammy started Louise on sewing and quilting at six. She was an excellent teacher and strict taskmaster who would rip out work that didn't meet her standards and make Louise re-do it. Louise soon learned to produce tiny, perfect stitches and to make a nice, smooth darn on socks to avoid getting blisters on her feet. All of her clothing was homemade during her elementary years, and most during high school, even underwear. Normally Louise used elastic in the underwear, but because it was expensive and scarce during the war she fashioned the items with ties instead. Although her dresses weren't made from old sacks, she did make quilts, and even bloomers, out of flour sacks with colorful flowered patterns.

For recreation, Louise's parents entertained neighbors and played cards with friends but also spent a lot of time with the girls, joining them for softball, croquet, and sledding. The family also enjoyed poker, bean bags, and board games like checkers, Monopoly, and Parcheesi, which they kept in a cupboard under a roll top desk. Louise's father didn't get any vacation, but sometimes on weekends they went on picnics by the brook, or went camping, bringing hamburg, onions, and big cans of Franco-American pasta so they could prepare American chop suey over their campfire. Occasionally Mrs. Hammond took the girls to Shirley Temple or Jane Withers movies in Norway. South Paris's own theater had been the silent-movies-with-piano variety and closed when the "talkies" came in. Mr. Hammond liked to box, and as he had no sons to spar with he taught his daughters. Their modern entertainment devices were a radio and a wind-up Victrola record player. Mrs. Hammond liked Rudy Vallee's voice, and his "Red Sails in the Sunset" was her favorite record. When Louise was very young they had to take turns listening to their old-style radio with its two sets of earphones.

There were several holidays Louise enjoyed. Her favorite was Christmas. In her stocking she received pennies, cookies, a small gift like a comb or a harmonica, and often an orange, which was a real treat. Her parents usually gave her handmade gifts such as doll furniture. Memorial Day was special as well. There was always a big parade. Just about all the kids in town marched in it, as members of groups like Campfire Girls or 4-H. And two kids' holidays were a lot of fun: May Day, when children hung baskets filled with candy on friends' front doors; and Halloween, when Louise and her friends played lots of tricks. One of the silliest involved a policeman they had nicknamed "Dick Tracy," and a hay rake. These large rakes were normally hitched to a horse, and a driver in the semi-circular seat held the reins while the horse pulled the rake through a field. The kids got hold of one from a friend who lived on a farm, brought it to the center of town, and dragged it down Main Street, the metal tines creating huge flying sparks. Dick Tracy took off after them, but the kids outran him and got away.

Every Saturday morning Louise made bread and rolls from scratch with her mother while Carolyn helped her father with outdoor chores. Summers, she also spent mornings doing chores. But she was free in the afternoons to go off with her friends and play, have picnics, pick berries, or help neighbors with haying. The nine or ten kids who lived in the neighborhood got together to play ball or "Indians." Louise also belonged to a 4-H club and played cymbals in the drum and bugle corps. She had plenty of outdoor equipment: ice skates, snowshoes, sidewalk skates, balls, a scooter, and skis that fastened with a leather strap to her boots. No bicycle, though, so she walked everywhere. It was about two miles to her cousins' home, at least two miles to 4-H club, a mile to church or school, and two miles to Norway for dances at the Grange Hall. In high school there were school dances, socials, and dancing classes. Swimming lessons were offered in the summer at Norway Lake, and a local man who owned a big touring car gave free rides to lessons to any kid who wanted to go.

Louise babysat regularly from the age of twelve. One summer she spent twelve hours a day doing housework and childcare for a working mother with a four-year old boy. At fifteen, she helped the sheriff's wife whose mobility was limited. One of her duties was churning butter, and she said that "cleaning out that churner was no fun!" The summer she was sixteen she took the bus to Norway to work in a shoe shop, but she hated it. The work was boring, and "the men at the shop were obnoxious." At seventeen Louise worked at a drugstore soda fountain for the summer. One or two summers during the war she also occasionally picked raspberries, cucumbers, beans, and strawberries, receiving all of one-and-a-half cents per pound for her labors.

Pauline had been a Methodist growing up, and Charles a Baptist, but they did not attend church themselves when the girls were young. Louise and Carolyn walked to the Baptist church for the service and Sunday school, and one day Louise came home and announced that the minister had tried to drown a woman during church. She didn't understand that she had witnessed a baptism. All the girls' friends attended the Congregational Church, and eventually the entire family started going there. The parents became members. The children attended the Sunday School held during the sermon in the morning service, and, when they were teens, the evening Pilgrim Fellowship youth group. Sundays were also a day for big dinners and family get-togethers. Sunday suppers were light. Occasionally Charles, who was a mess sergeant in his National Guard unit, prepared an oyster stew.

Louise started school when she was almost six. It was rarely canceled—never for snow—but was out for at least a few days after the Hurricane of '38. Her elementary school had four rooms, one each for grades one through four. Grades five through twelve were in the high school building. When necessary, teachers administered punishments in the hallway with a leather strap, and a second student was always present to count aloud the number of strokes. They had at least one recess a day, when they played tag, dodge ball, hopscotch, and marbles, and went on the swing and seesaw. Many dropped out before finishing high school, and Louise's class lost almost half its students, from fifty-four in ninth grade to twenty-nine by graduation in 1944. Louise was active in sports, playing on the basketball team and pitching for softball. A few teachers were memorable. Lila McAllister, her first-grade teacher, was a kind, motherly widow. The second-grade teacher, in contrast, "left a lot to be desired." In high school she had a crush on the football coach who supervised her study hall, and she took home economics for four years with a "wonderful" teacher. And then there was her new English teacher senior year. She was fired mid-year for dating . . . the senior boys.

In November 1942, when she was sixteen years old, Louise had one of the most exciting weeks of her life, every day packed with brand-new experiences. She and her 4-H partner, Janice, had won first place at both county and state level 4-H competitions in the Dairy Products category, earning them a trip to the 4-H National Convention in Chicago. On the day after Thanksgiving the girls took a train to Portland, where they were joined by their state leaders; another train to Boston, where they were joined by more students; a third to New York, where they spent the night and went sightseeing; and finally, an overnight Pullman car to Chicago. There they visited the stockyards and a museum and danced to famous big bands in the Aragon Ballroom. Author Lloyd Douglas addressed the convention, speaking about his work *Magnificent Obsession*. When it was all over, they returned by train through Canada. It was quite the trip for someone who had never even been out of Maine. To add to the excitement, Louise got to see her picture on the front page of the Chicago Sun, licking an eggbeater: she and Janice had taken second place in the entire country in their category.

Today Louise Hammond Bailey is an 86-year old widow living alone in her own home in New Hampshire. Enormously active and energetic, she tends a large garden and volunteers with several civic and church groups. After high school she trained at Massachusetts Memorial Hospital (now Boston Medical Center) and became a Registered Nurse. She had a long, happy marriage and three wonderful children and now has nine grandchildren and seven great-grandchildren. Looking back on a carefree childhood, she says, "What we didn't have my parents created, or we just made do with what we had. We had everything we needed."

51

Pumpie

PUMPIE IS NOW PEARL PERRY, a widow who, like **Bella**, could pass for twenty years younger. Growing up, she was known as "the quiet one," but today the family complains that the eighty-five-year old "talks too much." Maybe one reason for her quietness was her place in the birth order: a true middle child, she was the fifth of eight children, and the third of five girls. The family was, and still is, close and loving.

Her father, Caeser Quickley, was African-American and was born in Baltimore, Maryland. Little was known of his family—only that his mother, Mary Jane Quickley, still lived in Baltimore. Caeser's children loved him. He wasn't a harsh man at all, but he did expect to be obeyed. He had a leather paddle, and when the kids had been naughty enough to make him decide to use it, they would run under a bed and hide, squeezing way over next to the wall, out of his reach. Caeser would go in, lean over, and swat futilely under the bed for a bit. After he left, the little delinquents stayed put until he'd calmed down. When they finally emerged they would stay away from Daddy for a while, and this seemed to satisfy everyone. But if they got into trouble at school they could expect punishment at home. Their parents were serious about education; the kids were to behave, pay attention, and stay in school. And each one did graduate from high school, in a day when the dropout rate was very high.

Born *at home in Haverhill, Massachusetts in January 1928*

When I was your age, *school was different. The teacher was the boss, the authority.*

When I was your age, *I wore dresses made from flour sacks.*

When I was your age, *I never wore pants.*

What was your very favorite food to eat? *Smoked shoulder with a brown sugar glaze*

Did you or your friends ever eat out at restaurants or diners? *No*

You were required to attend church growing up. Is religion important to you now? *Yes, very*

Did you ever address adults by their first names? *No. Women who were close friends and neighbors were called "Aunt" So-and-so.*

What did you call your parents? *Daddy and Mom*

What was your first job while you were still in school? *Babysitting; then at 16, I started working after school in a shoe shop.*

How old were you when you went on your first date, and where did you go? *I was about eighteen. The fellow had a car, and we went to Salisbury Beach.*

How old were you when you got married? *I was 22, and he was 23.*

What was your first full-time job? *I worked in a shoe shop. When I was about nineteen, the machine I was using chopped off the tip of my left index finger. I was taken to the hospital, where a doctor repaired it using skin grafts from my thigh.*

What was your occupation for most of your working life?
I worked at Raytheon for thirty-four years, first as an assembly worker, then as an inspector, and later as a supervisor. I worked on both the Hawk and Patriot missiles.

Many things have been invented since you were a child. What has given you the most pleasure, or been the most valuable to you? *Modern washers and dryers*

Is there anything you wish had never been invented? *Perhaps computers*

What do you think you would most enjoy about being a kid today? *Having more clubs and activities available*

What would you most dislike? *Being inside so much. Kids aren't outside skating, sledding, and playing.*

By *today's standards*, did you have a lot of "stuff" growing up? *No*

In general, today we have many more possessions than when you were a child. Do you think this has affected our happiness? *Our possessions have overwhelmed us. Society is less happy. We're moving so fast we can't keep up. We've given up our privacy in some areas, but we trust others less. We used to know everyone; now we don't even know our neighbors.*

What is your name now? *Pearl Ellstine Perry*

Did you eat beans and franks for Saturday night supper? *Yes. And spaghetti on Wednesday and fish on Friday. Sunday dinner was a big meal. We had dessert only at Sunday dinner.*

Mr. Quickley worked as a custodian at the W.T. Grant department store in downtown Haverhill. The job didn't pay well, but he managed to support his large family on it. Sadly, when Pumpie was only eight years old he suffered a serious stroke and was unable to ever work again. Two years later he died at home of complications, and her oldest brother, still in his teens, became the man of the house. He took his responsibilities toward his younger siblings seriously. On one occasion, Pumpie was crying and crying because she wanted something so badly and her mother couldn't afford to get it for her. He took his own money and went out and bought it.

Mrs. Quickley—originally Viola Schencks—was born in Haverhill. Her mother was white, of English ancestry, and came from New Jersey; her father was African-American. Viola was home full-time when Pumpie was young. Housewives didn't need to drive in those days. The home was visited regularly by the bread man, the milkman, the iceman, the insurance man (weekly, for life insurance payments), and the vegetable man who came by in a horse-drawn wagon every Saturday. And Viola could get meat at the corner store. The kids adored her, but they knew her rule when playing in the neighborhood: they had to be "no further than my voice." If she called them in, they were responsible for hearing her and going home. They did. They didn't want to risk being sent to bed early, or being confined to the yard.

When Viola's youngest child was only about three, her husband died and she had to go out and find work. For many years she worked as a housekeeper in private homes; later she went to work in shoe manufacturing shops. She made her own root beer every winter. After being bottled and capped it was stored on the basement steps. She also made peach brandy from the fruit of a tree in her yard, but she used it only to settle sick stomachs.

Viola expected her children to take responsibility for their own actions. For a reason she no longer remembers, at around ten or eleven Pumpie enjoyed standing on a wobbly chair in the corner of the dining room while leaning against the wall. "Maybe it was a little warmer up there, as heat rises?" she wonders. Her mother told her again and again to "get down off that chair before you fall." One day, of course, it broke, and she fell. She wasn't hurt, but she cried. And received no sympathy from Viola.

The boys mowed the lawn and shoveled the snow, and the girls cleaned the house. There was some bickering between the girls over who was responsible to clean what, especially after their father died.

They were supposed to get the work done between the time they got home from school and their mother returned from work. This gave them plenty of time, but of course they often waited until the last minute. Once Viola walked in she started supper; she continued to do all the cooking and baking despite her outside job.

Supper was at six o'clock, and they ate together every night. Wednesday was spaghetti, Friday fish, and Saturday beans and franks. Other days might be baked ham; boiled dinner with cabbage, carrots, and potatoes; or fried potatoes and onions. On Sunday the main meal was at noon, and it was the only time all week they had dessert—a pie or cake. You didn't have to take food if you didn't like it—you were free to go hungry instead—but you did have to finish everything on your plate. Mrs. Quickley believed that liquid filled you up too fast, so she did not allow the children to drink anything until their meal was finished. There were never any snacks available.

Pumpie started school at six years old. In elementary school, everyone went home for lunch. Her mother walked home from work, over a mile, to be with them. Pumpie attended the Burnham School for grades one through four and the Fox for five through eight, each a quarter mile away. Her teachers—"dedicated old maids" Pumpie calls them, respectfully—had good control, and students who disrupted class were either sent to the principal or given "the ruler." She herself was very well behaved and never got it. She wasn't crazy about school, and she didn't start to really like reading until she reached high school. But she learned to just stick with it, get through it. One high school teacher in particular stood out: Mr. Freeman, her English teacher, who was not only a "nice guy" who treated everyone even-handedly, but a great teacher who made the material interesting. Looking back, she did wish she had taken some sewing and cooking classes in school, as her mother had been too tired and busy to teach her. She needed those homemaking skills after she became a wife and mother.

Christmas and Thanksgiving were Pumpie's favorite holidays, when the whole family and all the relatives were together. Her stocking was always stuffed with apples, oranges, and nuts. She would also have one or two gifts under the tree. Whatever gifts they received, though—dolls, trucks, games, stuffed animals—were expected to be shared with the others. The family had two bicycles—one girl's, one boy's—plus ice skates, a couple of sleds, and a wagon.

Your friends were *always* from your neighborhood, Pumpie said, even at school. You got along fine with kids from other neighborhoods, but you didn't play with them. The neighbor kids played group games like red rover, kick the can, and tag. Summers, they swam at Plug Pond. Winters, they skated on Round Pond or went sledding; sometimes the city even blocked off Windsor Street for sledders. Right at the end of their own street they could watch the many holiday parades that came down Main Street.

Mr. Quickley enjoyed listening to boxing on the battery-powered radio in the house. At about fifteen, Pumpie started listening to music on it when she allowed to, which wasn't often. Their piano was only for her sister Mary, dubbed "The Princess." She had been diagnosed with heart trouble and was supposed to rest and avoid anything strenuous. Exempted from housework and generally pampered, she was the only child to receive piano lessons and the only one to go to college, graduating with a teaching degree. It isn't known whether she actually recovered, or if her condition might never have been as serious as the doctors originally thought, but as of today Mary is going strong at eighty-eight.

Pumpie's first home on Ashland Street was a row house right next to their church. After her father's death they moved a little way up the street to a house that sat right on the "color line." On one side their neighbors were black; on the other, white. The white families had a little bit more money than the blacks, but not much. Everyone got along well, and all the children played together. There were no gangs, no fights. The Catholic girls Pumpie walked to Mass with were white, and some of the other white families attended Calvary Baptist, which was the heart of the black community in Haverhill, even though First Baptist was only a 3-minute walk away. They shared the same values; every adult was your parent and felt free to correct you, or to speak to your parents about you. They didn't judge each other by clothing, either; *all* the girls had dresses made from old flour sacks. There was only one car in the entire neighborhood, and it didn't belong to the Quickleys. There were some telephones, but her family didn't have one until she was in high school. Because their income was so low, the

Quickleys were eligible for some aid. There was some free sugar and flour, which came in sacks that eventually ended up as dresses, and Pumpie and her siblings received free dental care, and free fruit daily at school. They were resourceful, too, pulling their little red wagon over a mile to Railroad Square to fill it with scraps that had fallen to the street from coal bins.

Both of the Ashland Street houses had indoor plumbing, but water had to be heated on the stove for laundry, dishes, and bathing. Stoves burning wood, coal, oil, and/or gas provided heat in the kitchen and living room, and ceiling grates helped get warm air to the second floor. At fifteen Pumpie moved across the Merrimack River to the Bradford section of Haverhill, where they had gas stoves and a gas hot water heater but no central heating—not even any ceiling grates. In each house they had an ice box to keep food cool, and an electric washer with a hand wringer.

In childhood, race didn't seem like a big issue in Pumpie's day-to-day life. She didn't feel at all discriminated against by teachers or by other children. She didn't feel racial tension. But her mother prepared her for what was bound to come as she got older and left her neighborhood. In the South, she told them, you knew where you stood; you knew people hated you. Here in the North, you never really knew, because people weren't open about it. There were occasional slurs directed to her as a teenager, and she was taught to ignore them, to just keep walking as if she hadn't heard.

After graduating from high school and working for a few years, Pumpie married. She and her husband moved to Boston and brought up five children. After staying home with them for some years she went to work at Raytheon, first as a part-timer on a "mother's helper" shift and then full-time. In later years her husband got a job at AT&T, and they moved back to the Haverhill area. She continued to work at Raytheon until retirement.

What bothers Pumpie the most about life today is our selfishness and self-centeredness. She takes to heart what she learned from her mother: treat people the way you want to be treated. If you're not getting along with someone, have had an argument, don't ignore them: be polite, and even offer a greeting on the street. The most important thing in life is to get along with others.

52

Walt

WALTER—WALLY TO HIS PARENTS, Walt to his friends—was born in Boston. In his earliest years he lived with his parents and Swedish grandmother in a triple-decker on Conant Street, in the Roxbury section. His grandmother knew very little English, but little Wally was fluent in both Swedish and English when he was little, and he translated for her wherever they went, even as a toddler. Both of his parents worked at a residential hotel, Longwood Towers, just over the line in Brookline and within easy walking distance. His mother, Ellen, was a seamstress and his father, Matthew, an elevator operator. Ellen's brother John was Head Houseman, and they owed their jobs to his influence. In 1935, however, due to the economic effects of the Depression, Matthew lost his job. When he was unable to find anything else, he set off for Florida with Ellen and Wally, along with a cousin and his family. They did find work for a while, but eventually the economy caught up with them again, and Matthew was laid off. After returning to Boston in the spring of 1938 they lived with Ellen's best friend in Medway while they got on their feet. Ellen returned to Longwood. Medway was thirty miles west of the city, so she commuted by bus for half-day shifts and took sewing work home. Matthew joined the W.P.A. (Works Progress Administration), a New Deal agency created by President Roosevelt that put the unemployed to work on public works projects. Jobs usually involved manual labor, and Matthew got a

Born *at the Boston Lying-in Hospital in November 1932*

When I was your age, *I started a grocery hauling service with my little red wagon*

What was your very favorite food to eat? *Corn on the cob*

Did you or your friends ever eat out at restaurants or diners? *No, although I occasionally bought a soda or whoopie pie at the local store.*

You were not required to attend church growing up. Is religion important to you now? *Yes. I converted to Catholicism.*

Did you ever address adults by their first names? *Never*

What did you call your parents? *Dad and Ma*

What was your first job while you were still in school? *Usher at Fenway Park*

How old were you when you went on your first date, and where did you go? *I was about 16 and a junior in high school. My mother arranged a date for me for the Victory Dance.*

How old were you when you got married? *We were both 25.*

What was your first full-time job? *Pilot in the Air Force*

What was your occupation for most of your working life? *I spent 30 years in the military.*

Many things have been invented since you were a child. What has given you the most pleasure, or been the most valuable to you? *Television*

What do you think you would most enjoy about being a kid today? *Skiing*

What would you most dislike? *Manipulation of free time and being over-scheduled—Little League, etc.*

By today's standards, did you have a lot of "stuff" growing up? *No*

In general, today we have many more possessions than when you were a child. Do you think this has affected our happiness? *We are not happier. I have been accused of being abstemious, but delayed satisfaction is actually a good thing. And sometimes we give gifts to cover up the lack of real connection in our relationships. Give a big hug instead. We have too much and don't appreciate what we have. I'm not possessive, because I'm not afraid of having my stuff taken. I don't lock my house or my car.*

Did you eat beans and franks for Saturday night supper? *Yes*

horrible case of poison ivy while burning infested brush. Fortunately, in September of 1938 a job opened up for him again at Longwood. They moved back to their old neighborhood, this time to an apartment on Huntington Avenue. It was only a short walk to the hotel, and they lived there for the rest of Walt's growing-up years. [The entire neighborhood was later leveled as part of "urban renewal" in the early 1960s and replaced with high rises.]

Matthew worked at Longwood until about 1940, when he got a much better job at Lever Brothers, a soap factory, with not only higher pay but also paid vacation time, a benefit he had not ever had. Ellen left the hotel at the same time to do freelance work for drapers and upholsterers. The family upgraded their standard of living a bit: they got a telephone for the first time, and a car. They had had the car for less than a year when America entered the war, and with the subsequent gas rationing Matthew decided to get rid of it. He bought another after the war.

Matthew Uuno Kangas, Walter's father, was born and raised in Maynard, Massachusetts, in its Finnish community. As a young adult he legally changed his name from Uuno Matthew, to the slightly more American-sounding Matthew Uuno. He hadn't been called Uuno much, anyway. He and his three brothers all had permanent nick-names. His was Rosie and theirs were Biff, Kike, and Bilko. His father, Iussi (Finnish for John), worked in a mill in Maynard owned by American Wool, the largest woolen manufacturer in the country. He hated his job, and occasionally he would quit work and move his family to another part of the country, looking for some variety in life. He found it in places as diverse as Michigan's iron mines and Alaska's gold mines.

Both of Matthew's parents were born in Finland when it was controlled by Russia. Neither ever learned English, and Walt thinks that they were both illiterate even in Finnish. His mother, Hilja, was a milkmaid on her parents' farm in Piipola in central Finland, where Iussi worked as a woodcutter. Her parents, who owned their own land, discouraged their friendship, preferring that Hilja marry on her own social level; landowners were quite a few cuts above Iussi's "hired help" standing. Then Iussi was drafted into the army, but when he realized that Tsar Nicholas II was sending Finnish troops to fight on the Turk-ish border, he decided to desert, and ended up, probably illegally, in Maynard. Hilja eventually followed.

Walt's mother was Swedish. Ellen Victoria Samuelson came from Gothenburg, Sweden, the largest seaport in Scandinavia. Her own par-ents had met while they were employed on the same boat that traveled between their city and Denmark, he as a machinist and she as a cook. In the 1920s her now-widowed mother brought the family to America, but Ellen was denied a visa because she had had polio as a child and walked with a limp. She had to wait several years until the family could officially sponsor her; when they were finally established in Everett, Massachusetts, she sailed from Sweden to join them.

Even though there were no other children in his family Walt did not have his own bedroom. They had a tiny but fairly modern one-bedroom apartment, and Walt slept on the living room couch.

The stove and refrigerator were both gas-powered. There was a shower but no bathtub, and hot water came right through the faucets. Ellen did laundry in the kitchen sink with a scrub board. There was no yard, so she hung clothes from a line on the roof to dry. It would have been a long walk down to a yard anyway, since their apartment was on the sixth floor. There was no air conditioning, and the apartment could feel like an oven on hot summer days. Walt could sit out on the fire escape to get a little relief from the heat.

Living in an apartment building, Walt didn't have the traditional chores that many other boys had. There was no grass to mow, garden to weed, or chickens to feed, and the superintendent took care of clearing snow and tending the furnace. The only work Walt was responsible for at home was window washing. But he had many opportunities to work for pay. One was provided by his sixth-grade teacher and will be described later. Another came to him with the opening of a Stop & Shop supermarket on Tremont Street. Many housewives abandoned the local A&P in favor of this larger, less expensive store, but it meant a longer walk for them. Walt saw a brand-new need, and met it. He parked his little red wagon outside the store and offered to pull shoppers' groceries home for ten cents a bag. He soon built sides for the wagon so he could carry more bags on each trip. His service became popular, and before long he had competition from other boys with wagons. Everyone tried to be hired by those who lived in first-floor apartments; lugging bags up several flights wasn't anyone's first choice.

In high school, Walt shoveled snow in the rail yard at North Station whenever school was cancelled due to snow. He also caddied at Brookline Country Club and ushered at Fenway Park. He was very tall, making him a good candidate for crowd control in the right field pavilion where drunks and gamblers gathered during Red Sox games.

The Boston Public Schools had offered kindergarten since the 1870s, but Walt was still in Florida during the year he would have attended. In the fall of 1938, when he was nearly six, he started first grade at his neighborhood school. It was smaller than seemed warranted by the area's large population, but much of the heavily Catholic neighborhood attended parochial school. Walt remembers the teachers as being "very old, with neck-to-ankle dresses." Because his mother was working, Walt went after school and at lunchtime to a nearby house where the mother was home. At some point they dropped this arrangement and he became a "latchkey kid" who went home to an empty apartment.

During his grade school years Walt loved to read. His favorites were books about sailing ships, and adventure stories set in the past. He also liked to listen to radio programs, galloping around the table to the music from one of his favorites, The Lone Ranger. Walt joined the neighborhood boys in sledding, riding scooters, and playing ball. Their favorite sledding spot was Mission Hill, where they could slide all the way down to Huntington Avenue. Walt didn't have a scooter, so he built one out of a wooden board and roller skates. The boys were too small to be allowed to play real baseball at the playground, where they knew they would get kicked out by the bigger boys. So they made up their own ball games for empty lots or small spaces, with their own rules. In one version, they used a broomstick to hit a tennis ball against a square painted on the side of a brick wall. On Saturdays, the boys usually went to the movies in the morning and played in the streets in the afternoon. But on rainy days Walt often went alone to the Museum of Fine Arts, just a short walk up Huntington Avenue. He first went there because he had heard they had mummies in the Egyptian collection, but he found himself fascinated by all the other relics as well.

Walt was athletic and good at sports, and too tall and strong to ever be physically bullied. But he felt different in many ways. He was so much taller than his friends that he felt awkward. And he was teased for being the only Protestant kid in his Irish Catholic group. His friends were on the tough side. When his mother wanted him to take violin lessons, he absolutely refused—not because he wouldn't have enjoyed the instrument, but because of the social implications. He knew his pals wouldn't put up with a violinist in their midst. Walt had a stern father. He didn't allow him to have comic books and, more importantly, didn't let him play outside on summer evenings. As frustrating as this was for Walt, he admits now that it probably kept him out of a lot of trouble. As they grew older, his old friends starting getting even tougher. Sometimes Walt joined them to break into unlocked cars on Longwood Avenue and steal valuables. They were all headed for big trouble. Two years later, some of those same kids got involved with a murder. Fortunately, Walt was no longer running with them. One teacher had changed the course of his life.

In sixth grade, Miss McLaughlin had called his mother to the school. "Wally is a very, very good student, but he's getting in with the wrong crowd," she warned, and offered both long-term and temporary solutions. First, she recommended that he apply to Boston Latin School, the oldest public school in the nation and open only to those who passed a difficult entrance exam. Walt's parents had never heard of the school, which was only a few blocks away. Second, she said that she could use weekly help at her house in Jamaica Plain that she shared with several other teachers. She proposed driving him to her home after school to clean windows and floors. This was a brilliant plan. It not only got him off the streets for one afternoon a week but also pegged him as the teacher's pet and therefore a social undesirable. It had the immediate effect of separating him from his old friends.

If washing windows for his teacher started to make Walt a misfit in the neighborhood, going to Boston Latin completed it. In his required dress of shirt and tie, he stood out in sharp contrast to his former friends. There was only one other student in his class from his old elementary school: Barney Jones. One of only a handful of African-American students at Boston Latin, Barney was "an outstanding student" who went on to Harvard. Walt no longer had time to spend with neighborhood kids anyway. At Boston Latin he encountered homework for the first time and learned right away to not fall behind. It was a difficult school to be admitted to, but it was even harder to stay in. The flunk out/drop out rate for the six-year course was two out of three. At orientation they were told to "look at yourself and those sitting on either side of you. Two of you will not graduate." If you didn't study hard and keep up with your work, you didn't make it. And Walt wanted to make it. He was happy. He loved the new feeling of fitting in. The stress of being the odd man out was gone. Now his only stress was academic.

Both of Walt's parents had only an eighth-grade education, but Mr. Kangas was an avid reader. Mrs. Kangas read as well. She had been educated in Sweden and later learned to read English. They both enjoyed listening to classical music on the radio and tending their vegetable garden on public land in the nearby fens. Sometimes they went to Red Sox games at Fenway Park, as Walt's mother was an especially enthusiastic fan. They also frequently watched amateur baseball teams, sponsored by local businesses, play on fields in the nearby Fens. On Sundays they usually had ice cream for dessert at lunch. Ellen was not a great cook, but she did her best cooking for that meal. In the afternoon they might pack a picnic and take the streetcar or bus to an area of countryside in Dedham, or to Nantasket Beach. Or they would do something with Ellen's brother, John, and his family. John was doing very well and had a car. He was no longer a hotel worker but a master electrician, and he had invented a lighted Christmas tree holder. He had just one child as well, Marion, who was around Walt's age and was like a sister to him.

Matthew's parents were Lutherans, but Matthew considered himself an atheist. He and his brothers were ardent socialists and union activists. Ellen attended the Methodist church. However, she had Walt baptized in the Lutheran church and sent him there for confirmation classes, although he was never required to attend services. He converted to Catholicism as an adult.

Christmas was Walt's favorite holiday, with a Swedish smorgasbord and a big tree with perfect icicles. A close second was Midsummer, the celebration of the longest day of the year and one of Scandinavia's most important festivals. Everyone stayed outside until darkness fell, dancing and playing games. Uncle John and his best friend always played their accordions for the event. Walt also enjoyed holiday parades, including an extremely popular schoolboy cadet parade every spring. Military drill was required in the curriculum of Boston's public high schools, and the parade became a competition between schools, one that Boston Latin usually won. Walt marched as part of the school's Naval Reserves.

Sometime during his Latin years Walt developed a cultural appreciation of another area of the arts in addition to his interest in museum relics: opera. It happened by chance. One day, after he had left a movie theater and was walking home, he passed by the back of the Boston Opera House. There was a baby elephant outside, along with other animals in cages. He couldn't imagine why they were there. But a door was open, and nobody was around, so he went in and looked around, arriving just in time to view the Grand March from Verdi's opera *Aida*. He was hooked. He also realized that if he entered the opera house late, between acts, he could drift into the hall with folks returning for the next act and find an empty seat at the back without ever paying admission. He became a regular attendee and developed a great love for the art. But it wasn't until he was out of college, when he took a girlfriend to a performance of *Carmen*, that he ever saw Act I of any opera!

Because Ellen remembered the "starving days" in Sweden during World War I, she did not allow any food to be wasted. Walt had to eat everything that was served, and finish everything on his plate. There was a certain Swedish delicacy served on Christmas Eve that he and most of his fellow first-generation Swedish Americans partic- ularly detested. It was called "lutfisk"—meaning "fish cured in lye." Once the fish—usually cod—was preserved, it was inedible until it had been soaked for six weeks in water. Even then it turned the dinner fork black. Walt would much rather have been eating corn on the cob.

Some of the other special holiday foods were more appetizing: Swedish meatballs, pickled herring, potato sausage (korv), and smoked oysters. Christmas Eve they had a simple, traditional fish dinner. But after the church service that ended at midnight, the celebration started, with all kinds of meat and a special alcoholic drink. Straight alcohol and claret wine were heated in a pan. Then a grill was placed over the open top of the pan. Lumps of sugar were laid on the grill and then lighted, caramelizing the sugar, which would drop down into the pan. At this point there would be an argument between the men and the women over whether to cover it or not. The men wanted it covered, to keep more of the alcohol in, while the women fought to uncover it and let the alcohol burn off.

Every morning Walt was forced to swallow a spoonful of cod liver oil at breakfast, which was usually tomato juice and oatmeal, and maybe a hard-boiled egg. There was nothing available in the apartment to snack on after school, but the family ate a very early supper. Walt's father insisted that it be on the table when he arrived home from his factory job at 4:30 p.m. His mother always provided some kind of fruit for dessert.

Walt should have graduated from high school in 1950, but he took a slight detour and lost a year. In his junior year, he dropped out to join the Navy, lying about his age. Three months into his service the Navy discovered that he was only sixteen. Fortunately for him, they were kind enough to list his discharge status as "for the convenience of the government" instead of charging him with fraudulent enlistment. If they had, he would not have been eligible to later receive his Air Force ROTC commission and pursue a thirty-year military career as a pilot. He started college in the summer of 1951. Originally he was headed to Georgetown University on a football scholarship, but at the last moment the school dropped its football program and his scholarship disappeared. Walt could then have gone to Bowdoin College in Maine but was afraid of not fitting in. Instead he went to the University of Massachusetts, paying his tuition from football and ROTC scholarships and working both on campus and on local tobacco farms. He majored in sociology for his bachelor's degree and much later earned one master's in business administration from George Washington University and another in systems management from the University of Southern California. He is now eighty-one years old. His advice is to be relentless, stubborn, to stick with things to the end and not give up. Be your own person.

53

Elaine

FROM THE TIME she was born until the day she left for college, Elaine lived on West Hilton Street in Tiverton, Rhode Island, just two streets south of Fall River, Massachusetts. Both her mother's and her father's parents lived within her neighborhood. The population of the town was five thousand; today it has tripled to sixteen thousand.

Clarence Walmsley, Elaine's father, was born at home in Tiverton. By day he was an inspector for the U.S. government in Newport—probably, says Elaine, at the naval base. Evenings and weekends he worked for his father, Albert, who was a contractor and house builder. He and Clarence's mother had a home a few streets away. They were both born in England.

Doris Robertshaw, Elaine's mother, was probably born in Tiverton. She attended the Rhode Island School of Design in Providence for two years, quitting at nineteen to marry twenty-eight-year old Clarence. Her mother was Frances Donovan, and her father James Robertshaw, whose mother, Betsy Taylor, had emigrated with her husband from England. Betsy's husband died in his thirties, leaving her with five children, no support, and no welfare safety net. Fortunately, Betsy was "enterprising and spunky." She opened a fish-and-chips store in the Globe Corners section of Fall River and walked there every day from her home in Tiverton. One of her children had been born in England and the other four, including James, were born in this country. James

Born *at St. Anne's Hospital in Fall River, Massachusetts in March 1929*

When I was your age, *we played outside.*

What was your very favorite food to eat? *Hamburgers*

Did you or your friends ever eat out at restaurants or diners? *Yes, occasionally*

You were required to attend church growing up. Is religion important to you now? *Yes*

Did you ever address adults by their first names? *No*

What did you call your parents? *I called them Dad and Ma.*

What was your favorite holiday? *Christmas. I went caroling on Christmas Eve with my church and the next morning got loads of presents.*

What was your first job while you were still in school? *I worked at a soda fountain in a drugstore in Portsmouth.*

How old were you when you went on your first date, and where did you go? *At 14, I started going to Saturday night dances with different boyfriends who were in DeMolay. (I belonged to Rainbow, its sister organization.) I also went to youth group at the Congregational Church in Fall River with these boys.*

How old were you when you got married? *I was 19, and he was 21.*

What was your first full-time job? *Teaching school*

What was your occupation for most of your working life? *I was a fourth-grade teacher.*

What would you think about being a kid today? *I don't envy anything about it, especially the fast pace of life. I wouldn't be able to duplicate the childhood I had.*

By *today's standards*, did you have a lot of "stuff" growing up? *No*

In general, today we have many more possessions than when you were a child. Do you think this has affected our happiness? *We are less happy. The more we get, the more we want. Some of this is probably due to advertising.*

Today we hear that the lives of many American children are very stressful. Was yours stressful in any way? *No*

What is your name now? *Elaine Manchester*

Did you eat beans and franks for Saturday night supper? *Yes, as did all or most of the neighborhood.*

became a chicken farmer and also served as a senator in the state legislature.

Mr. Walmsley had little leisure time because of his two jobs. He was a Mason but didn't have time to attend meetings. Mrs. Walmsley was a Worthy Matron in the Eastern Star. She painted, taught a first aid class for the Girl Scouts, and enjoyed traveling by herself. Neither was a churchgoer. Doris read the Bible but didn't like to attend services; however, they insisted that their children go. Elaine went to the Primitive Methodist Church and her brother joined the neighborhood boys at the Baptist church. After church Elaine often went to Doris's mother's to have lunch and spend the afternoon with her cousins who lived upstairs, single women who were teachers. Both were air raid wardens during the war.

Elaine entered school when she was six. Her first school had three rooms, one for each of the first three grades. There were lavatories in the basement, so heading for them was referred to [both there and in countless other schools across the region] as "going to the basement." But her next two schools—one for grades four through six and one for seven and eight—had no lavatories at all but just outhouses out back. The four-through-six school had two rooms: one for fourth grade and half of the fifth, and the other for sixth grade and the remainder of the fifth. Elaine remembers one teacher particularly fondly: Miss Mary Ann Cullen. Miss Cullen kept "moving up" with Elaine's class, and she ended up teaching them from the fourth through the eighth grade! Elaine was very pleased to have this teacher for five straight years. She does admit that she was somewhat favored and the teacher's pet. Think of those poor souls Miss Cullen may *not* have liked who had her for those five years!

There was no high school in Tiverton. Instead, the town paid tuition for area public, private, or parochial schools of the student's choosing. Elaine chose the public Durfee High School, only a few miles away in Fall River and reached by a short bus ride. There she met her husband, who had quit school to enlist in the service and after the war had returned to finish. They were together in an English class, where she bested him in a debate on a topic along the lines of "a united way."

Most days started with a breakfast of juice and cereal, or sometimes eggs, but on Sunday mornings they had leftover beans from the previous night's supper. Supper, the only meal the family ate together, was served at about five. Because Clarence Walmsley had two jobs, the family lived at a higher standard than those around them. They had a car, which her parents both drove, a radio, and a telephone. They owned their own one-family house and had modern plumbing, oil heat, a gas stove, and a refrigerator as well as an electric wringer washer in the basement. There was one bathroom until 1943, when Clarence put on an addition that included a half bath. At about that same time they also bought a clothes dryer.

After graduating from high school in 1947, Elaine entered Rhode Island College. At the beginning of 1948 she left to get married, but she later returned to college for her bachelor's degree. In 1966 she graduated from California State College at Long Beach and became a teacher.

Looking back, Elaine's only remembered complaint is that she wanted to wear her hair in braids like one of her friends, but her mother, dreading the upkeep of long hair, made her keep it short. She had such a happy and carefree childhood that she wanted her own children to experience it, too—the camaraderie, wholesomeness, innocence, and freedom of her little town. When their children were still school-aged, she convinced her husband to move the family back to Tiverton from their home in California. She was disappointed, and so were they. Time hadn't stood still. Things had changed, and her idyllic world had disappeared. That disappointment, and others, led her into greater maturity in her walk with God and in her faith. She says that she has had "a good life, even with some heartbreaks as an adult."

54

Vicki

FRANK ELLSWORTH BRADLEY, who administered Vicki's one and only spanking, was a shoe cutter at the Knipe shoe factory in Ward Hill, a section of Bradford, Massachusetts. A few decades before Vicki's birth, Bradford had been annexed to the city of Haverhill, just across the Merrimack River to the north. Frank was "probably" of Yankee heritage. His father was a house builder who built the home Vicki was born in and lives in today. Lena Martha Ellis, her mother, was born in Nova Scotia and had worked at Knipe before marriage, perhaps as a shoe stitcher. Lena's mother was Jessie Carver. Most Nova Scotians were of Scottish descent, but Vicki thinks that her mother's family was English.

Vicki was the youngest of three sisters, and they had two older brothers. Jessie, four years older than Vicki, was closest to her in age, and the two were inseparable in spite of the age difference. There were only a few children in their neighborhood, so she and Jessie often walked a mile to visit friends on Neck Road. They liked hopscotch, marbles, jackstones [jacks], cards, jump rope, and long walks. Sometimes in the summer they picked berries for pay. Vicki had no riding or sliding toys: no bicycle, scooter, skates, sled, wagon, or even balls, but she did have some dolls she liked. She enjoyed radio programs like The Shadow and Amos 'n' Andy. In her teens she started listening to popular music. Neither she nor her friends played the piano or other

Born *at home in Bradford, Massachusetts in February 1925*

When I was your age, *I had a lot of fun, but I behaved myself.*

What was your very favorite food to eat? *Tomato sandwiches from tomatoes fresh from our garden*

Did you or your friends ever eat out at restaurants or diners? *No*

You were required to attend Sunday school growing up. Is religion important to you now? *Yes*

Did you ever address adults by their first names? *No*

What did you call your parents? *Dad and Mom*

What was your first job while you were still in school? *I occasionally picked blueberries, raspberries, and strawberries on the farm of our friends from church, the Chadwicks, whom we called Aunt Carrie and Uncle George.*

How old were you when you went on your first date? *I was in my 20s.*

What was your first full-time job? *My brother was a foreman at Knipe Shoe and hired me right after I graduated from high school. I worked there only a few months, while completing business school at night. I was required to join the union.*

instruments, but they bought the sheet music to popular titles and sang them together. Vicki had few chores to do. She and Jessie did the dishes together every night, but she wasn't expected to do much else at home. Christmas was her favorite holiday, even though gifts were few. And they had a special family tradition on the Fourth of July: a meal of canned salmon with fresh peas and new potatoes (if any were ready) from their garden.

What was your occupation for most of your working life?
I was a bookkeeper at a bank. I lived at home until moving to Boston about 1953, returning home on weekends. I moved back to Haverhill after retirement.

Many things have been invented since you were a child. What has given you the most pleasure, or been the most valuable to you? *Dishwashers and televisions*

What do you think you would most enjoy about being a kid today? *Having television*

By today's standards, did you have a lot of "stuff" growing up? *No. And it was much easier to clean the house, because it was less cluttered.*

In general, today we have many more possessions than when you were a child. Do you think this has affected our happiness? *I think that some things—like cars, TVs, washing machines, and dishwashers—have made us happier.*

Today we hear that the lives of many American children are very stressful. Was yours stressful in any way? *No*

Did you eat beans and franks for Saturday night supper? *There were always beans, and maybe also franks.*

Vicki's parents enjoyed playing whist or bridge with friends, and her father liked to sit by the radio smoking his pipe while he listened to ball games or organ music. He also enjoyed caring for his very large vegetable garden. He raised winter squash, potatoes, peas, corn, and popcorn (*lots* of popcorn, so the family always had a large stash). They also had a flock of chickens. Frank hired a man with a horse and plow to come break up the ground for planting every spring. He grew vegetables mainly for his own family's use, but if he had a bumper crop he would set up a vegetable stand in the front yard, which bordered busy Boston Road, and sell the extra. He also tended six apple trees on his property: two each of Baldwin, Macintosh, and Wealthy. They kept their surplus apples in cold storage in the cellar, giving them a year-round supply.

Lena belonged to the Ladies Aid Society at the nearby Congregational Church, Ward Hill Church of Christ. She and her husband did not attend services, but they sent their children to Sunday school every week. The church maintained a children's library, and every Sunday Vicki and Jessie checked out books to read on Sunday afternoon after their big dinner, while their parents rested.

Vicki was allowed to snack between meals on cookies if there were any around. She remembers that she wasn't required to eat food she didn't like, but she generally liked everything anyway. For breakfast she had oatmeal or cold cereal. For lunch, Vicki carried a sandwich to school; she had enough time to get home and back during the break but not enough to make the walk worthwhile. At Thanksgiving, Christmas, and the occasional Sunday dinner the family ate a chicken from their flock. Another special occasion treat was Lena's bread pudding.

When she was five-and-a-half, Vicki entered first grade at the four-room Knipe School, which she attended through eighth grade. There were two grades to a class, and typically fewer than twenty students to a room. Vicki remembers two of her teachers well: Miss Sullivan was "quite strict" and Miss Nudd, who taught her in grades seven and eight, was "very nice."

The family had two radios, one on each floor, and a telephone, but no car. Her father walked to work, and they reached stores by city buses that went right by their home. Lena did her laundry in the kitchen sink and wrung it out by hand before hanging it outside to dry. An ice box in the back hallway cooled their food until Vicki started working at a bank in the mid 1940s and bought them a brand-new yellow refrigerator. A furnace that could burn either wood or coal was later converted to gas. The kitchen stove also ran on both wood and coal. Until Lena's death of stomach cancer when Vicki was eighteen, all their hot water needs were supplied from water heated in a kettle on the stove. They had a copper hot water heating tank, but Lena was afraid it would explode if they used it. [She had probably heard of this happening; see **Adrianne**'s story.] After she died, Vicki got the tank hooked up and it never did explode.

After graduating from Haverhill High School in 1942, Vicki worked the day shift at Knipe Shoe and studied evenings at the Haverhill branch of McIntosh Business College. On finishing, she got a job as a bookkeeper at a bank. She looks back on her quiet childhood as a happy time. The one thing Vicki most disliked was having to get up in the morning to go to school. Of course, she later also had to get up for work. But once she retired she was able to start keeping the hours she had always wanted: late to bed, and late to rise. Nearing ninety and still in good health, it seems to be working for her!

55

Sports and Pews

WEEKENDS, SUMMERS, AND after school hours we wanted to enjoy ourselves. A few of us were especially burdened by very heavy chore loads at home, but even we had at least a little time to spend as we liked. On Saturdays, many of us worked around the house in the mornings but had the afternoon off; others had all day free. We spent our time playing, being with friends, seeing movies, reading, earning money, going to museums or the library, and taking walks. Charlotte, who was Jewish, sometimes attended synagogue in the morning but played in the afternoon.

On Sundays, most of us attended church, Sunday school, or both in the morning, and some also went to a church youth group or second worship service in the evening. (**Pumpie**, who was allowed *only* church-related activities on Sundays, regularly attended two Sunday schools, services at two different churches, and an evening youth group.) After church, there was often a big meal. In some families, parents rested after dinner while children played quietly or read; others had company over, visited relatives, or went on "Sunday drives." Some went on picnics, attended sports events, played together, listened to the radio, or just took it easy. Almost all stores and businesses were closed.

Movies and radio were very popular forms of entertainment. Several of us saw a movie at a theater almost every Saturday. When Rozzy went, she bought a ticket for a nickel and spent another five cents on a treat. Others saw films at their town halls. At some point typical prices doubled, to a dime.

Although most of us started listening to popular music in our teens, a few never became interested in it. Those who did usually also tuned in for the weekly Hit Parade on Saturday night. We enjoyed other types of radio programming as well: classical music; variety shows; big bands; and religious speakers. But what we liked most were the weekly serials, precursors of today's television sitcoms: mysteries, dramas, and soap operas that were aimed at audiences of children, adults, or both. Almost all of us remembered what our favorites were. "The Shadow" came in first, at ten mentions; "Amos 'n' Andy" and "The Lone Ranger" tied for second and third place, with six each. Others mentioned several times were Jack Armstrong, the All-American Boy; The Green Hornet; I Love a Mystery; The Inner Sanctum; and Ma Perkins. Some adults decried these programs as a waste of time, but in our defense, we had to use our imaginations to enjoy them. There were no images for us to passively watch; we had to visualize the scenes ourselves in our mind's eye as we listened.

Pianos were also extremely popular, and many households, even poor ones, owned them. Well over half of us had pianos. Some were able to take lessons, and the rest "fooled around" on the instrument or learned to play by ear. Half of those who had lessons learned to play well, and three went on to also play organ. A few of us enjoyed playing other instruments as well, including guitar, violin, and ukulele; and the fife, bugle, and cymbals in drum-and-bugle groups. **Walt**'s mother wanted him to take violin lessons, which he might have liked; however, that was a definite no-no in his tough-guy circle and Walt wasn't willing to commit social suicide.

When we were old enough, we started dating. There was a lot of variety within that "enough," however, as we ranged in age from eleven years old to our early twenties for that first date. Most of our first dates involved going with someone to a dance, and the next most common activity was seeing a movie. In third place was attending a church service or religious function, followed by roller- or ice-skating, a drive, or a walk. Kissing and cuddling was fair play on later dates. But sex definitely was not acceptable—not for nice girls. That was for marriage only.

Before we were old enough to date, there were toys, games, and sports to keep us happy. Toys were pretty simple by today's standards, but many have stood the test of time and are familiar to modern children: dolls, cards, toy soldiers, cars, trucks, trains, coloring books, blocks, and all kinds of balls. Even the poorest girl had some sort of doll, even if it was homemade or second-hand. Luckier ones had doll carriages, dollhouses, extensive wardrobes of doll clothing, and perhaps a real Shirley Temple doll; fortunate boys might have chemistry sets and powered trains. A few of our favorite playthings are still around but no longer as popular, such as paper dolls, marbles, jacks, and paddle balls. We had lots of board games. Some, like Monopoly, are commonly seen today; others, like Parcheesi, can still be found but are rarely played. Then there are the free toys, the ones that will never go out of style: ordinary objects that take on new identities in our imaginations. Clothespins turned into store goods, pine groves became houses, and sticks were imagined into steering wheels.

Some of our other toys required us to be creative, and some did not, but all of them had one characteristic in common: they couldn't be enjoyed by just being *watched*. They didn't "do" anything. We couldn't just press a button and be entertained; we had to physically participate. We arranged soldiers, dressed dolls, kicked balls, pushed trucks, drew pictures, played songs.

We spent a *lot* more time playing outside than inside. Some things we could use indoors or out: dolls, trucks, marbles, jacks, even books. In bad weather we might be inside with toys, games, and books, and maybe be allowed to listen to the radio. But usually when we had free time we were outdoors, whether we lived in the country or the city. We explored woods, fields, streams, and city streets; went on walks and hikes and picnics; picked berries; played pranks; and (on the Fourth of July only) set off firecrackers. We rode bicycles and scooters and we pulled wagons. We sledded, swam, and ice-skated. We roller-skated, even if we had to make the skates ourselves. We played hopscotch, jacks, and marbles; enjoyed the neighborhood snow on skis and snowshoes; swung on swings; played with our pets; flew kites; turned cartwheels; walked on stilts; jumped rope. There were games of base-ball, softball, football, dodge ball, basketball, hide 'n' seek, red rover, giant step, red light, badminton, croquet, capture the flag, ringalario, and kick the can. (Everything under the sun, except soccer.) We orga-nized everything ourselves, and the older kids were the authorities. No adults supervised or nagged us. We didn't carry water bottles so we could "hydrate." Nobody told us how to play, whom to play, how to pick teams, or anything else. We just had a lot of fun.

56

News and Views

NEW ENGLAND WAS still feeling its way toward being a true melting pot. As one immigrant group became assimilated, the next was fighting for full acceptance, and the newest was dealing with rejection and discrimination. No single ethnicity was responsible for the harassment. Suspicion of newcomers and doubts that they would ever become "real" Americans was by no means limited to the older Yankee population. Groups that had fought their way in—"paid their dues"— often tried to prevent others from succeeding. And while some city areas became multi-ethnic, others were enclaves of only one ethnicity.

Lucy's Fall River neighborhood was mostly Irish, and she was sometimes chased by kids calling her names. "Portugee Stink Fish! Portugee Stink Fish!" they'd yell. But times were already changing. In neighboring rural Westport, Yankees had started to intermarry with the Portuguese—**Ellie**'s sister, Esther, for example.

Walt had a couple of good friends who were African-American, including the son of his apartment superintendent. The superintendent's daughter, June, "passed" for white and had an office job downtown. They were the only blacks in the mostly-Irish neighborhood.

Pumpie grew up African-American in a predominantly white city. Her neighborhood was in the heart of the black community, but it wasn't segregated. Just "sort of" segregated: blacks lived on the end of the street closest to their church, whites at the other, and they met in the middle—right at Pumpie's house, which sat on the dividing line. Her neighbors on one side were black and on the other white. However, everyone got along well, and the children played together. Some of the white families attended Pumpie's mainly-black church, even though another Baptist church was only a 3-minute walk away. Race didn't seem like a big issue to her as a child in either her neighborhood or her school, but her mother worked to prepare her for the day when it would be. In high school, she was able to "just keep walking" and ignore slurs that were occasionally directed at her.

Most of our growing-up years were between two major world wars. It was largely a time of violent upheavals in some parts of the world, a worried peace in the rest, and financial uneasiness everywhere. In the U.S., aviation and aviators were big news: the transatlantic flights of Charles Lindbergh and Douglas "Wrong Way" Corrigan; the kidnapping of Lindbergh's child; the disappearance of Amelia Earhart. We also heard about civil wars and invasions, and sensational stories about disasters and murders. And in 1935, the identical quintuplets born to the Dionne family in Canada were a worldwide sensation.

What news stories—from the radio, newsreels, newspapers, or family talk—do you remember?

Beena   *I remember the Lindbergh kidnapping, because I prepared a speech on it for class but was too nervous to deliver it.*

Edith   *The Hindenburg disaster, the Lindbergh kidnapping, Amelia Earhart, Wrong Way Corrigan. And the New York World's Fair. I went to it nine times!*

Elaine   *The events leading up to World War II, and the invasion of Poland.*

Ellen   *I remember the presidential campaigns.*

Ellie   *I don't remember now, but we did get a daily Boston newspaper.*

Louise   *The double murder in 1937 of our doctor, James Littlefield, and his wife. They lived right across the street from us. Also, the Lindbergh kidnapping.*

Okie *I remember hearing about the Lindbergh baby.*

Shirl *I remember the New York World's Fair—first, because I went to it; second, because when I was in the fifth grade, our class walked to the railroad station to see a train being brought from Scotland pass through town on its way to the Fair. I also remember hearing about fighting in Ethiopia.*

Sonny *News of World War II: battle results, Mussolini, the liberation of France, bad reports from Iwo Jima.*

Tom *Amelia Earhart.*

Vicki *The kidnapping of the Lindbergh baby.*

Walt *The Cocoanut Grove fire in Boston in 1942, when almost 500 people died in the city's most popular nightclub. D-Day, which also happened to be Enrollment Day for me at Boston Latin.*

In 1937, everyone in the country heard about the Hindenburg disaster, where a luxury German passenger blimp burst into flames as it tried to land in Lakehurst, New Jersey, killing almost half of those on board. The cause of the tragedy is still disputed, and theories include weather, sabotage, and mechanical or structural failures. **Shirl** had actually seen the airship earlier in the day as it passed through her town:

I remember seeing the Hindenburg on May 6, 1937, when I was in the third grade. The ship was to pass through the center of our town as it traveled south, following the train tracks, and students from all the Sharon schools—which were all near the town center—were allowed to go outside to view it. In the late morning it came through, just over the treetops. It was large and silver, had a very loud motor, and was flying so low that we all felt as though we could almost touch it. The cabin hung down below the blimp, and we could actually see the people inside. It was a pretty exciting few minutes for us. It has been said that the people of Sharon were the last to see the Hindenburg, because soon afterwards cloudy, foggy weather blocked the view. It was truly something never to be forgotten.

Franklin Delano Roosevelt, the only president many of us grew up with, was a particularly polarizing figure. The country was deeply divided over the approaches he implemented for economic recovery from the Depression. Two of his programs were the W.P.A. (Works Progress Administration) and the C.C.C. (Civilian Conservation Corps), which employed some of our family members for a time. His successful run for an unprecedented third, and then *fourth,* term as president alarmed so many that it led to Congress passing the twenty-second amendment to the Constitution in 1947, limiting presidents to being elected twice to office. [During the ratification process, Massachusetts voted against the amendment.] Our own families were about equally divided in their feelings toward Roosevelt.

Did your parents have strong feelings about FDR?

Adrianne   *Yes; negative ones.*

Beena   *I can't remember, but my father was a Republican so he probably didn't care for him. On the other hand, his mother loved him!*

Bella   *Yes. They liked him.*

Butch   *No.*

Charlotte   *No strong opinions.*

Claire   *My father liked him.*

Edith   *Yes; negative ones.*

Elaine   *I know that they did not vote for him.*

Ellen   *They didn't like him at all.*

Ellie   *Not that I remember, but they were Republicans.*

Helen *No.*

Louise *Yes, and they liked him.*

Lucy *Yes. They liked him.*

Nancy   *Yes. My folks had very little regard for him. They were extremely upset about Social Security and called it "the beginning of the end of this country."*

Okie   *They liked him very much, and they liked his programs, especially the C.C.C and the W.P.A.*

Pumpie   *No.*

Rosanna   *They never mentioned any.*

Rozzy   *My mother didn't like him. I don't know how my father felt.*

Shirl   *Yes. They liked him.*

Shirley   *No, but they were Republicans.*

Sonny   *My parents didn't speak about politics much, but I think they liked him.*

Stillman   *I don't know, but my brother, who was a Republican, didn't like him.*

Tom   *They liked him very much.*

Vicki   *I don't know.*

Walt   *Yes. They loved him.*

Finally, there was the Hurricane of '38, also known as the Great New England Hurricane of 1938 or the Long Island Express. Although there had been a couple of very destructive hurricanes in New England in previous centuries, the last one had been so long ago that people had come to think it could never happen here again. So the region was taken completely by surprise on September 21, 1938. The weather community had effectively silenced the few forecasters who correctly predicted the path and speed of the storm. Its rain and winds hit Long Island, then crossed into Connecticut and pummeled New England's southern shorelines before continuing north. It eventually died out in Canada after causing great destruction with huge coastal surges, inland flooding, and extremely high winds. The "Express" nickname referred to the storm flying up the entire east coast without any stops, to its first landfall on Long Island.

Where were you during the Hurricane of '38?

Adrianne *It struck the Connecticut shoreline in the afternoon. When I got out of school the storm was already raging, and things were getting worse. My mother was nearly hit by a falling tree as she walked home. Then the "eye" passed over us, but nobody realized what it was. We still didn't know we were in a hurricane; we thought the storm was over, when in reality the worst was yet to come. Our family even got in the car and drove down to the beach to see what the surf looked like. Fortunately, the storm didn't start up again until we were safely home! Then a tidal wave—now called a storm surge—came in and swept away all the beachfront summer homes, even those built high up out of the water on stilts. School was out for weeks afterward.*

Bella *I was married and living in Andover. I watched from my front door as the roof of Tyer Rubber was lifted up and off, then set back onto the building.*

Butch *Main Street in Bennington was flooded by the river, and a boy slipped and fell into the river and drowned.*

Charlotte *I was working on Essex Street in Lawrence. The door of a dress shop flew off. Everything was blowing. I held on to lampposts on my way home.*

Claire *The water was so high and so rough that officials closed the bridge connecting South Lawrence and Lawrence.*

Edith *I was at school, in my fifth grade classroom on the second floor. We could all see the trees bending in the terrific wind, and we watched as a limb came down on a teacher's car. We were let out early so we could get home before it got any worse, and we didn't realize it would be weeks before we returned. I got a ride with the father of a friend who had come for his daughter. Trees were down everywhere. We couldn't get down my street, so I told him to go around to the block in back of my house. After he let me off, I got into my own yard through* *a gate from the neighbor's property. I had to climb over a downed tree to get into the house. We lost power almost as soon as I arrived. Then a big apple tree in the yard went down as well. But due to the physical geography of the area, no water reached our street in spite of how close to the harbor we were. Meanwhile, my father was at work on low-lying land right on New Haven harbor. When he and his fellow workers realized they needed to evacuate, they found the only street out blocked by downed trees. The tide was rising fast, so Daddy said to those around him, "If you want to get out of here tonight, follow me." Then he grabbed an ax that belonged to the company and chopped a hole in a fence separating its property from Kimberly Avenue, and they were all able to drive their cars out to safety. Later, when the tide came fully in, the water flooded all the inventory in the building.*

Elaine   *When we marched out of school at the end of the day we saw the biggest tree in the schoolyard topple. It barely missed us. There was no power for a long time after that.*

Ellen   *I was ten years old and living in Holliston. One or two friends had come over after school on the day of the hurricane. Mother put us in my sister's large closet to keep us away from flying glass from windows that might get blown in. We played happily and were not alarmed. However, there was a tremendous amount of damage in town. Dad had to abandon his car and pick his way over fallen trees to reach the house.*

Ellie   *I had just moved with my mother into our present house in Dartmouth. Trees were bending in the wind. Mother decided she wanted to go down to Horseneck to see the waves. We returned home via the Hix Bridge, crossing it only an hour before it was washed away. Horseneck was stripped bare of all its homes and cottages.*

Helen   *I can't remember. Perhaps it wasn't too bad for us on the Cape? It wouldn't have mattered that we lost power, since we had no electricity anyway!*

Louise   *I was living on Brook Street in South Paris. Hailstones started coming down the fireplace and bouncing off the floor, so we closed the damper. Some of the neighbor's chickens were killed by the hail,* *and nine windows were broken in our house. Wind twisted the big elms out front. The clothesline broke, and the clothes on it had to be rewashed.*

Lucy *We watched the river come up almost to our street. There was bumper-to-bumper traffic on the bridge from Portsmouth over the Sakonnet River. The bridge was very low, and when it was rebuilt after the storm it was set much higher. Some cars were washed off by a huge wave, and everyone in those cars drowned. One contained our next-door neighbors—mother, daughter, and son. The son had picked up his mother and sister from work in Portsmouth, and all three died.*

Nancy *The day of the hurricane I got out of school at the usual time, which was 3:40 p.m. I noticed that it was extremely windy. It happened to be Mother's forty-seventh birthday, and she had gone to Boston for a church meeting. Dad was in Providence on business. I was ten years old and in the sixth grade. My sister Lucy, who was a senior in high school, was to be in charge of me until my parents got home. Trees were being uprooted all around. Seawater from Buzzards Bay was being pushed onto land and into ponds, which overflowed in turn. Water came up my street to within two houses of us. The next-door neighbor had us come over to her house.*

Okie *I was living in a home in Braintree, outside of Boston, working as a mother's helper while I attended school. My employer's husband had a hard time getting home from work in Boston.*

Rosanna *Our house was on a slight incline, so we got only a little water in our basement. But others were being flooded out. My brothers went out to help people get to shelters. There was one in Armstrong Hall at St. Joseph School.*

Rozzy *In Lynn, my sister Connie had returned from work early because of a severe headache. We were looking out the windows in the front room, watching trees being bent way, way over by the wind. My mother was worried that the windows might shatter. She said, "Come away from the windows, come away from the windows" and made us stay away from them. School was out for at least three or four days.*

Shirl   I was in the fifth grade in Sharon. The eye of the hurricane passed right over us as we were getting out of school, but nobody realized what was happening. So we drove over to Norwood to buy my brother a new football, and on the way home my mother had to drive around pine trees that were being uprooted and falling onto the roads. A teenaged Sharon boy, Robert Davis, was killed when a tree fell on him. There was no school for two or three weeks.

Shirley   When I looked outside, I saw trees going down. Mother was not at home.

Sonny   There were no trees on our street in New Haven, but our parlor faced Sylvan Avenue and we could see trees falling there and on other streets. I also heard about the extensive flooding on the shore.

Stillman   By the time the hurricane reached Haverhill it had lost much of its strength but still did plenty of damage. Downtown, the Merrimack River flooded. My father was so concerned about the weather that he came to pick me up after my piano lesson instead of letting me walk home. The clouds looked yellowish, and the wind was roaring in gusts. Apples were all over the yard from our Greening apple tree. The power went out, and we lit kerosene lamps. The storm blew the chimney off; it crashed through a skylight window and landed in a bedroom. A big locust tree my grandmother had planted fell over. Many trees were uprooted because the ground was soft from so much previous rain.

Tom   I was outside my house, watching as a huge tree in the yard swayed but did not topple. It survived, but so many others were lost all over Lowell.

Vicki   I was in high school, and walking home from the bus stop I felt the strongest wind I'd ever experienced. It didn't do much damage that I saw, though.

Walt   We had just moved to Boston. When we opened the door to the apartment, the change in air pressure shattered one of our windows. We secured the window, maybe with a roller shade. There were sheets *and sheets of water coming down. The street lights stayed on, so it's possible we never lost power. The next day, we went to the Fens. Many of the big old oak trees were down. My father was just amazed; it had taken a hundred years for them to grow, and then—poof!*

57

Shirley

SHIRLEY WAS BORN in Pelham, Massachusetts in 1922 in a "private home for deliveries." She was the third of seven surviving children, four girls and three boys, born over a 25-year span from 1917 until 1942. Another two babies died at birth.

Lawrence Gale, Shirley's father, was of Yankee descent. He grew up on a farm in Charlemont, Massachusetts and went on to "Mass Aggie" in Amherst—Massachusetts Agricultural College, which eventually became the University of Massachusetts. Lawrence became a farm manager, drawing on both his formal training in agriculture and his own experience, and managed several farms in southern Vermont and western Massachusetts. During Shirley's childhood the family lived in Pownal and Shaftsbury in Vermont, and Bernardston in Massachusetts.

Edice Eastman, Shirley's mother, was also a Yankee. She was a distant relation of Emily Dickinson and, like Emily, had grown up in Amherst. Her first name was bestowed on her under somewhat peculiar circumstances; someone gave her parents a gift in return for naming her Edice!

Shirley remembers her childhood well, and fondly. Although Mr. Gale made his living through outside work, he always maintained a small farm at home as well. There was plenty of work to keep the children busy—haying, feeding livestock, milking cows, gardening. It was

Born *at a private "delivery home" in Pelham, Massachusetts in August 1922*

When I was your age, *things were much simpler.*

What were your very favorite foods to eat? *Chicken, vegetables, and fruit*

You were sent to Sunday school when you were a child. Is religion important to you now? *Yes*

Did you ever address adults by their first names? *No*

What did you call your parents? *Mother and Dad*

What was your first job while you were still in school? *I did lots of babysitting, starting early on.*

How old were you when you went on your first date? *I was 18 or 19*

How old were you when you got married? *We were both 21, though I was a few months older.*

What was your first full-time job? *I was a clerk at Tap & Dye in Greenfield, Mass.*

Many things have been invented since you were a child. What has given you the most pleasure, or been the most valuable to you? *Central heating! No more having to fill the wood box from the woodshed.*

What do you think about being a kid today? *Life was simpler then. We had less money, but we managed. There was much less stress. We did more things with our families.*

What is your name now? *Shirley Sweet*

Did you eat beans and franks for Saturday night supper? *Yes* a perfect environment for 4-H activities, and Shirley once raised Banty hens as a project. Both parents were active in the Grange and the Community Club, and in church organizations. They didn't actually attend church themselves, but they sent the children to Sunday school. Edice had grown up with a Baptist father who went to church and a mother who was active in the Baptist women's group but "too busy cooking a big dinner" on Sundays to attend services. In Bernardston, Shirley and her sister started going to the Congregational Church because they liked the minister, who was a neighbor. Today, at the age of ninety, she is still a Congregationalist.

The Gale children played mostly outside. Shirley had ice skates, sidewalk skates, and a sled, and at sixteen she bought herself a bicycle. Hide 'n' seek was the kids' favorite game. On Sunday afternoons, after a big dinner, they went on long hikes or nature walks. They also enjoyed board games and cards. Shirley sometimes quarreled with her siblings and parents, but only "once in a while" and not as often as some of her brothers and sisters. In the summer, she spent one or two weeks with her mother's parents and was quite attached to her grandmother. Christmas was her favorite holiday, even though there were not many presents. She does remember receiving a doll once or twice. Often her mother and Grandma Eastman would make doll clothes for presents.

Mealtimes involved eating everything whether you liked it or not, because you didn't get dessert until it was finished. For Shirley, the not-likes included anything with any fat on it, especially pork. For breakfast they had hot cereal—oatmeal or cream of wheat. Supper was meat, potatoes, milk, vegetables—sometimes in a salad—and always a dessert. They weren't allowed to snack between meals, but sometimes they succeeded in "sneaking" something.

The Gales lived in rural houses, sometimes renting and sometimes owning their homes. They had a radio and a telephone, and also a car, which both parents drove. Food was kept cold in a closed pantry in the winter, and in an ice box in the summer, with ice delivered a couple of times a week. Two wood stoves provided heat—one in the kitchen and another in the living room. In at least one of the houses the only indoor water source was a pump at the kitchen sink. Faucets were added later, and still later, indoor toilet facilities to replace the outhouse. On

Saturday nights the tub was hauled into the kitchen from the shed and water for their baths was heated on the stove. When Shirley was ten they got a modern Maytag electric washer. Even then, they had to heat water on the stove to put into the machine.

Shirley started school in Vermont at the age of six and walked almost a mile to the schoolhouse. She moved to Bernardston for second grade and stayed through high school, graduating in 1941, at almost nineteen, as the valedictorian of Powers Institute, the local public school. (She had repeated seventh grade because of an illness that had kept her out of school for most of the year.) There were sixteen in her graduating class. In grades one through five she attended one-room schools with about thirty to a room. There were two short recesses each day, plus an hour for lunch. She started getting homework in seventh or eighth grade, but she says it was strictly voluntary! In high school she was given "real" homework assignments.

After high school Shirley did a short stint at Greenfield Commercial School to brush up on office skills. She then got a job at Greenfield Tap & Dye and stayed for three-and-a-half years, first as a clerk and later as a secretary. These were the war years. Greenfield was the largest tap and die company in the United States, and it was considered so vital to the war effort that anti-aircraft guns were placed on its grounds for defense in the event of an air attack by the Germans. She continued at the job after marrying, but after the war she left to raise a family.

58

Lucy

LUCY'S FAMILY WAS LIVING in Somerset, Massachusetts when she was born. Her father walked a mile in a December blizzard for the doctor, but she was born before they got back to the house. Of the twelve children born to John and his wife, only six survived childhood. Following tradition, they named their oldest son and daughter Joseph and Mary. Joseph—Joe—was thirteen years older than Lucy, Manuel—Manny—was eleven, Gil four, and Mary—Mamie—two-and-a-half. Ermelinda, named for her mother and called Emily, came four years after Lucy. Later there would be two half-siblings, a girl and a boy.

John Santo Christo, Lucy's father, was born on St. Michael, the largest island in the Azores, an island group in the Atlantic that was uninhabited when the Portuguese discovered and claimed it in the 1400s. John's father was from a wealthy family but was disowned for marrying far below his station. That was only the beginning of the troubles for his wife and three sons. John was the middle child. When the youngest was very young their father died. His widow had no way to support them all, so she sent John to live with a childless farming couple to work in exchange for room and board. The only family help she got was from her husband's brother, a doctor, who later paid for their passage to America. John lived with the farmer and his wife for quite awhile. They loved him as their own, taught him to read and write, and wanted to keep him. John wanted to stay, but his mother insisted that the family go together to America.

Born *at home in Somerset, Massachusetts, in December 1923*

"When I was your age, *I paid a lot of respect to my elders."*

What was your very favorite food? *Chicken feet*

Did you or your friends ever eat out at restaurants or diners? *No*

You were required to attend church growing up. Is religion important to you now? *Yes, but I am a Protestant now and no longer Catholic.*

Did you ever address adults by their first names? *No*

What did you call your parents? *Ma (for both my mother and stepmother) and Pa*

How old were you when you went on your first date, and where did you go? *I started dating my future husband, Rudolph, when I was almost 18. He didn't have a car, so we went on long walks—down Main Street to window shop, to the park, or even all the way from Fall River to Somerset.*

How old were you when you got married? *I was 22, and he was 21.*

What was your first full-time job? *Sewing machine operator*

What was your occupation for most of your working life? *Sewing machine operator*

Many things have been invented since you were a child. What has given you the most pleasure, or been the most valuable to you? *Electric washing machines. When I was first married, I had just a tub and a hand wringer.*

Do you think you would enjoy being a kid today? *No, I don't think I would like it much. Now children are indoors, at computers, instead of playing outside. I liked my own world a* *lot better. There wasn't as much bullying. We took pride in our schools: if someone saw a piece of trash on the floor he would pick it up. There was no graffiti.*

You were abused and beaten. Would you have been happier being removed by social services—taken from your family? *No. I wasn't suffering alone. I had my two sisters. And I was tough.*

In general, today we have many more possessions than when you were a child. Do you think this has affected our happiness? *It has not made us happier. I feel sorry for today's babies. We have too much. We used to appreciate everything, because we had so little.*

What is your name now? *Lucy Morris*

Did you eat beans and franks for Saturday night supper? *No*

As they were moving into a tenement in Fall River, Massachusetts, tragedy struck. John's older brother was carrying his mother's sewing machine up a narrow, steep staircase when he stumbled and fell, and he died a few days later of his injuries. His mother had counted on this boy, who was in his early teens, to find work in the mills. Now that fell to John. Because he was still below the legal age his mother made him use his dead brother's name and birth certificate to get a job. His younger brother went to school and learned English, but John never got beyond broken English and couldn't carry on a conversation. Resenting his brother greatly, he grew into a bitter, uncaring man.

Ermelinda Fernandez, known as Emily, was Lucy's mother, and she died when Lucy was only 12. She came from the Azores with her parents when she was a child and worked in the mills before marriage. She and John bought a house in Somerset, a country town just to the west of Fall River, and John took a trolley to Fall River to work as a spinner in a cotton mill there. He was very good at his job and also popular among the other Portuguese-speaking workers, partly because he was the only one who could read the Portuguese-language newspaper. This paper carried dramatic stories in serial installments, and the others would gather around him to hear him read the latest episode. Then the Depression came, mills started to close, and John lost his job. He could no longer pay the mortgage on his house, and in 1930, when Lucy was in the first grade, they moved to Fall River. John owed only $1100 on the house, and the bank never foreclosed on it. Years later, when the economy was better, the bank offered it back for only the amount he had previously owed. For reasons unknown, he turned down this opportunity and didn't tell his family until the offer had expired. His grown sons were very upset, as they could have, and would have, bought it themselves through him.

There was no electricity at the Somerset home. The kitchen had an indoor pump, their only source of water. There was no toilet; just an outhouse. Water for baths was heated on the wood/coal stove every Saturday night and poured into the aluminum laundry washtub. The tub was placed in front of the stove for warmth, but it was still very cold. The three boys bathed by turn while more water was heated for the girls. Lucy loved the house, loved living in the country. Some of her happiest times after the move were the occasional visits to her mother's sister, who still lived in Somerset. She had an annual clambake at her home, which was "just wonderful," and there were fireworks at her church on July 4.

The third-floor tenement apartment had no electricity for the first several years because Lucy's father either couldn't or wouldn't pay the one-dollar-a-month cost to provide it. Finally, Joe, who was working, paid to get electric service. It consisted of light from a single bulb hanging from a ceiling. They had running water and a toilet, but no bathtub, and the wood/coal stove in the kitchen was the apartment's only source of heat. Lucy's mother either scrubbed the laundry in the sink or sent it out, paying by the pound. A man picked up dirty laundry on Monday and returned it on Friday, wet and still needing to be hung to dry. For refrigeration, John built a little wooden chest and nailed it to the pantry window, his own original version of an ice box. Down on the street, children would start running when they heard the cry, "Ice! Ice!" Lucy joined them, chasing the truck and picking up fallen chips to suck on. Farmers drove carts with meat and produce up and down the streets, calling out what they selling. Pastry trucks made rounds as well, and sometimes drivers gave kids free pastries they couldn't sell because they were several days old.

In spite of added income from Joe and Manny, who was also working, the Santo Christos had very little. To help pay off Emily's hospital bills, they sold their player piano. Joe and Manny brought some cheer by purchasing a Zenith floor model radio, and Lucy loved listening to The Shadow and to singer Eddie Cantor. But they were crowded. All three girls shared one bed, sleeping in their underwear because they couldn't afford pajamas. Nor did they have boots or warm winter coats. Lucy walked to school in the snow in sneakers, with only an unlined leather coat and thin gloves to keep out the cold. In her first year of high school, a slightly warmer green coat just appeared one day in her locker. She waited several weeks for someone to claim it. Nobody ever did, so she started wearing it with a clear conscience.

Lucy's family was Catholic, and the children were expected to attend church. Their father and Emily were religious, but their later stepmother never went to church. Lucy and her siblings were expected to be very respectful toward adults, especially their parents, including their stepmother. Whenever they left the house they put a hand to their mouth while saying in Portuguese what is roughly translated as "Bless me, Father" to their mother or father. They repeated this on returning home, and when passing their parents in the street. This was probably spelled Pai, abençoa but they pronounced it as "passabenss."

The outward respect paid to their parents wasn't always felt inwardly. Their true reverence was reserved for Joe, who became a loving substitute for his demoralized father and who supported them both emotionally and materially. After John lost his job in the Depression he refused to apply for welfare, even though Joe's job could not cover their expenses. So Joe went over his father's head and applied for the little help that was available. At specified times, Lucy and her sister pulled their brothers' homemade wagon to a food distribution point and were given powdered milk, powdered eggs, and butter. Sometimes workers were dishonest, moving friends to the head of the line or cheating large families. If the girls were supposed to get two pounds of butter they would give them only one and put the other aside for themselves. They knew there was nothing young girls could do to stop them.

The family's favorite celebration was the annual Santo Christo feast. Not only was it a very big deal in the Portuguese community, but they shared a common name with the holiday. It was even more fun than Christmas, because John gave them each a penny, which bought about eight pieces of candy. They didn't really celebrate Christmas, not receiving presents or having a tree until their father remarried. Even then presents were given only to their stepmother's children.

Before the remarriage the children often played games of tag, kick the can, hopscotch, and marbles; after the marriage they worked almost constantly. One happy memory is of a time the whole family went to the Crescent Amusement Park in East Providence, Rhode Island, for a picnic. An uncle worked for a farmer who let him take his truck; the adults sat in the cab while the kids rode in the open back and sang. Lucy liked to play with paper dolls she made herself from pictures cut out of the Montgomery Ward catalog. When she played "school" with them she rapped the knuckles of naughty dolls, just like her teacher did. She had only one other doll, one her mother had made for her by stuffing and twisting a stocking. The only "real" toy she had was a pair of roller skates. She had received five dollars—a huge sum—from her godparents at confirmation when she was seven years old. Lucy turned the money over to her mother, who asked if there was anything she would like. She asked for roller skates, and her mother bought them. They cost only forty-nine cents! The only other presents she remembers getting were from Joe. Once he gave her some crayons and a coloring book; another time, writing paper and a pencil.

There was no snacking, because there was barely enough food for regular meals. Lucy was skinny, and always hungry. Her parents bought a live chicken off a street cart every Saturday, and John wrung its neck and put it in boiling water. Then his wife hung it from a hook in the kitchen until it was drained and ready for her to pluck and cook. It was used the next day in "Portugee soup" for Sunday dinner. Weekday suppers were soups of rice or potatoes, with cabbage, kale, or peas flavored with onions and garlic, and rarely contained meat.

Lucy started first grade in Somerset when she was five years old, but before the year was out she moved to Fall River. She knew no English on entering school but learned very quickly and was fluent within a few months. The "Santo Christo" last name was a continual source of confusion at school. The children had to constantly fight teachers who insisted that both words could not possibly be in their last name because there were "two capital letters." They refused to believe them and recorded it incorrectly as only "Christo." But Lucy appreciated school and everything she was able to learn. She was especially grateful that she learned to sew and cook. She was not good at arithmetic, which she thinks was probably due to trouble seeing the blackboard. She had had complications from measles and been left with weakened vision. She needed glasses, but her father wouldn't get them for her. When Lucy was fourteen she finally got a pair for free. They were distinctly recognizable as "welfare glasses," so after she started earning her own money she bought herself a new pair.

She remembers her teachers mostly as "impatient, cranky old maids who played favorites." One seated her in the back of the room despite knowing she couldn't read the board from there. Another, Miss Fitzler, was crabby and not well-liked. However, Lucy remembers her fondly. Somehow she had learned that Lucy's mother was dying of cancer. Miss Fitzler responded by inviting Lucy and her sister to go out with her to a soda fountain, where she bought them ice cream sodas. This was an unheard-of treat for the girls.

In the sixth grade Lucy caught up to her brother Gil, who had stayed back enough times to land in her class. He was quite intelligent, but not interested enough in school to pay attention. Their family did not consider education important, so he had no encouragement from home to do well. Gil had a friend about the same age—fourteen or fifteen—who was also in class. Both of them were just putting in time at school, waiting until they could drop out at sixteen. During a geography lesson, his friend was making noise and not paying attention, so the teacher told him to come to the front of the room and show her where a certain country was on the map. He slouched forward saying,

"Why should I show you? You know where it is." He was promptly sent to the principal for punishment.

When Lucy was ten and her younger sister only six, Emily developed breast cancer and was in and out of the hospital for the next two years and bedridden for her last year. Emily's mother moved in with the family to care for her and the children, but in June 1935, when Lucy was twelve, she died at home, screaming in pain. Lucy's grandmother remained with them for another six months but went to live with a different daughter when John remarried. Their new mother was thirty-five years old, only ten years older than Lucy's brother Joseph, and had never been married. At first the children were excited. They missed their mother but were happy about the prospect of having a normal family life again. They had no idea what they were in for.

Olivia and John married in January. She was nice for a while, and everyone was happy. But the following July, with Olivia five months pregnant, everything changed. She turned abusive and cruel toward her step-children, although she was always loving and kind to both of her own once they were born. She stripped all remnants of joy from their home. Lucy cannot even remember what her stepmother's first name was. She has suggested "Olivia" as a pseudonym. They suffered both verbal and physical attacks from her. Lucy loved to read, but she had to sneak books into the house, keep them hidden, and read only at night by the light of the street lamp outside her window, because Olivia did not allow books. She once found a library book buried in the closet, where Lucy had hidden it. She burned it.

John never defended his children against his wife's verbal abuse, but Lucy assumed he was unaware of the beatings. Later she learned he had known of at least one. She was fifteen and watching Olivia's young daughter outside, when the girl fell and started crying. Her mother rushed out and immediately started beating Lucy with the handle of her broom, without asking what had happened. A neighbor witnessed the attack and notified the authorities, who visited her father at work and told him it had to stop. Nothing changed. It's possible he didn't care, considering he had once done almost exactly the same thing to Lucy. Emily, sick and in pain, had sent her to the store for something she needed right away. Lucy hurried home with the purchase, but when she reached her building's gate, a neighbor girl was standing on it and wouldn't get off. Repeated pleading had no effect, so she finally just pushed hard enough on the gate that it opened. The girl was thrown off balance, fell, and evidently broke a tooth. Later her father came by to complain to John, armed with only his daughter's dishonest account. John was embarrassed at losing face and didn't care about the truth. He beat Lucy for it.

School ended for Lucy at the end of 1939, when she turned sixteen. She was in her junior year and would have graduated from Durfee High School in 1941 if her father hadn't forced her to leave, but it was now time for her to help support the family. Fortunately, she had taken evening classes in sewing machine operation, enabling her to get work as a skilled operator. Every week she turned her paycheck over to Olivia, who returned ten percent of it to Lucy for her own use. Initially she made $7 a week for full-time work. When America entered the war two years later, she found a job for almost five times that: $34 a week on the assembly line at Firestone, making gas masks and cementing parts of airplane fuel tanks. She had money for herself for the first time, and every Wednesday, on "dish night," she treated herself to a movie. But she still hated to go home. She sensed "a darkness, a pall" over the apartment. When she was sick she went to work anyway, just to get away.

Two years after leaving school, when she was almost eighteen, Lucy met the love of her life. A friend introduced her to Rudolph Souza, who was a year younger and lived a few streets away. They dated until he was drafted. When she was twenty-one, and he was still in the service, Olivia gave Lucy's sister Emily such a severe beating that the sisters moved out together. When Rudolph returned they married, but their happiness was short-lived. Lucy was four months pregnant with their first child when Rudolph died of a ruptured appendix. He had been a popular, good, and well-liked man, and a VFW post in Fall River is named for him. Lucy was a widow for seven years before remarrying and having another son and two daughters. She lived in Warren, Rhode Island, where she continued to work as a sewing machine operator while raising her children.

Lucy is now eighty-nine and lives independently. After a stressful, traumatic childhood, a wonderful marriage that ended tragically, and an unhappy second marriage, she finally found lasting happiness thirty years ago in an encounter with Jesus one morning in her own living room. She was immediately and permanently healed of emotional burdens and fears, and of two chronic health conditions. She found peace and love, saw blessings and beauty all around her for the first time, and was filled with the certain knowledge that God loved her. Lucy has fully enjoyed life ever since.

59

Stillman

WHEN STILLMAN WAS BORN in February of 1929, he truly was the baby of the family. His sister, Evelyn, was twenty; his brother, Guy, eighteen. Evelyn was a teacher at the Fox School in Haverhill. Old enough to be his mother, she was a real second mother to him, helping to train and discipline him and later paying for the first few years of his piano lessons.

His father, Guy Moses Haynes, was a dairy farmer and milkman until he "retired" at the age of seventy-two to take a job working in a mill. He stopped that at seventy-seven after breaking a hip. Guy was born in 1870 and was already fifty-nine years old when Stillman was born. Of Yankee ancestry, he had grown up on the twelve-acre farm in Haverhill where he kept cows, chickens, and hens and cultivated three vegetable gardens, a small flower garden, and fruit trees. Guy's mother, who still owned the farm, lived with them until close to her death at the age of ninety-eight. Her maiden name was Hammond, and she was born in 1842 in Lincoln, Maine.

Minnie Sargent, Stillman's mother, also a Yankee, was born in 1885 in West Newbury, Massachusetts and was forty-four when Stillman was born. She grew up in Newburyport and married Guy in 1908. Her mother, Evelyn, was the daughter of Stillman Higgins Riley, her son's namesake. Minnie's father was born about 1841 and had fought in the Civil War.

Born *at home in Haverhill, Massachusetts in February, 1929*

When I was your age, *things were quite different.*

What were your very favorite foods to eat? *Wheaties, and homemade applesauce*

Did you or your friends ever eat out at restaurants or diners? *Very seldom*

You were taken to church growing up. Is religion important to you now? *Yes, very*

Did you ever address adults by their first names? *No*

What did you call your parents? *Pa and Mother*

What was your first job while you were still in school? *I just worked for my father on the farm.*

How old were you when you went on your first date, and where did you go? *I was 18 or 20. I don't remember where we went.*

What was your first full-time job? *I worked at a woolens mill.*

What was your occupation for most of your working life? *I was a factory worker, first in a wood heel shop and later in textiles.*

What do you think you would most enjoy about being a kid today? *I would rather be a kid back then. Life was slower.*

Today we hear that the lives of many American children are very stressful. Was yours stressful in any way? *Not really*

Did you eat beans and franks for Saturday night supper? *We had canned beans (Friends' or B+M) and brown bread.*

It must have seemed strange for Stillman to study the Civil War as something that had happened a long, long time ago; had ended seventy years before he entered school. Strange, because at least three of his grandparents had been adults at the beginning of the war. At least one grandfather had been a Union soldier. The grandmother he threaded needles for—whose failing eyesight did not stop her from sewing—was already nineteen years old when the fighting started. He literally grew up with an eyewitness to history at his side. Put another way, she was born only fifty-nine years after the end of the American Revolution! She may well have known some who fought in it.

On Saturdays Stillman helped his sister clean the house, but most of his chores involved farm work, especially in the summer. Although he didn't milk the cows until his late teens, he regularly cut hay, gathered eggs, and worked in the vegetable and flower gardens. In his free time, Stillman listened to radio programs such as Amos 'n' Andy, adding Hit Parade in his teens. In winter he liked to sled down the big hill off Carlton Street. He also enjoyed going to parades on some of the patriotic holidays. In 1940, Haverhill celebrated its three-hundredth anniversary with a big pageant at the stadium. Stillman attended this commemoration—"Drums of Freedom"—and remembers it well.

Minnie was an excellent cook, and Stillman especially loved her homemade applesauce. For breakfast he liked bread spread with either honey or molasses. Dinner, around noon, was the day's biggest meal. Guy picked him up from school, about a mile-and-a-half away, so he could eat with the family. Supper was fairly light and was served around six or seven, after milking was over. Saturday's menus never varied: hamburgers, boiled potatoes, and homemade gravy for dinner, and beans and brown bread for supper.

Guy and Minnie attended West Congregational Church regularly, and were active and involved, but Stillman isn't sure whether their religion was actually important to them. "We just went," he says of church. In his own adult life it is very different. "To be born again and be able to go to Heaven" is the most important thing in the world, he says.

Stillman talked too much in school and sometimes got into trouble for it. He liked spelling, English, geography, American history, and science, and was especially good at English and spelling. He didn't care for ancient history, and he had just an awful time with arithmetic.

The Haynes family might have been described as middle class. They owned a motorized vehicle—first a Model T truck for the farm, and later, a car. In the 1930s they bought a Silvertone radio that lasted eighteen years. They also had a telephone, but all calls, even local ones, had to be placed through the operator; direct dial was not implemented in Haverhill until 1949. Many other improvements occurred during his childhood. Indoor plumbing was installed in the 1930s. In 1937 a coal furnace replaced their former heat sources of a kitchen oil stove and wood stoves in the living room and his grandmother's bedroom. In 1939, a refrigerator replaced the ice box in the back entryway, but they still used an ice chest in the milk room for the dairy operation. The farm had a separate ice house to store its own ice supply. At some point they got an electric Kenmore washing machine from Sears, with a motor underneath and an electric wringer on top. Because of the demands of the farm they didn't get away much. Once in a great while they were able to take a day trip to a place such as Hampton Beach, Benson's Wild Animal Farm, or the Topsfield Fair.

Stillman attended Haverhill High School but quit before graduating to join the U.S. Army. He was in the service when the Korean Conflict broke out but was stationed in Europe and never saw combat. After leaving the army he attended trade school on the G.I. Bill, and he started taking organ lessons. Stillman lived at the farm until he was twenty-eight, when it was sold following his father's death. A condominium complex, Hunters Run, was built on the land, while the house was moved elsewhere. He greatly enjoyed being able to play the organ and piano and is grateful that his family provided lessons for him. He worked hard in a factory all week, but on Sunday mornings Stillman was a church organist, playing at West Congregational for twenty years and later substituting at area churches.

60

Nancy

THE GIRLS RE-FORMED their lines after offering their flowers, and the parade turned around, came off the bridge, and turned left onto Main Street to proceed to Riverside Cemetery. There they stood for a memorial service and the reciting of the Gettysburg Address by the president of the high school's senior class.

Nancy spent her childhood in Fairhaven, Massachusetts, a coastal town bordering both New Bedford Harbor and Buzzard's Bay. Born the youngest of four girls in 1928, she never knew her oldest sister, Barbara, who had been born in 1917 and died of meningitis in 1926. Janice had followed in 1919 and Lucy in 1921. Before Nancy was a year old the family moved from Easton to Fairhaven, and in 1933 they bought a home at 118 Pleasant Street.

Wendell Tripp Eldredge, Nancy's father, was born in Chatham on Cape Cod and traced his lineage back to the Mayflower through Elizabeth Tilley and John Howland. At least one ancestor had fought in the American Revolution, and Wendell's grandfather, Zelots Kinney Eldredge, a Union soldier, was at Appomattox when Lee surrendered. Wendell was exempt from the draft in World War I because he had a child. He eventually enlisted anyway, but before training started the Armistice was signed and so he was no longer needed. Wendell had not graduated from high school. He supported his family as a salesman, first for the Atlantic Refining and Amoco oil companies and

Born *at Goddard Hospital in Brockton, Massachusetts in July 1928*

When I was your age, *I didn't think I'd live this long.*

When I was your age, *I was happy.*

What was your very favorite food to eat? *Seafood!*

Your least favorite? *Sweet potatoes*

Did you or your friends ever eat out at restaurants or diners? *Yes, but my family did this more than my friends' families.*

You were required to attend church growing up. Is religion important to you now? *Yes, it's very important.*

Did you ever address adults by their first names? *No. My family was dear friends with the Jacksons in Acushnet, so they were Uncle Leo and Auntie Ruth, but we used formal titles for all other adults who were not relatives.*

What did you call your parents? *Dad or Daddy, and Mother or Mama*

What was your first job while you were still in school? *Salesclerk at the Star Store in New Bedford*

How old were you when you went on your first date, and where did you go? *I was 15, and we went to a movie.*

How old were you when you got married? *I was 19, and he was 21.*

What was your first full-time job? *Receptionist*

What was your occupation for most of your working life? *Farm wife, and secretary or receptionist*

Many things have been invented since you were a child. What has given you the most pleasure, or been the most valuable to you? *Automatic transmissions. They were invented before I was born but were not in common use until I was well into my adult years.*

By *today's standards*, did you have a lot of "stuff" growing up? *No*

In general, today we have many more possessions than when you were a child. Do you think this has affected our happiness? *"Stuff" doesn't make people happy. A smile, a kind word, caring for and about others is more important, although I do enjoy having a dependable car. I like to drive and it has given me a lot of freedom.*

Today we hear that the lives of many American children are very stressful. Was yours stressful in any way? *Yes, but only when my father was out of a job, with no money coming in.*

What is your name now? *Nancy Houghton Chapel*

Did you eat beans and franks for Saturday night supper? *Is the Pope Catholic? Of course we did! My mother would slow-cook the beans in a big brown bean pot. In winter, she would place it on a ledge in the coal furnace. She always used molasses rather than sugar. We put homemade piccalilli—relish—on the franks.*

later for a construction company that repaired and re-pointed industrial chimneys.

Lucy Forbush Houghton, whose earliest Yankee ancestors arrived in 1630, was Nancy's mother. She was born in Newtonville, Massachusetts and grew up in North Andover. After high school Lucy took two years of teacher training at Salem Normal School, commuting daily by train. She started teaching in Dennis on Cape Cod at eighteen and by nineteen was the principal of a two-room school. Lucy's father, Eugene Coolidge Houghton, had been born in 1844 and orphaned at seven when his brother and parents died in an epidemic of either smallpox or typhoid. He was a Civil War veteran.

Nancy and her sisters had few chores—made their beds, did the dishes, and occasionally vacuumed or dusted—but Nancy wishes that her mother had taught her to cook. The family owned one radio, positioned next to her father's chair in the living room. Nancy remembers that they listened to Amos 'n' Andy, "because that's what my father liked." She learned to play piano as a child and continued with it into adulthood. Until just a few years ago she was the organist for her church.

She grew up in a safe world. Nancy was allowed to play alone outside by the age of two and to go next door or across the street by herself by three. When she was very little she had a wonderful peddle car given to her by an aunt. Nancy later progressed to scooters, sleds, and skates. She also liked to play with dolls. The neighborhood kids played kick the can together, with children from early teens down to seven-year olds in the group. On Saturdays she might go to the movies or on a hike with friends, taking along a picnic lunch. On Sunday mornings Nancy attended Sunday school at Grace Episcopal Church in New Bedford. After dinner, the family usually visited close friends in Acushnet, "Uncle" Leo and "Auntie" Ruth Jackson and their two daughters, staying through supper. Her father enjoyed helping Leo gather eggs from the thousand hens in the two-story, ten-room hen house and working in the large apple and peach orchards while the wives visited and the girls played together. On Christmas Eve Nancy hung a stocking, one of her mother's old nylons. The next day she always found an orange at the bottom and the rest filled with useful, rather than frivolous, items such as toothpaste or hand lotion. The tree was decorated a few days before the 25th and left up until Twelfth Night, or Epiphany.

Fairhaven children had to be only five years old to enter first grade, so Nancy started just two months after her fifth birthday. Students in the first seven grades had an extraordinarily long lunch break—just ten minutes short of two hours—whereas grades eight through twelve at the high school had only twenty minutes! Nancy remembers that the high school cafeteria meal cost only ten cents. She also remembers that her teachers were only very, very rarely absent; she doesn't recall having any substitutes until high school. On the rare occasion an elementary teacher was absent, classes were combined. Students sometimes had to double up and sit two to a seat.

One person Nancy remembers with the greatest admiration was Mabel Hoyle, the "best teacher I ever had," who taught English and public speaking at the high school and directed the senior play. "Everyone who had her loved and feared her." Miss Hoyle had emigrated from England to Haverhill, Massachusetts at the age of seven. She told Nancy that they originally had booked passage on the Titanic but rescheduled due to some last-minute business. Miss Hoyle went to Tufts College at the urging of her high school English teacher, Dorothy Houghton, a Tufts graduate who, coincidentally, was Nancy's aunt, and then taught in Fairhaven for her entire career, retiring in 1974. Nancy later attended Tufts herself.

Because of the Depression, Nancy's father was sometimes out of work. "He could get despondent when he had no job and no money," she says. But normally he had both. They owned their home and had both a car, which he needed for his job, and a telephone. The house had a coal/wood furnace and a gas stove, and a bathroom with toilet, sink, and claw foot bathtub. The couple had bought a modern Frigidaire refrigerator in 1928 which lasted for over twenty years, but Mrs. Eldredge had no washing machine. She laundered everything by hand, even sheets, in a "good-sized enamel dish pan." She also followed the same weekly sheet rotation as **Ellen**'s mother: wash the bottom sheet, move the top sheet to the bottom, and add a fresh top one.

After graduating from Fairhaven High School in 1945, Nancy studied at Tufts for two-and-a-half years before marrying Byron Chapel and moving to his family's land in Parma, Michigan. With the exception of a period the family spent in California, she has lived on their farm ever since. Nancy looks back with fondness on her childhood and her hometown, where, she says, she was raised to be honest, love God and her country, and honor her family.

61

Claire

CLAIRE WAS BORN AT HOME in Lawrence, Massachusetts, the eighth of her parents' fourteen children—eight boys and six girls. Both of her parents, Ludger Dube and Clairina Lafond, had also been born in Lawrence. Ludger worked as a truck driver for Railway Express and also as a part-time policeman. His wife, Clairina (for whom Claire was named) stayed home but was always busy. In addition to the usual duties of a housewife, she cut all of her children's hair herself and made all their clothing, even their school uniforms. She also taught each daughter to sew so skillfully that they could make anything at all, even a wedding gown, which Claire later made for own daughter's wedding. The couple did well. In spite of having to provide for sixteen people, Ludger was able to save enough to buy a home in December 1941. He drove a company-owned truck for his job but also owned his own car. Sometimes the family took Sunday drives in it.

All of Claire's grandparents were French Canadians who had been born in Canada. Her mother's parents lived across the street when Claire was little, but she didn't really get to know her father's parents, who had returned to Quebec. Her family did travel to Canada to visit relatives, but only a few times.

Her growing-up years were happy ones. The Dube children liked to fool around on their piano, although nobody took lessons or could read music. They played a lot of cards—whist, 45s, scat. Sang along

Born *at home in Lawrence, Massachusetts in July 1927*

When I was your age, *things were very different.*

What was your very favorite food to eat? *Chicken*

Your least favorite? *Green beans*

Did you or your friends ever eat out at restaurants or diners? *No*

You were required to attend church growing up. Is religion important to you now? *Yes*

Did you ever address adults by their first names? *No*

What did you call your parents? *Pa and Mum*

What was your first job while you were still in school? *I was a store clerk at J.J. Newbury, then W.T. Grant's.*

How old were you when you went on your first date, and where did you go? *I was around 19. We went to a movie.*

to music on the radio. Fought with each other. Argued over chores. (Claire admits that the younger children, including her, had to do a lot less work than their older siblings.) Sometimes she went to the movies with friends. Mostly, she went outside to play. After school, Saturdays, all summer long. Baseball with the other kids in the neighborhood. Sledding in the winter.

With fourteen children to feed, Ludger and Clairina were strict about not wasting food. Claire had to eat everything served, whether she liked the food or not. She also had to finish everything on her plate. There were no snacks. Supper was served around 5 or 6, and usually everyone was home for it. They typically had a meal of mashed potatoes, vegetables, and meat, often chicken. She came home from school

How old were you when you got married? *I was 24, and he was 23.*

What was your first full-time job? *Grant's, when I became full-time at 16.*

Many things have been invented since you were a child. What has given you the most pleasure, or been the most valuable to you? *Microwaves*

Is there anything you wish had never been invented? *Telephones, especially cell phones*

By *today's* *standards*, did you have a lot of "stuff" growing up? *No*

Today we hear that the lives of many American children are very stressful. Was yours stressful in any way? *No*

What is your name now? *Clairina Currier*

Did you eat beans and franks for Saturday night supper? *Yes*

at lunch for a peanut butter and jelly sandwich. Breakfast was toast, milk, and hot cereal, usually oatmeal.

Two months after turning six, Claire started first grade at St. Joseph's School, about a fifteen-minute walk from home. She went there through the eighth grade and then attended Lawrence High School. Nuns taught all classes. There was the usual range of teachers—good, bad, in-between, but Sister Mary Ellen, who taught her in the eighth grade, was "very mean." Her school uniform was a navy blue jumper and white blouse, and Claire changed into play clothes after school. There was one distinctive of St. Joseph's that made it slightly unusual even among parochial schools: language. The school was for Lawrence's French-speaking Catholic community, a population that didn't want its children to lose their heritage. Every day, only half the students' instruction was in English. The rest of the day they were taught in French.

Claire attended Lawrence High for two years and worked after school as a department store clerk, first at J.J. Newbuy and later at W.T. Grant. At sixteen she went full-time at Grant's and transferred to the school's "Night High" evening program to complete the rest of her credits, graduating in 1945. Claire went on to be a hard-working wife and mother, helping her husband in the tavern he owned in South Lawrence while raising her family. Today, at eighty-five, she is recovering from a recent stroke but has graciously consented to an interview. She sums up the difference between now and the times in which she was raised very simply: "When I was a girl, things were *very* different."

62

Rich, Poor

OVER HALF OF US described ourselves as "poor." This covered a wide range of actual family incomes, including some kids who had barely enough to eat and others whose families owned their own homes. Four of us felt that we were a little—but just a little—better off than most others in our community, and one felt solidly better off. Eight thought they had about the same as others, and another eight felt that they had less, or a little less. **Rozzy**, who had access to beautiful hand-me-downs through her aunt's job as a housekeeper, kept a positive attitude: "We had less, but we dressed as if we had more!" Many of us had friends who had more than we had, or less, or both. Nobody felt that it affected friendships in any way, and we felt neither superior nor inferior. For others, all our friends were neighbors, and all the neighbors were pretty much at our level. **Pumpie**, for instance, said that her friends—both black and white—were *always* from her own neighborhood. She went to school with children from other sections of town, and while they were cordial to each other, they didn't form friendships. The only class distinction problems mentioned were by **Ellen** and **Bella**, and they are detailed in their chapters. For Bella, there was a rift at school between the haves and have-nots. In Ellen's case, the mother of a potential playmate prevented the friendship on the grounds of Ellen's higher status.

The Great Depression started in 1929 and lasted until World War II, and New England was suffering from its effects while we were growing up. Thirteen of us distinctly remembered people talking about it at the time. Here's what some recalled about the situation:

Beena   *I didn't hear talk about the Depression, but I do remember once or twice getting food that was handed out at Town Hall.*

Bella   *I heard talk about "tightening your belt."*

Edith   *I don't remember talk about the Depression, but I remember my church helping the poor in its midst.*

Lucy   *I remember hearing about the Depression. Unemployed men hung around corners talking about it.*

Nancy   *I'm not sure my mother talked about the Depression, but I do remember that she spent only five dollars a week on groceries.*

Rozzy   *I remember my mother talking about it.*

Tom   *I heard a lot about the Depression, but our family never went hungry.*

Walt   *My grandparents lost their home in Maynard, Massachusetts when the mill closed due to the Depression. At first my father took it over, but he couldn't keep up the payments either. He vowed to never, ever take a mortgage again. It meant we had to live in a cramped apartment for my whole childhood while he saved up for a home, but he eventually reached his goal. After I left home he was able to buy a piece of land in Framingham for cash, and two years later he completed a two-bedroom house there, paid for entirely with cash.*

Even in the midst of economic hard times, however, our standard of living gradually rose. Only half of us had telephones in our homes while we were children, but by the time we were in high school eighty percent of us did. One family even had two. The five still without them were among the oldest of us—those who graduated from high school before the country had started to recover. Almost everyone started life with a radio, and by the end of high school we all had at least one in the home, even if it was battery-powered because we had no electricity. Five homes had more than one. About half our families owned a car or truck, but usually only our fathers drove them. Only six of our mothers had learned to drive.

One effect of the Depression and resultant unemployment was a huge rise in men who adopted the "hobo" lifestyle, traveling the country looking for work, often riding as stowaways in freight cars. Nine of us said that hobos had come to our doors looking for food. Five were sure that they had been given something; the other four couldn't remember. Here are some of our memories:

Adrianne   *Once in a while a hobo would come by. We would always give him something to eat, but not inside the house. Food was brought out to the back step.*

Edith   *We had hobos come by. My mother always gave them a job to do, and then some dinner. The first ones probably marked our house. [Hobos would make some sort of mark to signal to those coming after them where they might find a friendly reception.]*

Ellen   *We saw hobos fairly often during the year we lived in the center of North Dana. The railroad tracks went right through the village, and men would jump off the freight cars and go looking for food. Mother always gave them something. They probably had the house marked.*

Rosanna   *We lived next to the railroad tracks, and hobos came to the house. My mother gave them food until my father put a stop to it.*

Tom   *We didn't get any hobos, but once my father brought home a fellow he'd met on the street who was dressed as a priest. My mother immediately recognized him as a fraud. I think they may have had to call the police to get rid of him.*

Walt   *Nobody actually came up to our apartment, but hobos and bums frequented nearby land owned by the Beth Israel Hospital. They slept there in the summer, and Jimmy, our building superintendent, let them into the basement at night in the winter.*

63

War

MANY OF OUR FATHERS had fought in World War I, which was supposed to have been "the war to end all wars." It was not, of course. World War II was sparked in Europe in 1939, and the United States became involved after December 7, 1941, when Japan bombed Pearl Harbor and other U.S. interests. People often remember exactly where they were when they heard something particularly shocking and important, and most of us were no exception. Here's what we were doing when we learned of that attack:

Adrianne   *I was on my way out of the house when I passed by the radio and heard the announcement of the bombing of Pearl Harbor.*

Beena   *I was pregnant with our second child and living in West Upton, Massachusetts. I was in one of the other apartments in the building with my husband, Doug, and one or two other men and their wives. Doug and the men had trapped some foxes and raccoons for their furs a while back and were preparing them for sale. When that announcement came over the radio, Doug said that they'd better get the furs to market right away. He was worried that the price might plummet with news of war.*

Bella   *I was married. I just couldn't believe it.*

Butch   *I was at my aunt's house and heard it on the radio.*

Charlotte   *I was working in a store on Essex Street when I heard it over the radio.*

Claire   *We were actually moving into our new house at the time.*

Edith   *I was listening to One Man's Family, which was on the radio from 3-4 p.m. on Sundays.*

Elaine   *I was at my mother's parents' house that Sunday afternoon, and someone called on the phone to tell us the news. Then we turned on the radio to hear about it ourselves.*

Ellen   *I was walking downstairs from the second floor to the first. Half-way down, at the landing, I heard the radio announcement.*

Ellie   *I was a grown woman of twenty-seven, but I don't remember when I heard it.*

Helen   *I was at home.*

Louise   *I was at home and heard it on the radio.*

Lucy   *I was with Rudolph, whom I'd just started to date, at my aunt's house in Somerset.*

Nancy   *I was walking home when a neighbor came out on her porch to tell me. I went home and told my parents.*

Pumpie   *I don't actually remember.*

Okie   *I was in Concord, New Hampshire when I heard it on the radio.*

Rosanna   *I was already living in the convent. Someone came running around, giving everyone the news.*

Rozzy   *I heard about it over the radio. The next day, everyone at the high school was talking about it.*

Shirl   *My family was on the way to Peabody to visit my father's World War I buddy, and in Peabody Center we stopped at a drugstore to ask for directions. My mother heard it on the radio while she was in the store and came back to us with the news.*

Shirley   *I can't remember when exactly, but I know I did not hear it on the radio.*

Sonny   *I can't remember, although my family usually listened to an Italian music program on Sunday afternoon so we probably heard it on the radio. I remember everyone talking about it.*

Stillman   *I was lying on the living room couch, listening to the New York Philharmonic on the radio.*

Tom   *I was out in the yard, doing something with my wagon. My father heard it on the radio and called me in to tell me.*

Vicki   *I was a senior in high school, but I can't remember exactly when I heard the news.*

Walt   *We were visiting Uncle John, and I was playing outside with my cousin Marion when we were called inside to be told. The adults were hunched over the radio. The drive home was very somber, partly because my father was afraid that he would be drafted. One of his brothers did get drafted.*

With the war, life changed in many ways for us—some small, some not so small. **Tom** entered the Navy in 1945 and was sent to the Pacific. He was on Okinawa when the war ended. **Okie** enlisted in the military as well, in the Women's Army Corps, and served in Europe. Our other four men—**Butch, Sonny, Stillman, and Walt**—were all too young for the war but served in the armed forces in the years following it.

During the war years we had periodic "blackout" drills. Every neighborhood or city block in America had someone designated as an air raid warden. This person patrolled the streets in a set area after an air raid siren sounded, looking for violations of blackout rules. He or she checked to make sure that no light from any home could be seen from outside. People could either extinguish all lights, or use blackout curtains or roller shades to keep light from escaping. **Butch**'s and **Shirl**'s fathers, **Ellen**'s mother, and **Elaine**'s adult cousins all served in this capacity. [With the exception of a couple of minor incidents on the West Coast, there never were any air raids on the continental United States. The sirens were sounded for drills so that the population could practice the procedures of preparing for a real attack. The concept was the same as that of fire drills in schools.]

At school, we bought stamps for war bonds. We had rationing, with restrictions on how much we could buy of certain things. Gasoline, tires, shoes, sugar, butter, and meat were among the items requiring coupons. **Ellen** says that when she was in high school, gas rationing made them very careful about how much they drove. It didn't really inconvenience her, as she could walk or take a bus anywhere she needed to go, but she didn't get a chance to learn to drive. She was married and had three children before she got a license. Here are some of our other wartime memories:

Adrianne   *Even before the United States entered, the war had become very real to me. Soon after it started in Europe I began to correspond with a distant cousin in London, England. We kept it up for several years, and she wrote about friends, school, and air raid shelters. But at some point her letters started coming back undelivered. Her home had probably been bombed in the Blitz—the relentless air attack on London by Germany—and her address no longer existed. She never wrote again, not even after the war. We all assumed that she had died in the bombing.*

Beena   *Doug and I had two small children, and he was employed at Bath Iron Works as a machinist. He worked on ships the Navy was building for its fleet, so he kept getting deferments from service. In 1944, because the Bath job was such a long commute from our home in Rockland, he transferred to a shipyard in Camden and then was immediately drafted. In expectation of his being called up to service, we moved back to Port Clyde so I could be near my mother, and he took a job at a brand-new sardine company in the village while wait-ing. His new boss liked him so much that he gave him a series of pro-motions and somehow kept getting him deferred from duty. He never did go into the service.*

Bella   *After Pearl Harbor, my husband joined the Navy. He stayed in for twelve years, rising to the rank of Chief Petty Officer. He was on the U.S.S. Massachusetts when it was hit.*

Ellen   *Soon after the war started the government appointed my father head of Fairhaven's draft board. He was already extremely busy with his job as school superintendent, and this position meant a lot of extra work and yet more evening meetings. He was out almost every night.*

My brother enlisted in the army when he graduated from high school in 1942. He saw combat in Europe, where he was so badly wounded that the medics caring for him didn't expect him to live. To ease his pain while he died, they pumped him full of morphine. But he lived, and he struggled for the rest of his life not only with chronic pain from his injuries, but with a drug addiction brought on by the morphine he had been given.

Okie   *I enlisted in the Women's Army Corps in 1942 when I was twenty-five years old. I was trained as a radio operator and stayed in the military for four years.*

Pumpie   *Every week my sister and I took a special bus to Fort Devens for a U.S.O dance, where we talked and danced with the soldiers.*

Sonny   *My parents were from Italy, but they were not Italian sympathizers; they disliked Mussolini. After Pearl Harbor, my two older brothers both joined up. One was sent home because of problems with his feet, but the other served a couple of years and saw action.*

Tom   *I served in the United States Navy.*

Walt   *One of my father's brothers served in Patton's Third Army. My father was afraid that he might get drafted, because he was only thirty-two years old. It's possible that his job at Lever Brothers saved him, because they manufactured soap. A by-product of soap production, glycerin, was used in making nitroglycerin, the main substance in dynamite, and dynamite was vital to the war effort.*

64

More

WE HEAR A LOT these days about how stressful the lives of American children are. When asked if ours had been stressful in any way, over half of us said No. A few others cited academic pressure, or home stress due to parental abuse or unemployment. **Ellie** was particularly thoughtful. She recalled only peaceful times but was wise enough to know that she "probably" felt it *was* stressful at the time, even if it didn't seem that way looking back. In general, we're pretty happy that we were born when we were. We envy a little about opportunities today's kids have, but not much! We appreciate some modern creature comforts but worry that children are over-scheduled and don't have enough free time.

To close, we share some of the wisdom we have accumulated over the years. We're all over eighty years old, so we've had a while to think about these things. Notice that many of us address money or possessions in the final question.

What is the most significant insight you have gained so far?

Adrianne   *Life is pretty fragile.*

Beena   *Salvation is in the Lord.*

Bella   *Be happy and enjoy things.*

Butch   *Learn to control your temper.*

Charlotte   *Have faith in yourself. You can do more than you think you can. I started out bashful but became a top seller for Avon.*

Claire   *Work hard.*

Edith   *Be responsible for your own actions. Actions have consequences. Be responsible and respectful.*

Elaine   *There has to be a Creator. There has to be a means of redemption, and forgiveness is the first step in that process.*

Ellen   *If you want to get something done, just keep putting one foot after the other. You'll get there eventually.*

Ellie   *Keep my mouth shut.*

Helen   *You have to be true to yourself. If you want something, you need to work for it. You can do anything you want if you work hard enough.*

Lucy   *Knowing God. I didn't enjoy life until I knew him.*

Nancy   *Be tolerant of others' views.*

Pumpie   *Don't be selfish and self-centered. Treat people the way you want to be treated.*

Rosanna   *Take one day at a time. Don't let anything overpower you.*

Rozzy   *Money is not important, but God is very important.*

Shirl   *Be friendly, and know how to say No, which I'm finally beginning to learn how to do.*

Tom   *The best thing I ever did was marry my wife, Jean Ann. And she died of cancer when she was only forty-nine.*

Vicki   *It's good to work on friendships, to make friendships that last.*

What is the most important thing in life?

Adrianne *Love.*

Beena *The Lord, the Church, salvation in Jesus. Next my family—my children and grandchildren.*

Butch *Family, kids, grandchildren.*

Charlotte *The most important things for me were having my four children, and helping others.*

Claire *Be happy, and get along with people. It's not worth it to fight.*

Edith *My faith, and my family.*

Elaine *My faith.*

Ellen *Love.*

Ellie *Take each day as it comes; there's nothing you can do about it anyway.*

Helen *Friends.*

Louise *Family and husband.*

Lucy *Love.*

Nancy *My family.*

Okie *Health.*

Pumpie *Get along with others, and mind your own business.*

Rozzy *My children.*

Rosanna *To accept what you can't change. Don't try to accomplish the impossible.*

Shirl *Having friends.*

Sonny *Knowing Jesus, who he is, that he died for us, that there is life after death.*

Stillman   *To be born again and be able to go to Heaven.*

Tom   *Family.*

Vicki   *Having people you're close to and care about—your family and friends.*

The least important?

Adrianne   *Money.*

Beena   *Shopping.*

Charlotte   *Money.*

Elaine   *Material things.*

Ellen   *Money.*

Helen   *Money.*

Louise   *Material things.*

Okie   *Money.*

Rozzy   *Money.*

Shirl   *Having more money than you need to enjoy yourself.*

Sonny   *Being rich.*

Tom   *Liquor. After my stroke I went on a medicine that made it unwise to drink more alcohol than one glass of wine a week, rather than the one daily plus a shot of whiskey that I was used to. I really used to enjoy Jameson whiskey, but I miss it less and less.*

Vicki   *Money. I know that sounds silly.*

No, it doesn't, Vicki! Just about everyone else said the same thing. And it's a great note to close on.

Hmm...

*Because this book is meant for people of varied ages,
I have included ideas, comments, and questions for
different interest levels ranging from child through
teen to adult—from ages 7 to 97 and beyond.
If one doesn't appeal to you, move on. Maybe
the next will be fun to think about or discuss.*

Once Upon a Time

Have older people talked to you about what life was like when they were your age? What kinds of things did they tell you?

Did you identify with anyone in this book as you read about their thoughts and experiences? What did you have in common?

Our New England (map)

Maps are so much fun to look at! Don't skip over this one. See where all the kids lived.

Kids Back in the Day—Ch. 26

Did it surprise you that more than half of the kids were born at home? It's rare now, but a growing trend in some segments of the population. Do you know anyone who was born at home?

In Our Families and Homes—Ch. 27

In some ways, the people featured in this book were very much like today's parents and children. But they also lived different lives in quite a few ways. Had you realized . . .

— that so many of them married young?

— that there were so few divorces?

— that so many of them had brothers or sisters who died?

— that most of the mothers worked (very hard) at home and did not have paying jobs?

— that a lot of them did not have hot running water or indoor toilet facilities?

— that so many of the women washed their laundry by hand?

Okie—Ch. 1 and Ch. 28

Okie remembered her childhood as a wonderful time in spite of how very isolated she was. Do you think that you would have liked having Okie's childhood? What would bother you the most, and what would you enjoy?

Adrianne—Ch. 2 and Ch. 29

Adrianne's mother, Mrs. Gray, came up—on the spot—with an astonishing solution to a very difficult problem. My admiration for her is immense. Unbounded. Were you impressed, too?

Adrianne was able to shorten her walk to school by cutting through yards, which was perfectly acceptable at the time. It no longer is. Do you think it should be? Why, or why not?

Sonny—Ch. 3 and Ch. 30

Some of you may identify with Sonny. Some definitely will not. What a rascal! It was good to see that he settled down in high school. What might happen to you if you got caught skipping school? or snatching donuts from the bakery?

Shirl—Ch. 4 and Ch. 31

Halloween is one of those holidays whose celebration has changed *a lot* from Shirl's day to yours. People used to expect some minor vandalism and pranks. You might ask an older person this: "Do you miss the old Halloween, or is it Good Riddance?"

Shirl's mother's laundry system may seem bizarre to you, but it was very effective at rinsing the clothes well. Although none of the other kids mentioned having the same setup in their basement, it wasn't an uncommon one at the time.

Bella—Ch. 5 and Ch. 32

Bella's advice to today's kids is probably not what you would expect: "Be happy and enjoy things." What do you think about that? Any idea why she might have said it?

Eating, Treating—Ch. 33

Were you very surprised to read that twenty of the twenty-five people interviewed ate beans and franks, or at least beans, every single Saturday night? Any idea why that meal was on Saturday, and not a different night? And why beans and franks in particular?

Meeting—Ch. 34

Meeting up with friends often meant walking or biking to their houses. And many not only walked to and from school, but also home and back every day at lunch. On top of that, they usually played outside after school. That added up to plenty of exercise, but nobody thought of it that way. It was normal, taken for granted, just like being driven places and playing indoors is normal today. Can you think of any ways to give kids some "normal" exercise opportunities in their busy lives?

Beena—Ch.6 and Ch. 35

Beena's resourceful parents were able to meet their family's needs with very little money. Her mother fashioned new garments out of old clothes, and her fisherman father supplemented his income by shooting sea ducks and hunting fox and other game. This allowed him to provide a few more comforts for them, such as ice cream bars for Beena. She passed away in July of 2017, at the age of 97. Perhaps her two-bowl-a-day coffee ice cream habit was responsible for her long and happy life? Then again, maybe it was because she "liked dried fish even better than candy!"

Helen—Ch. 7 and Ch. 36

Helen had to fight her way to college. She battled her own doubts, low expectations from the community, and strong opposition from her family. She might have given up without the aggressive support and encouragement of her minister and her high school principal, and their wives. This was a Big Thing for Helen. But anybody, even children, can find ways to support and encourage others in Little Things. Maybe you can find ways to do this yourself.

Butch—Ch. 8 and Ch. 37

If you search the internet, you'll be able to find an image of Butch in Norman Rockwell's "The Coin Toss" (sometimes titled "The Referee"). He's the player on the left.

Butch accomplished something that is probably impossible everywhere in the U.S. today: registering himself at the public school without his parents' knowledge. I guess there were no forms for his parents to fill out and sign. Today there are. Lots of them! See if you can find out what documents and forms are needed now to enroll a child in school.

Ellen—Ch. 9 and Ch. 38

In this story, there was an example of a child participating actively in an area that is now restricted to adults: Ellen's 8-year old brother helping the firemen empty their house of almost all their possessions—*while it was burning*. That would be considered too dangerous now, even in a slow fire like theirs. Do you think that's a good change in our thinking? bad? mixed?

Rosanna—Ch. 10 and Ch. 39

Sixteen people under one roof. Interesting. Fourteen rooms. *Very* good. One bathroom. Now *that* must have been a challenge. If you had to share a bathroom with fifteen other people, what kinds of rules and policies might you have to have in place?

Responsibility and Respect—Ch. 40

Rosanna, who taught school for quite a few years, said that her students didn't behave as well on days when outdoor recesses were cancelled. Maybe you're very lucky and get several a day, like most of the children in this book. If not, do you wish you had more recess time? What's your favorite thing to do at recess?

Carefree Liberty or Neglect?—Ch. 41

If you have less independence and freedom than these children, have you ever wished you had more? Or are you happy with how things are? You could argue that children were in more danger back then, and you could also argue that we overprotect them now. Do you agree with one side or the other, or somewhat with both?

Ellie—Ch. 11 and 42

Do you recall what Ellie's "school bus" spent most of the day transporting? I wonder if the hosings got rid of the odor. Hmm. Probably not completely.

Rozzy—Ch. 12 and Ch. 43

Rozzy's home life was more complicated than that of almost all the others, due to her father's drinking and gambling when she was a child and his abandonment of the family when she was thirteen. Today, homes headed by single mothers are pretty common, aren't they? They weren't at the time, though. Most kids lived with both their parents.

Tom—Ch. 13 and Ch. 44

As a five-year old, Tom was understandably terrified at the prospect of being left in charge of his younger sisters for the evening. His parents weren't really as neglectful as it might seem, as the neighbors had been told and would have been available in an emergency. However, it's something that certainly is frowned on these days! It might even lead to the children being removed from the home. What do you think about their plan? Was it wise?

Edith—Ch. 14 and Ch. 45

Speaking about how we have many more possessions now than when she was a child, Edith said, "People don't realize that we can get along very nicely without a lot of what we have, since marketers have convinced us otherwise." I think she put her finger on something very important by mentioning "marketers." Can you think of some techniques they use in advertisements and commercials to influence us? If you can't, try watching ads with that in mind. It's hard to do at first, but see if you can learn to spot ways they try to persuade us without even using words.

Charlotte—Ch. 15 and Ch. 46

Does selling candy all day sound like a dream job? Maybe, but Charlotte had really, really wanted to go to college and become a phys. ed. teacher. Unlike Helen, she had nobody to help her navigate the mysterious process of getting there, and she became a candy clerk in a department store instead. Sometimes lemons become lemonade, however, as she met her future husband in that candy department. Has there ever been a disappointing event in your life that ended up leading directly to something wonderful?

Learning, Yearning—Ch. 47

Six of the girls spent at least a year attending a school where there were three, four, five, or six different grades within their classroom.

Do you think you would enjoy that? How would it make school very different for you?

Also, did you notice that over half of the boys—three out of five—stayed back at least once? And there were mentions of other boys who had stayed back. Yet only two of the twenty girls ever did, and for both it was because of prolonged absences due to illness (which was the case for only one of the boys). Certainly girls were also kept back a grade when it was necessary, but it was much more common for boys. It might be interesting to try and figure out a possible reason for this. [HINT: Look for information on brain development.]

Times of Earning—Ch. 48

Earning your own spending money has a lot of benefits besides putting cash in your pocket and making you feel more independent and grown up. It provides an education about life that you'll never get in a classroom. Many of the children in this book, especially the boys, had jobs even before they were teenagers. Thinking about those jobs, what do you think they might have learned?

Here's a Look at What We Wore—Ch. 49

Can you imagine playing softball wearing a dress? Many of these girls did just that.

Louise—Ch. 16 and Ch. 50

Louise was one of several who said she had loved playing outdoors and wouldn't enjoy having to be in the house as much as kids are today. What are your favorite things to do outside? Would you play outside more if your friends joined you?

Pumpie—Ch. 17 and Ch. 51

Pumpie was raised in a neighborhood in which everyone was poor but shared a feeling of tight community: they had the same values, and every adult was their "parent" and felt free to correct them, or to speak to their parents about them. Your own neighborhood probably isn't like this, for many reasons. What are some of those reasons?

Walt—Ch. 18 and Ch. 52

Walt had a very caring sixth-grade teacher who went out of her way to open up a new world to him. She may literally have saved him from a life of crime. If he had had a different teacher that year, he might have ended up leading a very different kind of life. Her actions had major consequences for him. But even small deeds can influence others. And a kind word, or a cruel one, can make someone's day brighter—or ruin it.

Elaine—Ch. 19 and Ch. 53

When Elaine moved back to her Rhode Island hometown with her own children, she hoped that they could experience the idyllic childhood she had had. But although only about twenty years had passed, nothing was the same. We can't blame video games or smartphones, as they hadn't been invented. Nobody even had cell phones at that time. Or computers. What do you think might have changed to disappoint her so badly?

Vicki—Ch. 20 and Ch. 54

Had you ever wondered where popcorn came from? Now you know! Okie's family grew it as a cash crop, but Vicki's raised it for fun in their garden. *Lots of it,* she added, so they always had a "large stash" to enjoy. That makes me think about maybe planting some myself next spring. Maybe you could try that, too.

Sports and Pews—Ch. 55

Do you have a lot of fun playing a sport in an organized league? There are many benefits to this. There are also advantages to the way most kids used to play, with no adults to supervise, instruct, or nag. The older kids were the authorities and the experts. You organized yourselves, and your game rules fit your space and your players. Do you sometimes get a chance to do this? What games or sports have you played like this?

News and Views—Ch. 56

What news stories have you heard in *your* life that you might always remember?

Shirley—Ch. 21 and Ch. 57

Shirley and her sisters got caught. Have you ever tried to do something you knew you weren't supposed to do? Well, of course you have. Did you get away with it?

Lucy—Ch. 22 and Ch. 58

Have you ever noticed how many fairy tales feature a wicked stepmother? *Cinderella, Snow White,* and *Hansel and Gretel* are three of the best known currently, but there are *lots* more, and the stories come from all over the world. Maybe one reason for this unfair portrayal—for there are many, many loving and kind stepmothers—is that it's usually very difficult and stressful to be a stepmother, no matter how nice you are and how hard you try, especially if your new stepchildren wish you'd just go away. It seems a little different with Lucy's stepmother, as she started off well, and everyone was happy. Only after her own children were born did she turn cruel. But Lucy survived, and she was very glad that social services never removed her from her home, where she had the love and support of her brothers and sisters.

Stillman—Ch. 23 and Ch. 59

Stillman sometimes got into trouble for talking too much in school. Ellie did as well. Does this sound familiar?

Nancy—Ch. 24 and Ch. 60

In Nancy's town, the Memorial Day parade ended at the cemetery, where the president of the high school's senior class recited the Gettysburg Address. Many communities across the country still observe similar traditions. Do you know why this particular speech became important in celebrating the holiday? If not, find out!

Claire—Ch. 25 and Ch. 61

At her parochial school, Claire was taught in French for half of every day, and in English for the other half. In this way her immigrant community maintained its identity without depriving its children of becoming fluent in the language they needed to succeed in their new country. Bilingual education is a controversial subject now. But one important difference between today's issues and Claire's situation is that *everyone* at her school came from a French-speaking background.

Rich, Poor—Ch. 62

Nobody in these stories was wealthy; everyone was middle class, lower middle class, or poor. What kinds of differences *and* similarities did you notice between them?

"We're not poor. We just don't have any money." This saying isn't used much now, as it doesn't apply to as many people as it used to. Those who said it viewed themselves as belonging to the mainstream of local society in terms of culture, education, expectations, values, and dignity. It describes several of the families in this book. The Depression in the U.S. had greatly increased the number in that position, as jobs disappeared and families went quickly from living comfortably to barely surviving. They became poor, but only in the sense that they had little money. Thanks to government entitlement programs, today's poor are usually better fed and clothed, and have better health care and more comforts, than yesterday's poor (or even middle class). But they are more likely to be culturally impoverished and live on the edges of society rather than in the mainstream, and in more dangerous neighborhoods.

War—Ch. 63

World War II brought rationing on many items, including gasoline. Children were already used to walking where they needed to go, or taking public transportation. But kids today spend a lot of time being driven places by their parents. How might your life change if gas rationing had to be brought back?

More—Ch. 64

The people I interviewed were asked to look back over their more than eighty years of experience on this planet and decide what was and what was not important. Just about everyone said, more or less, *and unprompted*, that **money was not the key to happiness**. They are passing this insight on to you. Treasure this gift by never forgetting it.

Hmm . . .

Many said that they wouldn't want to have to be a kid today, *but* that they did enjoy various modern conveniences, like dishwashers or power tools. Do you think there's a way we can take the best of the old and combine it with the best of the new?

What advantages do kids in your day have over the kids in the book? If you're glad you were born when you were, lay out your reasons for feeling this way. On the other hand, if you wish you'd been part of the generation you just read about, explain why.

Acknowledgments

Ellie, Jim, Linda G., Linda J., Matthew,
Nathan, Stephanie, Suetta, Tom,
and Mom for their assistance
in finding participants

Tami, Annalia, Helen, Hannah,
Eden, and Ben for providing
initial feedback

Ned, for his indispensable support

Sarah, Nancy, Ellie, Alex,
and Susannah for their critical
support and feedback

About the Author

After her own New England childhood in the 1950s and 60s, **Anne G.D. Smith** earned a degree in music, taught school, worked as a medical secretary, homeschooled her six children from birth until college, and fell in love with Sudoku. Dubbed "The Old Lady on the Bike" by a child on her daily route, she spends her rides designing houses that will never be built and devising solutions for national problems that would be sabotaged if ever implemented. She and her husband, Edward, live in northern Massachusetts.

Printed by BoD™in Norderstedt, Germany